Praise for *The Impactful Vegan*

"The stories of animal advocates and effective animal charity organizations in *The Impactful Vegan* will inspire you to take your animal advocacy to the next level. This is a refreshing and superb display of compassion in action."
—**Carleigh Bodrug**, *New York Times* **bestselling author of** *PlantYou*

"What I love about Robert is that he helps us realize that we are all in the position to make an impact for animals, for the planet, and humanity."
—**Tabitha Brown, #1** *New York Times* **bestselling author of**
Feeding the Soul (Because It's My Business), **Emmy Award–
winning actress, and "America's favorite mom and auntie"**

"Robert Cheeke drives a stake through the common approaches to reducing animal suffering with his bold, straightforward argument that we can't just be well-intentioned, but we must also be highly impactful with our actions. *The Impactful Vegan* is a provocative guide with an indispensable framework to help animals, making it a must-read for everyone."
—**Rich Roll, author and host of** *The Rich Roll Podcast*

"Robert Cheeke is one of the great plant-based evangelists! Science has settled the question: eating a whole food, plant-based diet stacks the deck in favor of longevity. In this new book Robert gives us several more beautifully argued reasons to eschew the bacon and chew more plants. It belongs on every bookshelf for those of us who want to live a longer, more ethical life."
—**Dan Buettner, National Geographic Fellow and #1** *New
York Times* **bestselling author of** *The Blue Zones*

"*The Impactful Vegan* by Robert Cheeke is a testament to the tangible change we can all contribute to now. It goes beyond theory, offering actionable, humane strategies that resonate with the immediacy of our mission at Plant Based News—to foster a compassionate and informed community. With nearly three decades of vegan advocacy, Cheeke's seasoned perspective is a beacon for those navigating a life of meaningful impact. His book is more than a manual; it's a rallying call for harnessing our collective skills, talents, and resources to champion animal welfare effectively. Cheeke's work serves as a beautifully articulated guide, empowering us to extend our reach and deepen our commitment to a world where empathy towards all beings is the norm."
—**Robbie Lockie, cofounder of Plant Based News**

"In this book, Robert Cheeke really drives home the truism I have discovered in life: that when something is right, it's right for everyone. Eating animals and animal products makes humans sick, harms the planet, and it's cruel to the animals. Conversely, when we eat plants, it's better for all of us. Being vegan is the best thing I have ever done. Because of my plant-based Goodbye Auto-immune Disease protocol, I have been lupus-free for 18 years now, after living with terrible chronic illness for 12 years of my life, including kidney failure, arthritis, and mini-strokes. I am not only disease-free, I am fit and strong in my late 40s, whereas most folks my age are getting sicker and sicker. My greatest joy is giving that same benefit to my clients and patients around the world. However, the benefits I have experienced extend far beyond my health. I love living a life where I can feel great and cause no harm to others or the planet. Also, it's a beautiful experience for my husband and I to raise compassionate vegan kids who feel connected to their fellow humans, animals, and the planet. In this book, Cheeke takes you through the steps to understanding the benefits of veganism, the reasons it's so hard for many people to embrace it, and how to create the mindset and habits that will help you fully embrace becoming vegan and proud of it! Thank you, Robert!"

—**Dr. Brooke Goldner, author of** *Goodbye Lupus*

"Robert Cheeke writes a clever and practical guide to advocate for animals, with unique strategies that are designed to make the greatest impact. Follow his example to level up your advocacy, helping animals in the most meaningful ways."

—**Kathy Freston,** *New York Times* **bestselling author of** *Quantum Wellness, Veganist,* **and** *The Lean*

"With *The Impactful Vegan*, Robert Cheeke has created a one stop shop for information on all things vegan, the impact of diet on the environment, the tragic animal suffering, and everything the modern age vegan and non-vegan alike can reference in an instant. Robert is also a plethora of information on veganism as a complete diet; busting myths about protein deficiency and of being an incomplete source of nutrition. With Robert's vast experience as an athlete and vegan bodybuilder he can back up all the information with his personal experience."

—**Phil Collen, co-lead guitarist of Def Leppard**

"If you want to make a positive difference for animals, for our planet, or for your own health, a plant-based diet is a great place to start. And if you want to inspire others, too—and be part of the solution—then this book is just what you need. Robert Cheeke delivers a clear and engaging evidence-based guide to maximizing your impact. *The Impactful Vegan* will give you a serious dose of grounded hope—and show you how easy it can be to make the world a better place."

—**Ocean Robbins, cofounder of Food Revolution Network and author of** *Real Superfoods*

"Robert Cheeke is PlantStrong for the animals, and he exemplifies, in all the best ways, the meaning of an impactful vegan. As a longtime vegan athlete and crusader, Robert understands the levers that lead to behavior change, and he shares these beautifully in this highly anticipated new book. Check out *The Impactful Vegan* to make a difference in the lives of others."

—**Rip Esselstyn,** *New York Times* **bestselling author of** *Plant-Strong*

"It's not enough to merely long for a more healthful, compassionate society— we must summon it into existence through our thoughts, words, and most importantly, our deeds. Calling upon the higher vision and vast inner resources that we all possess, in *The Impactful Vegan* author Robert Cheeke provides the map and the blueprint to help transform our world profoundly for the better. *The Impactful Vegan* will inspire and guide you into a new, fulfilling chapter of your life—and we will all benefit from the impact. It's hard to ask more from a book than that."

—**Michael Klaper, MD, author of** *Vegan Nutrition: Pure and Simple*

"With decades of firsthand experience, Robert Cheeke offers a refreshing and inspiring approach to effectively helping animals in *The Impactful Vegan*. His passion and dedication are infectious, making it feel impossible to not participate in some form of advocacy. Regardless of where you are on the 'vegan' continuum, you will learn fascinating insights and gain hope from this insightful book."

—**Julieanna Hever, the Plant-Based Dietitian® and author of** *The Choose You Now Diet* **and** *Plant-Based Nutrition (Idiot's Guides)*

"Robert Cheeke makes a compelling case. Highly recommended!"

—**James Wilks, winner of the UFC's** *The Ultimate Fighter* **and producer and narrator of** *The Game Changers*

"Robert Cheeke's happiness and compassion are well known. And it is no sur- prise that both have been poured onto the pages of *The Impactful Vegan*. The thoughtful strategies he employs to reduce animal suffering are so practical that many of us can incorporate them immediately, and spare lives today! Robert is ruthlessly consistent with his intuitive connection between our actions and the measurable impact they have on others."

—**Chuck Carroll, host of** *The Exam Room Podcast*

"A must-read. Robert Cheeke delivers a thoughtful, data-driven approach to the often emotional conversation of changing diets in *The Impactful Vegan*. This book is certain to move the needle for a better world for people, planet, and, of course, animals."

—**Jennifer Stojkovic, founder of Vegan Women Summit**

"Robert Cheeke, with his refreshing new approach backed by data-driven evidence and a lifetime of experience, presents *The Impactful Vegan* as a highly engaging and deeply thoughtful book. With practical strategies to reduce animal suffering, Cheeke effortlessly connects our actions to the measurable impact they have on others. As a vegan advocate for nearly three decades, his breadth of experience and insightful interviews with change-makers in the vegan community make this manual a must-have for navigating an impactful vegan life. *The Impactful Vegan* not only presents a comprehensive case for doing the most good for animals but also lays the foundation for a more compassionate and plant-forward future for all of us. Cheeke's expertise and guidance empower readers to make a profound positive impact using the skills and talents they already possess."

—**John Lewis, CEO and founder of Badass**
Vegan and author of *Badass Vegan*

THE
IMPACTFUL
VEGAN

Also by Robert Cheeke

Vegan Bodybuilding & Fitness

Shred It!

Plant-Based Muscle
(coauthored with Vanessa Espinoza)

The Plant-Based Athlete
(coauthored with Matt Frazier)

THE
IMPACTFUL
VEGAN

How YOU Can Save More Lives and Make the
Biggest Difference for Animals and the Planet

ROBERT CHEEKE

BenBella Books, Inc.
Dallas, TX

BenBella Books, Inc.
10440 N. Central Expressway
Suite 800
Dallas, TX 75231
benbellabooks.com
Send feedback to feedback@benbellabooks.com

BenBella is a federally registered trademark.

Printed in the United States of America
10 9 8 7 6 5 4 3 2 1

Library of Congress Control Number: 2023053370
ISBN 9781637744581 (hardcover)
ISBN 9781637744598 (electronic)

Editing by Claire Schulz and Gregory Newton Brown
Copyediting by Michael Fedison
Proofreading by Sarah Vostok and Jenny Bridges
Indexing by Amy Murphy
Text design and composition by PerfecType, Nashville, TN
Cover design by Morgan Carr
Cover image © Adobe Stock / raquel
Printed by Lake Book Manufacturing

"I argue that there can be no reason—except for the selfish desire to preserve the privileges of the exploiting group—for refusing to extend the basic principle of equality of consideration to members of other species. I ask you to recognize that your attitudes to members of other species are a form of prejudice no less objectionable than prejudice about a person's race or sex."

—Peter Singer, *Animal Liberation*

"Do we, as humans, having an ability to reason and to communicate abstract ideas verbally and in writing, and to form ethical and moral judgments using the accumulated knowledge of the ages, have the right to take the lives of other sentient organisms, particularly when we are not forced to do so by hunger or dietary need, but rather do so for the somewhat frivolous reason that we like the taste of meat? In essence, should we know better?"

—Peter Cheeke, PhD, *Contemporary Issues in Animal Agriculture*, 2004

VEGANISM has an official definition, but it's hard for anyone to live up to it due to the nature of the world we live in. Veganism is defined by The Vegan Society, which, along with Donald Watson, coined the term "vegan" in the 1940s, as *"a philosophy and way of living which seeks to exclude—as far as is possible and practicable—all forms of exploitation of, and cruelty to, animals for food, clothing or any other purpose; and by extension, promotes the development and use of animal-free alternatives for the benefit of animals, humans and the environment. In dietary terms it denotes the practice of dispensing with all products derived wholly or partly from animals."*

CONTENTS

INTRODUCTION

More animals are being killed for food today than at any other time in our history. The number of animals being slaughtered for our burgers, sandwiches, pizzas, burritos, tacos, sushi, nuggets, wings, school lunches, holiday meals, and other dining experiences is astronomical. Annually, more than a trillion sea animals and ninety billion land animals are killed for food globally.[1]

Our human population is growing at a record pace, too, with an estimated ten billion people globally by 2050. Our appetite for eating animals outpaces even our population growth, however. Eating animals has become desirable for those who were previously unable to afford that opportunity. While a rise in human prosperity should be a good thing, it has become bad news for animals, our planet, and our physical health as well. Studies show a rise in eating meat and a decrease in bodily and planet health. The world's leading health organizations explain this correlation across a number of quantifiable factors. The key drivers include the act of eating animals contributing to an increased risk of heart disease, cancer, type 2 diabetes, hypertension, strokes, obesity, and other diet-related diseases that increase risk of early mortality; elevated levels of methane and carbon dioxide emitted into our atmosphere from animal production; and the pollution of air, land, and water due to factory farming, labor, transportation, and distribution of farmed animals for food.

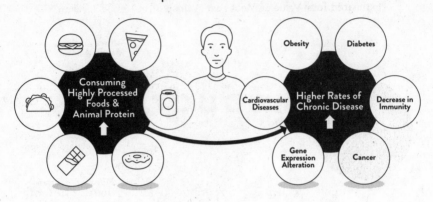

Health Impact of Diet on Western Disease

Tragically, as many as 30 percent of animals killed for food are not consumed by humans and are instead tossed out as waste, rendering their slaughter an unnecessary evil.[2] Furthermore, industries (particularly the fishing, chicken, and egg industries) are riddled by diseases that wipe out millions of animals. Tens of millions of other animals are destroyed because of viruses or illnesses resulting from their cramped living conditions on industrial farms. Other widespread causes of unnecessary death include: undesirable sea animals caught in large fishing nets and then discarded as waste and animals dying during transportation to slaughterhouses, which happens on large shipping vessels and in livestock trucks regularly. Additionally, environmental factors, such as heat waves, floods, tornadoes, hurricanes, freezes, and other climate disasters, contribute to the total number of animals originally raised for food but not consumed as food for humans.

All the while, nearly a billion people go to bed hungry at night, according to global hunger statistics from the World Health Organization.

It is well documented that we grow enough food to feed every human on Earth, but most of the food we grow goes to feeding animals, which further pollutes the planet, while we get only a fraction of the calories in the form of animal protein and fat that we would have consumed (due to the above attrition rates and the more undesirable parts of animals that are rejected as food) had we eaten the plants that we instead fed to the animals.

Total Food Waste in the Meat Sector
(Estimated Total Value of Meat Lost in the US Is Over $83 Billion)

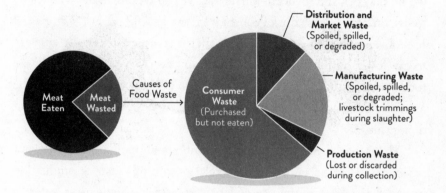

Data sources: Katie Flanagan, Kai Robertson, and Craig Hanson, "Reducing Food Loss and Waste: Setting a Global Action Agenda," World Resources Institute, August 28, 2019, https://doi.org/10.46830/wrirpt.18.00130; Małgorzata Karwowska, Sylwia Łaba, and Krystian Szczepański, "Food Loss and Waste in the Meat Sector—Why the Consumption Stage Generates the Most Losses," Sustainability 13, no. 11 (2021): 6227, https://doi.org/10.3390/su13116227.

The Feed Conversion Ratio examines the energy efficiency of animal agriculture, evaluating the percentage of caloric energy inputs as feed to an animal that is effectively converted into consumable animal products. We usually get just 10–20 percent of the calories we feed to animals as edible calories for humans, revealing a staggering inefficiency from caloric use alone. This doesn't include the massive amount of water needed to raise crops for animals, and the amount of water that animals drink while they are farmed to be turned into food. We're breeding, killing, and eating more animals than ever before, with seemingly no end in sight. And in addition to being an utterly inhumane practice, it is wildly inefficient as well.

My father, Peter Cheeke, an animal scientist and professor at Oregon State University for thirty years, explained the following: "For each 'step up the food chain' there is about a tenfold loss of efficiency. When chickens or pigs are fed a plant-based diet of corn and soybean meal, the typical diets of broiler chickens and pigs, it takes ten times as much corn and soybeans to produce meat, which humans then eat, than it would if we ate the corn and soybeans ourselves. We could do that, but who wants to live on corn flakes? But of course we don't have to eat just corn flakes! It is obvious to even a fourth grader that it is more biologically efficient to eat 'lower on the food chain.' If we can effectively utilize plant-based foods, what is the point of feeding them to animals and then eating the animals? From a biological efficiency point of view, there is no point in doing this."[3]

My father continued, with a point about inefficiency with our resources, when he said, "Another relationship of livestock production to water resources is the use of large quantities of irrigation water in the production of feeds and forages. Alfalfa, a major feedstuff in dairy production, is, for example, extremely inefficient in use of water. With climate change, as distribution of water availability changes, production of crops like alfalfa may become unfeasible. Air pollution caused by large-scale animal production includes methane, ammonia, and odors. Swine odor is particularly offensive." There are plenty of other inefficiencies that we see all around us, whether it's sharks, dolphins, and other large sea animals and birds caught in nets as a result of large-scale fishing, or water pollution from hog farms that flows into the Mississippi River, which empties into the Gulf of Mexico, making the water so toxic, it is uninhabitable. Lingering here for a moment, those areas are aptly named "dead zones." These are areas of the ocean where there are such low levels of oxygen that essentially no life exists beneath the surface of the water.[4]

For most of us, the animals we eat don't come from small farms or family farms like in the old days. Today, 99 percent of animals slaughtered for food are grown in so-called "efficient" factory farms, where the objective is to breed, feed, house, and slaughter as many animals as possible, in as small of a space as possible, as quickly as possible, in order to maximize profits.[5] This means that tens of thousands of chickens share a single barn together, with hundreds of thousands of chickens cramped

Feed Conversion Ratio

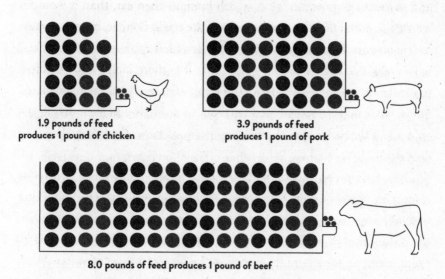

1.9 pounds of feed
produces 1 pound of chicken

3.9 pounds of feed
produces 1 pound of pork

8.0 pounds of feed produces 1 pound of beef

Data from M. Shahbandeh, "Feed conversion ratio of selected meat and fish worldwide," Statista, August 3, 2023, https://www.statista.com/statistics /254421/feed-conversion-ratios-worldwide-2010.

into many barns on an individual industrialized farm, unable to spread their wings due to the density and confinement. This is common practice in today's factory farm–focused animal agriculture. Factory farms, feedlots, and confinement operations are responsible for producing the vast majority of the animal protein we consume as a society in the United States, and in many places around the world.[6]

Indeed, we have reached the highest number of animals consumed on a daily basis in history, particularly because of the rise in popularity of eating smaller animals—fish and chickens. This causes more total suffering than the result of eating larger animals—it takes more than one hundred chickens to produce the same amount of edible meat that a cow produces. Paired with the fact that, of our growing human population, 98 percent of all babies will (at the current rate) grow up to be omnivores, based on a global statistic of just 1 to 2 percent of humans following a plant-based diet (while likely raising their children to do the same), this makes for an uphill battle for the vulnerable animals among us who are the most likely to end up as menu items on dinner plates.[7]

This might look like a battle that is destined to be lost, but there are plenty of reasons to be hopeful that positive change can and will take place for animals—especially farmed animals—to experience better lives. Where do we find hope in the wake of such staggering statistics? We look to books, like this one, movements that are underway and being led by people like you and the people profiled in these pages, and we draw on history, which has often shown brighter days ahead— consider how far our own human struggle for independence, sovereignty, autonomy, safety, and freedom has come, even if we have far to go still. Believing in a brighter future is crucial, but *taking action* to create a brighter future is what will get us fully there. We also look to experts for insights. My father shared the following speculation: "My prediction is that 'factory farming' of animals will be a temporary blip in agricultural history. It is simply not sustainable to confine huge numbers of animals in a small space."[8] Combined with technological advancements in food production, perhaps my father's predication will come true, hopefully sooner rather than later.

There are measurable ways to effectively reduce animal suffering— approaches that have been evaluated based on diverse criteria of efficacy and have been determined to be efficient, impactful, and demonstrably influential. What if I told you that these very methods are part of the driving force behind a potential *decline* in meat consumption in America where these particular animal advocacy strategies have been implemented? For example, the dairy industry in America is declining at a record pace, while plant-based milk alternatives have experienced record profits, to the tune of more than $2 billion in annual sales in the United States alone.[9] Plant-based and alternative protein sales are at an all-time high, encompassing alternative meat, milk, eggs, and other foods, with more than $8 billion in annual sales in America in 2022.[10] The reshaping of the grocery store refrigerator and freezer sections is taking place before our eyes in America and in other parts of the world, like the UK, where tactics to reduce animal suffering are being utilized. In 2022, meat consumption fell to a thirty-four-year low in Germany, when they experienced a 9.8 percent drop in pork (pig) production, an 8.2 percent dip in beef and veal (cows and calves) production, and a 2.9 percent dip in poultry (chickens, ducks, and other birds) production.[11] In the fall of 2023, various media outlets reported the UK had reached its all-time lowest level of meat consumption since the 1970s (when official records began to record and track that data).[12]

People might not be willing to give up eating meat anytime soon, and that's okay, because through innovative technological break-throughs, and effective animal advocacy, we're changing the way meat is made, which can now be done without substantial animal suffering. A change in food consumption is afoot, even if at the moment you're reading this more animals were killed for food today than were killed yesterday. That shouldn't deter us from impacting the number of animals that will be killed for food tomorrow, or a year from now, or five years from now, or twenty-five years from now. Change takes time, and revo-lutions take perseverance.

As a vegan advocate for nearly three decades, I have been preoccu-pied with being effective for animals. Early on, I thought that being the "perfect" vegan was the key to reducing the most animal suffering—you know, not eating at restaurants if there was slight cross contamination with animal protein, refusing to sit on leather car seats, and judging everyone else around me—turning many people away from veganism. I later realized that effectively contributing to the reduction in ani-mal suffering extends far beyond vegan purity. This is a story about my discovery and what the evidence and data say about making the most significant impact for animals. My assumption is that you care about animal suffering, and given the option for your animal advocacy to be ineffective or highly effective, with essentially the same effort, you would choose the latter every time. One of the biggest obstacles in our pursuit of nearly anything is that our personal biases tend to get in our way of doing the most good or being the most effective. We all have preferences and knowledge we've acquired from our experiences. We have our own systems and patterns of doing things, and we prefer to maintain those habits without considering changing them for the better—because we often think what we're currently doing is already the best way to do it.

What I've learned over the years as an animal advocate trying to make the greatest impact for animals is that some approaches are more impactful than others, and if we evaluate what the evidence says is most effective, and apply those strategies, we can have a more significant influence on the reduction of animal suffering, getting closer to a shared goal of extending compassion to others. I've also learned that we don't know what we don't know, and our confirmation biases—assuming that our actions are very effective, while having those perspectives reinforced by our peers, without being challenged or scrutinized—might very well be holding our advocacy back, and therefore contributing to more animal harm.

If you want to do the most good for animals, you may have to do what I did, and set your ego aside and embrace how to help animals the most. The answers to our most effective animal advocacy might not be what you suspect, or what you want to hear, and the solutions to reducing animal suffering might challenge your beliefs. I've concluded that it is far more beneficial for animals that our actions are effective, rather than trying to prove that we're right. Yes, it is possible to be effective and to be right, but rarely do we land at that destination on our own without the help of evidence-based practices guiding us to those conclusions.

How do we determine that one approach to animal advocacy is better than another? We have to look at the net impact, establishing which forms of advocacy really are best at reducing suffering. That is what this book will explore in detail. Thankfully, many organizations and individuals have dedicated their lives to figuring that out, so we'll hear directly from some of the most influential people in the world in the areas of amplifying veganism and reducing unnecessary animal suffering, learning from those who have made the greatest impact. To be clear up front, these will not just be nonprofit animal advocacy founders and presidents advising the rest of us on what we should do to help animals. In fact, not all of the advice about how to most effectively reduce animal suffering will come from vegans. Some non-vegan philosophers, entrepreneurs, and venture capitalists have been effective at reducing animal suffering, and you'll learn about their approaches later on. Collectively, through their innovation and far-reaching impact, they have had a significant influence on reducing the need for animals in the food and beverage industry, and therefore have helped animals mightily despite the fact that they themselves still eat animals. That might sound counterintuitive, but if we're striving for serious change, we have to think outside the box.

Some might be upset that I would give oxygen, in the form of recognition, to the non-vegans that help animals, rather than shining light on the real vegan heroes in the world. That, again, is a result of ego, rather than efficacy. Our goal is not to applaud vegans alone. Our goal is to uncover and figure out what really contributes to the greatest reduction in animal suffering, to learn from it, apply it, and improve upon it.

You will read stories of influential companies, nonprofits, animal sanctuaries, and individuals who are committed to what I am calling effective vegan altruism, a term we will explore in the first chapter. Briefly, effective altruism is about figuring out how to do the most good for others, and implementing those actions, whatever they turn out to be. Effective *vegan* altruism is about figuring out how to do the most good for animals (and, in particular, farmed animals killed for food, which are the most abused animals in the largest quantities), and implementing those actions, whatever they turn out to be. Effective vegan altruism is a practice, like leadership, mentoring, or yoga—it will never be perfect—but it will continue to evolve with the constant exploration of what does the most good for animals.

I am going to plant this flag right here and say that I am an effective vegan altruist, which I have been for the entirety of my adult life, even if it took me decades to understand there was a term to describe my type of vegan advocacy. For as long as I can remember, dating back to my early teenage years of veganism, decades ago, I wanted to be *effective* in my outreach for animals, and I was committed to making a measurable difference. I wasn't satisfied by merely being a vegan, avoiding contributing to unnecessary animal suffering, and I was hell-bent on being *effective* for the cause. This manifested in many ways and took on different shapes and forms throughout my life, ultimately leading me to realize that writing, public speaking, leading by positive example, and creating what I have called The Vegan Strong Method are all part of the most effective ways to help animals.

Nearly all "new vegans" are passionate about their lifestyle, but in addition to passion, I had *effectiveness* on my mind. I used athleticism as my vehicle to drive the message of compassionate veganism home. By becoming a champion vegan athlete, I showed that I built my body without consuming animal protein, and that is something I have been sharing with audiences for nearly thirty years, showing millions of others that they can do the same. My motto was "anything you can do, I can do vegan," which has become cliché in the vegan world at this point, because so many vegans have proven this to be true—from Olympic gold medalists, to award-winning scientists, to successful entrepreneurs, to parents raising vegan families, vegan living has never been easier or more practical.

I grew up on a farm and became a vegan for the animals at age fifteen, in 1995, weighing just 120 pounds as a five-sport high school athlete. I was primarily a long-distance runner, but also played soccer, basketball, and tennis. I wrestled, competed in track and field, cycled recreationally, and dabbled in weight lifting. After adopting a plant-based diet, I continued to excel as a vegan athlete throughout the rest of high school, and then I ran for the cross-country club at Oregon State University the following year. I went to school in Salt Lake City, Utah, to become a licensed massage therapist, and during that time, I discovered the sport of bodybuilding, in 1999. I pursued competitive bodybuilding for a full decade, from 2001 to 2011, becoming a champion vegan bodybuilder, and producing and releasing a documentary (*Vegan Fitness:*

Built Naturally, 2005). I grew from 120 pounds to 220 pounds through the years, with a natural, drug-free approach to bodybuilding, showing clearly that we can build our bodies without eating animals. I wrote and published four books on the subject, including the *New York Times* bestseller *The Plant-Based Athlete* (which I cowrote with Matt Frazier), and have been on a speaking tour for nearly two decades, sharing my story of transformation from skinny farm kid to champion vegan bodybuilder.

My journey to effective vegan altruism has taken me around the world. I speak at plenty of vegan events, empowering those audiences with many of the advocacy principles you'll find in this book. But most of my time these days is spent interacting with people who are not vegan, aiming to have a meaningful influence on them, leading to an effective reduction in animal suffering by inspiring people to change their eating habits.

Left: As a skinny new vegan in my high school days.
Right: As a champion bodybuilder and longtime vegan in 2023.

I've had many great role models, teachers, and colleagues who have paved the way and led by example, focusing on results, not on ego or being "right." Any contributions I have been fortunate enough to make to the vegan movement are a result of those who came before me, like my older sister, who carved out a path for me to follow. I wrote this book to be a useful tool for *you* to incorporate proven strategies into *your* approach to effective animal advocacy. Together, as effective vegan altruists, we can make an incredible impact on our planet.

CHAPTER 1

WHAT IS EFFECTIVE VEGAN ALTRUISM?

"Effective altruists don't give to whatever cause tugs most at their heartstrings, they give to the cause that will do the most good, given the abilities, time, and money they have available."
—Peter Singer, *The Most Good You Can Do*

What does it mean to be an effective altruist? You might be familiar with the word "altruism," and you probably even know some people who identify as altruists.

Altruism is the act of doing good for others without expecting anything in return, or without the hope or expectation of benefiting as a result of contributing to the well-being of those you are supporting. It is, in essence, authentic generosity that comes from a place of empathy and compassion for others. *Effective* altruism is about doing the "most good" for others in an effort to make the most significant impact on those who are experiencing the greatest amount of suffering.

I first learned of effective altruism when reading *The Most Good You Can Do: How Effective Altruism Is Changing Ideas About Living Ethically*, a 2015 book by the renowned and iconic animal rights philosopher Peter Singer. Singer's book is all about using practices of effective altruism to make the greatest impact on our world. (It's worth noting that Singer didn't start the effective altruism movement; he just added weight behind it as one of the world's greatest contemporary philosophers and one of *TIME* magazine's one hundred most influential people in the world.)

Whether we like it or not, the world revolves around money, and the bulk of Singer's book focuses on how to use our financial resources in the most effective ways. Whether we're trying to save the oceans, save the rainforests, save starving children, save animals from going extinct, or prevent billions of farmed animals from being bred and born only to be slaughtered for human consumption, accomplishing those goals will require financial resources. The book makes some classic arguments on behalf of effective altruism. For instance, for a set amount of money, say $1,000, you could make a far greater impact in sub-Saharan Africa purchasing mosquito bed nets to protect people from contracting malaria and dying than spending $1,000 to feed the hungry in a developed part of the world, such as in the United States.[13]

Effective altruism pushes back against the tendency to think of our own communities first. Most of us probably have a regional bias toward our town, our state, our country, and our continent. But often, especially for readers in the Euro-American world, we forget about how impactful our financial resources can be beyond our country's borders. The reality is that for the same amount of money, one can make a significantly greater impact on lives for those living in developing countries. That's just the way our global economy works, particularly because of currency strengths and exchange rates that allow for funds in US dollars to be more impactful in specific regions. In Africa, particular parts of Asia, South America, and Central America, resources from the Western world can extend to a greater number of individuals, therefore making a more significant influence on more lives. Poverty and oppression extend far beyond those locations, and are present in North America, Australia, and Europe, too, but we can all agree that people in some regions of the world suffer more than those in others.

In his book *Doing Good Better*, William MacAskill, a cofounder of the effective altruism movement, put it this way: "The fact that we've found ourselves at the top of the heap, globally speaking, provides us with a tremendous opportunity to make a difference. Because we are comparatively so rich (in the United States), the amount by which we can benefit others is vastly greater than the amount by which we can benefit ourselves. We can therefore do a huge amount of good at relatively low cost."

Kilograms of Apples That Can Be Purchased for $10 USD in Each Country

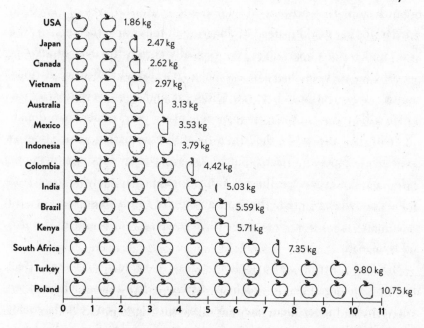

USA	1.86 kg
Japan	2.47 kg
Canada	2.62 kg
Vietnam	2.97 kg
Australia	3.13 kg
Mexico	3.53 kg
Indonesia	3.79 kg
Colombia	4.42 kg
India	5.03 kg
Brazil	5.59 kg
Kenya	5.71 kg
South Africa	7.35 kg
Turkey	9.80 kg
Poland	10.75 kg

Data from "Price Rankings by Country of Apples (1kg)," Numbeo, accessed November 2023, https://www.numbeo.com/cost-of-living/country_price_rankings?itemId=110.

To frame decisions when using effective altruism to do the most good, MacAskill prompts us to ask the following key questions:

1. *How many people benefit, and by how much?*
2. *Is this the most effective thing you can do?*
3. *Is this area neglected?*
4. *What would have happened otherwise?*
5. *What are the chances of success, and how good would success be?*[14]

Action is the key here. Intentions are great, but actions can be life changing. Effective altruists do good deeds all year long without fanfare—not just giving during the holiday season, or posting photos or videos online to show one's generosity when helping those in need. It's a genuine desire to want to help, not a reaction once someone asks for help. Effective altruists also focus on the most impactful ways to make a difference in the lives of others. This is why they donate to organizations that prevent starvation and spare the lives of people in the developing world instead of donating to museums, theaters, or "the arts," which don't spare lives, but typically enrich the lives of affluent people who are in less need of assistance. It's also why effective altruists support organizations that cure blindness and help prevent diarrhea, which kills more than a million people every year, rather than donating to organizations like the Make-A-Wish Foundation, which doesn't spare lives or prevent death, but brings short-term enrichment to one individual (and their families) at a time for approximately ten thousand dollars per wish granted. The same amount of funds could prevent a lot of human and animal deaths in the developing world where so much aid is needed.

Effective altruists also look for areas of neglect, and they reject donating to organizations such as disaster relief funds, which often receive more money than they need, because "everyone else is donating to them." The same is true for the largest and most well-known charities in the country, which often work with major grocery stores to "round up" purchases or to add a donation. Those organizations are not experiencing neglect in the ways that many international aid organizations are, and that same approach and discernment can be applied to how effective altruists determine how to most effectively give to reduce animal suffering.

Effective altruists don't want or need anything in return either. They get all they need from the joy that comes from helping others and making a difference in the lives of those who could use a little more compassion sent their way. They help because others are genuinely in need of help, and they are compelled to take action. Effective altruists are not perfect, though, and as a movement, there have been missteps, but the goal is still there: to most effectively impact the lives of others in positive ways without expectation of return or validation.

This applies to both human and nonhuman animals.

We're naturally drawn to want to support our pets. But an *effective* altruist would evaluate the pros and cons of using finite resources to help all types of animals. Is it better to focus on domesticated companion animals like dogs and cats, or to use our efforts to help chickens, pigs, cows, and other animals who are often far more abused than pets? (Singer released a 2023 book entitled *Animal Liberation Now*, which reminds us of the ongoing struggle that all animals face in today's world.) An effective altruist might come to the conclusion that it would be more altruistic to invest in saving chickens than dogs, because for the same amount of money, one might be able to save far more lives. This is one example of how effective altruism and ethical veganism go hand in hand.

Within ethical veganism, we don't help the abused pig because we hope the pig will return the favor and help us out someday. We help the abused pig because we oppose abuse and we're empathetic to her suffering. We help the chickens because they are worthy of being helped; like us, they want to live their own lives free of fear, pain, and suffering. We help the cows so they won't have their babies taken away from them while being turned into milk-producing machines because we oppose that level of exploitation.

Sources of Animal Suffering

99%
Food System

1%
All Other Sources Combined: Cosmetics, clothing, wool, leather, fur, rodeos, zoos, fighting, vivisection, etc.

By focusing our efforts on animals in the food system, we are choosing the most effective path to sparing the most lives.

INTRODUCING EFFECTIVE VEGAN ALTRUISM

Effective vegan altruism's goal is to use our time, energy, skills, talents, and resources to make the greatest impact *for nonhuman animals and the planet*. There are myriad nonprofit organizations aimed at bettering the lives of humans (approximately one million of them in the United States alone, in fact, with new organizations sprouting up all the time, according to Singer's preface in *The Most Good You Can Do*). Humans are almost always given priority over nonhuman animals.

Yet animals have the same capacity to suffer that we do but are treated far worse than us, particularly those animals who are factory farmed or in vivisection animal testing laboratories. Every effort to help animals at home and abroad is something that I want to celebrate under the umbrella of **effective vegan altruism**. The easiest way I can describe effective vegan altruism is: doing the most good for animals by contributing to organizations that reduce the most animal suffering, prevent the most unnecessary animal deaths, and save the most animal lives using our own unique talents, skills, connections, and resources to achieve that goal.

Since traditional effective altruism focuses so much on impacting humans, and animals often get overlooked, neglected completely, or continue to be exploited even by those doing effective altruistic work for humans, as an **effective vegan altruist**, it is my responsibility to bring awareness and support to helping animals most in need—animals such as fish, chickens, pigs, cows, turkeys, goats, sheep, and other commonly factory farmed beings, as well as monkeys, rabbits, rats, mice, and others that are being experimented on. All of the above endure far greater suffering than domestic pets or wild animals.

For instance, consider the feel-good emotional response from donating to cover the veterinary bills for a friend's cat that got hit by a car. Then think about how those same funds could drastically help hundreds of farmed animals in America, or perhaps even thousands of farmed animals in developing countries.

Is it better to use the same amount of resources to help one animal rather than potentially thousands of animals just because we're emotionally connected to or proximity biased toward the one? Is it better to help one particular animal because of their species? Are some animals simply more deserving of our attention and support because we view them with awe and amazement, such as elephants and tigers, compared to those we view as pests, such as rats and mice? If we remove proximity, species, personal preference, and emotional biases, which animals do we choose to help and which ones do we ignore? These and other questions about morality, speciesism, utility, and net impact for animals are ones we'll be evaluating. Many of the most effective animal charities in the world have data to support their answers to these difficult questions.

Most of us don't take the initiative to go out and actively make a difference for animals on a daily basis (aside from our food choices), but many of us have the ability to contribute to organizations that specialize in doing the most good for animals daily. That's something effective vegan altruists focus on. Many animal rights and vegan advocacy organizations have already spent years doing the legwork to establish strategies, programs, and initiatives that are designed to make the greatest impact for animals. They've done the research, learned from trial and error, and determined the most effective paths toward aid, from education to liberation, to habit change, to diet change. Animal organizations also know how to make money stretch and how to responsibly use financial resources to reduce the most suffering. Whereas many of us might wonder which animals to prioritize—helping chickens, cows, pigs, fish, or others—the best vegan-friendly nonprofit organizations will know which approaches to take to make the most difference.

Of course, effective vegan altruism is not all about contributing financial resources, but also about how we communicate compassionate veganism to others, what we put on our dinner plates, how we represent ourselves as vegans or animal advocates, and how we vote with our dollars with every purchase we make.

When it comes to helping animals, I would much rather that people do something, rather than nothing at all. At the same time, I don't want to encourage you to take the easiest route or do the bare minimum when there are real lives at stake every moment of every day. Therefore, I will continue to evaluate how to do the most good for animals, using available evidence and data. However, I will deviate from traditional effective altruism a bit, which is evident from my "do something" approach compared to the effective altruism position of "do the most good" at all times. I hope that the ways I embrace effective altruism and effective vegan altruism are more practical, actionable, and accessible to a larger number of people, and therefore create a greater net impact for animals than a traditional effective altruism position: prioritizing humans and being focused on performing only the most effective actions.

We have to crawl before we can walk, and we have to walk before we can run, and my objective is to instill habit-forming, sustainable behaviors that will help reduce animal suffering for the long haul, without being overwhelming or intimidating. Consequently, I will celebrate small steps, reward consistent progress, and embrace good intentions, as well as honor outstanding results. As a community committed to reducing animal suffering, we can achieve amazing results when we come together and stick together, fighting for a common cause, and seeking a shared vision and outcome that saves lives and prevents suffering.

EFFECTIVE VEGAN ALTRUISM IN ACTION: FARM SANCTUARY

Gene Baur's commitment to helping animals led him to create what is very likely the world's most well-known animal sanctuary, Farm Sanctuary, which he cofounded in 1986. His unique approach to promoting compassionate veganism is a story worth telling.

Gene used to travel around to the Grateful Dead concerts selling vegan hot dogs out of a Volkswagen bus in the mid-1980s as a way to raise money to help rescue animals. His serving table was draped in vegan literature, sharing the plight that farmed animals endure, leading to conversations about how to extend our empathy and compassion to the most vulnerable among us. With his long hair and beard, he often talked animal rights with Dead Heads for twelve to sixteen hours per day, during multi-day concerts.

Gene was determined to change the conversation about how animals should be viewed as individuals rather than objects and to normalize interacting with nonhuman animals with compassion and grace. He wanted to help the everyday person see animals as friends, not food. This approach, led with compassion and optimism, enabled Farm Sanctuary to grow into an organization that would inspire farm animal sanctuaries to pop up all over the world.

Under Gene's pioneering advocacy, Farm Sanctuary grew from a refuge for abandoned, sick, neglected, injured, or unwanted animals (or those that were rescued, or were lucky to escape the miserable fate destined for them on a traditional farm) into a source of information and inspiration to help all animals live better lives. Beyond that, Farm Sanctuary got directly involved with petitioning policy change to make farmed animals' lives better and also raised awareness among the general public, with thousands of annual visitors to their farms meeting the inquisitive and intelligent animals that most people only know as food.

Today, there are hundreds of accredited farm animal sanctuaries that house tens of thousands of rescued animals. They receive hundreds of thousands of annual visitors, reach millions of people with collective in-person and online campaigns, and raise hundreds of millions of dollars every year to help animals live better lives.

I visited both of the Farm Sanctuary locations more than a decade ago (one in upstate New York and the other in Southern California), and I have known Gene for just as long. He is one of my favorite people in the vegan movement, exuding happiness and optimism. In his own words, this is how he measures the lifesaving work his nonprofit organization has been able to accomplish for animals:

"Beginning in 1986, we've worked to end the abuses of animal agriculture, saving individual animals from inhumane circumstances, as well as passing laws to lessen suffering and working to raise awareness and advance legal and corporate policies to encourage eating plants instead of animals," he told me when I interviewed him. "Over the decades, Farm Sanctuary and other shelters have rescued tens of thousands of farm animals from egregious suffering and provided them with peace and freedom at sanctuaries. Farm Sanctuary's efforts to restrict the slaughter of downed animals and to ban the confinement of calves, pigs, and hens in cages and crates where they can't even turn around is reducing the suffering of millions (including more than eighty million hens)."

Gene explained that in the 1990s Farm Sanctuary campaigned successfully to get Burger King to sell the BK Veggie nationwide. They now sell the (plant-based) Impossible Whopper, and in some parts of the world, such as in Germany, the Impossible Whopper accounts for 20 percent of all Whopper sales, according to Plant Based News. Options like these have made it easier and more convenient for consumers to eat plants instead of animals.

"I believe many consumer habits are encouraged and enabled by convenience," Gene said. "I also believe it's important for the food system to be reformed to make ethically produced foods more convenient and affordable. Part of creating a more resilient, transparent, and diversified food system involves connecting citizens more closely to the source of their food. This can help lessen the myriad harms that tend to come from a consolidated mass-production system when consumers unknowingly support practices that are in conflict with their values or interests."

Among their accomplishments, Farm Sanctuary has helped lessen animal suffering by getting 3 percent of sows out of gestation crates, which accounts for 180,000 of the 6 million breeding sows, and by getting 26 percent of laying hens out of battery cages, which amounts to 84.5 million of the 325 million commercial layer hens.[15]

Beyond the policy successes, Farm Sanctuary has played a huge part in opening the doors to hundreds, if not thousands, of other animal sanctuaries worldwide. The collective successes of those animal sanctuaries stands on the shoulders of the foundation that Gene and his cofounder laid when they found Hilda, a sheep left on a pile of dead animals, and rescued her from the stockyard in Lancaster, Pennsylvania.

Hilda would become the first Farm Sanctuary resident.

According to Farm Sanctuary, "Thrown just inches from a rotting carcass, flies and maggots were crawling all over her seemingly lifeless body. When she picked up her head, we lifted her into our van and rushed her to the nearest veterinarian. Hilda had collapsed because of the brutal transportation conditions—she was not suffering from any injuries or diseases. Twenty minutes after we arrived at the veterinary hospital, she stood up and started eating and drinking."

Hilda spent eleven years roaming the green pastures of Farm Sanctuary's New York shelter. During her life, she touched the hearts and minds of millions of people, from legislators and policymakers, to individuals who learned of Hilda's plight in dozens of national news stories, to visitors of all ages who met and learned through Hilda that farm animals feel pain or sorrow just like dogs or cats.

Hilda passed away peacefully in her sleep, dying from old age on September 25, 1997. She is buried in a beautiful garden grove on the farm, with a memorial plaque that will continue to reach and teach people for years to come.

I have been to Farm Sanctuary's cemetery, where Hilda and other residents have been buried, and I've never been able to walk away with a dry eye. I always take a few moments of silence to remember the lives rescued, the lives lived to their fullest, and the lives who have since passed on. It's a moving experience, and not that I need extra encouragement or reinforcement to continue on my vegan journey, but I do feel reinvigorated to make an even bigger difference for animals when I visit Farm Sanctuary, a model of my definition of effective vegan altruism for their dedication to making a continued difference and their commitment to pushing the movement forward.

I know that I am not alone in my appreciation. Many other vegans and non-vegans alike have felt inspired to create effective change for animals after seeing animals flourishing on the farm and being confronted with the cemetery remembering those who have passed. It is refreshing to see animals honored in that way, with cemetery stones and plaques, rather than being tossed in the trash and forgotten about. Memorialization normalizes compassion toward animals and reinforces that animal lives are important, just like human lives.

Whenever we're able to put animals in situations that many people associate with humans, we extend our hand of compassion with a wider reach. Decades ago, many people left their dogs outside, not allowing them in the house, and certainly not on their furniture. Today, dogs are not only in our homes and on our furniture, they often have their own furniture, their own toys, and, in some cases, their own wardrobes. Many dogs sleep in the same bed with us. We started to associate dogs as members of our family, and that provided dogs with better living conditions. The same is true for cats and birds, in many cases, and for a growing number of companion animals that we share our homes with today. It should also be true of cows, pigs, sheep, goats, chickens, turkeys, and other animals commonly found at shelters and often relegated to farmed life.

With Gene as perhaps the quintessential effective vegan altruist, focused on animals, not accolades, I'd like to reflect on his accomplishments for a moment. Farm Sanctuary has done a lot since 1986. As we've seen, a whole lot. Millions of animals have been spared, saved, and impacted directly because of Farm Sanctuary's commitment to their core belief of spreading kindness and compassion. It is no surprise that Farm Sanctuary's efforts have also impacted millions of people, encouraging them to open their hearts and minds to the beauty of what a compassionate future could look like for all animals, from everyday people to celebrities like Jon Stewart, whose wife, Tracey, read Gene's first book, *Farm Sanctuary: Changing Hearts and Minds About Animals and Food*, when it was left in a vacation rental where they stayed, leading them to contact Farm Sanctuary to learn how to start their own animal sanctuary; Ellen DeGeneres; Joan Jett; David Duchovny; the late Betty White; the late Mary Tyler Moore; Alicia Silverstone; Moby; Sarah Silverman; Rainn Wilson; and many other pillars in the animal rights movement.

The altruist in me is happy to share that "millions of animals have been impacted" and that "millions of people have been inspired by Farm Sanctuary to change the way they view animals," as Gene and his organization say, but the *effective* altruist in me wants to see the evidence for these huge numbers.

How do we measure the impact that Farm Sanctuary has year after year? Is their impact growing or shrinking? Show me the efficacy so I can decide if I can really throw my support behind Farm Sanctuary. What's the evidence that Farm Sanctuary does indeed make a significant impact? Thankfully, smart organizations like Farm Sanctuary have all of that data.

Here are some of Farm Sanctuary's 2021 highlights:

- 1,027 farmed animals received temporary or permanent sanctuary under their care
- 1,573 placement requests for 10,689 animals in need
- 163 lifesaving animal rescues
- 95 placements for animals through direct and referral adoptions
- 18,580 miles traveled to rescue, place, and/or transport animals
- 27,614 students engaged in their various missions
- 1,122 humane education presentations delivered
- 943 curriculums downloaded by educators
- 484 schools and summer camps served
- Expanded national program presence to 44 states, plus DC and Puerto Rico

And many more meaningful highlights, including their advocacy and outreach through the Farm Sanctuary community, which has the potential to impact a massive number of animals through corporate and legislative policies and winning legal battles to protect animals. Farm Sanctuary is encouraging state and federal legislatures to restrict factory farms and to encourage more just and compassionate plant-based agriculture. For example, they've endorsed the Farm System Reform Act, which, if passed, would mean no new large factory farms or expansion of existing factory farms; phasing out the largest factory farms by 2040; holding corporations responsible for pollution and other egregious harms; and $10 billion per year over ten years for farmers who transition out of factory farming.

Farm Sanctuary also claims that in 2021, 53,799 people took 80,918 actions to help animals through their various programs and campaigns. They reached an aggregate audience of 1.9 million people globally through their public awareness initiatives, and they had more than one million unique visitors to FarmSanctuary.org in 2021. On the social media front, they gained 207,447 new followers across the five major platforms, raising their new total to 1.7 million followers, while getting

15.9 million online engagements (likes, shares, comments) to wrap up the year.[16]

Having data like this, and much more, which is effectively shared in an impact report, helps us understand the efficacy of an organization, and to some degree, lets us know how our donation dollars are being put to use to help animals.

The more data an organization has to demonstrate the impact they are making, the more likely they are to be able to communicate their efficacy for helping animals to potential donors, as well as philanthropists and major financial contributors. As you can see from just some of the statistics that I shared from Farm Sanctuary's impact report, they were able to reveal the number of animals that were saved, rescued, or helped, as well as detail initiatives that are admittedly harder to quantify, such as education, research, legislation, and calls to action for potential policy changes.

At the end of the day, veganism is about doing the most good, and the implications of veganism extend to human and nonhuman animals, our forests, our rivers, our oceans, our air, and our planet at large. And by looking through the lens of effective vegan altruism, we can evaluate our advocacy and adjust in order to make the greatest difference and save the most lives. Use these altruistic examples, like Gene's Farm Sanctuary, and their effective impacts, to guide your desire to help animals in ways that matter most to you, and in the ways that make the biggest difference for those who are waiting for us to answer the call of solidarity and support. It takes nothing away from us to extend kindness and compassion to others. Today is a great day to change someone's life for the better.

Gene asks a simple, but profound question: "If we can live well without killing others, why wouldn't we?"

In the following chapters, you will read many more stories of effective vegan altruists as you explore how to become the most effective vegan altruist you can be. It is my hope that together we can change hearts, minds, menus, and meal plans, and help animals live and let live. To do that work, we must first be clear about our personal whys around veganism and advocacy.

CHAPTER 2

FUELING YOUR ADVOCACY

WHEN YOU FIND YOUR WHY, YOU'LL FIND YOUR WAY

"Today, more than 90 percent of the world's large animals are farm animals: cows, pigs, sheep, and chickens. Billions of animals with a rich world of feelings, emotions, sensations, needs, and fears pass their lives as machines for producing meat, milk, and eggs in industrial production lines. It is the responsibility of each and every one of us to be aware of the immense suffering that we humans are causing these animals and to do our best to reduce this suffering."
—Yuval Noah Harari, author of *Sapiens: A Brief History of Humankind*, from the foreword of *Why We Love Dogs, Eat Pigs, and Wear Cows* by Dr. Melanie Joy

Why be vegan in a world where the vast majority of people are not? That can be a hard question to answer, and a question that continually comes around on our vegan journey, which, like any journey, is not immune to doubt.

Whether you're trying to continue and deepen your dedication to veganism or looking to embark on a vegan lifestyle and start your journey, finding your *why* can be crucial.

I never lose sight of my why, despite obstacles the real world presents every day—from food marketing, to clothing, to everyday items that contain animal by-products. It is through my why that I have found meaning in staying the course. And it's your own personal why that I want to help you cultivate in this chapter.

I grew up on a farm, surrounded by animals that are typically turned into food, and I got to know them as individuals. Those unique experiences inspired me to avoid hurting animals or contributing to their suffering. I saw animals as individuals, not things, and it changed my life forever. It's been decades since I made my decision to dedicate my life to helping animals live better lives, and that is what drives my *why* to continue to help animals today.

Take a moment and consider your current relationship to veganism. What compelled you to change your lifestyle, to adopt a new way of thinking, and a new way of living? Sometimes our why is rooted in the ethical or moral—like not doing harm. Other times it has practical origins—the desire to not eat animals for personal health reasons. Other times, it comes from a place of planetary health—what can I, as an individual, do to alleviate planetary resource drain? Sometimes our whys come from a combination of motivations, as we'll see in several following examples.

VEGAN WAYS AND WHYS THAT LAST

It's easy to fall prey to temptations of highly processed, cheap, accessible animal foods. And it's easy to struggle with circumstantial amnesia. In fact, much of our capitalist society has been built on those very two things.

Simply put, by knowing why you *choose* to live a vegan lifestyle, and never forgetting it, even during times of temptation, you may soon discover that not only are you not tempted by the animal foods that used to dominate the space on your plate, but that you'll actually be repulsed and repelled by them once your nutritional and consumer program shifts to plants.

Once you have determined your why, your habits will reflect your priorities, and you will be on track to live in alignment with your authentic self.

But how do we do this?

Through small, consistent actions, we develop new habits, and those new habits become our new normal, our routines, and our second nature. Studies show that we're more likely to be successful when we take small, incremental steps, adapt to our new routines, and practice them daily.

If you want your vegan lifestyle to stick, you need to practice it consistently. Ultimately, if willpower fades (and it will), or your priorities change, or your moral perspectives are shifted, it is your consistent practice of vegan living that will help sustain a long-lasting commitment to reducing animal suffering. In essence, we are the sum of the actions that we most often take. Athletes exercise. Entrepreneurs work. Musicians play. Vegans eat plants. Your habits define you, so choose them wisely.

It also helps to know how an animal goes from living on a farm to ending up on your plate. When you understand that the only way for an animal to be turned into food is through slaughter, and that most animals we eat are babies who are just weeks or months old, it helps us make more compassionate choices for our meals, develop new taste preferences for plant-based foods, and encourages us to avoid the enticement of returning to old eating patterns. By aligning your moral compass with compassion, equipping yourself with plant-based nutritional knowledge, and developing a sense of our relationship with our planet—which actions, foods, beverages, products, practices, and resources contribute most to the erosion of the place we all call home—you can find a true vegan North Star.

WHAT MOTIVATES YOUR DESIRE TO CHANGE YOUR FOOD CHOICES TO HELP ANIMALS?

How does it make you feel to see a dog chained up in a yard for hours, days, weeks, or months on end? How do you react to someone kicking a cat or a dog? Do you feel the desire to join in and participate in the assault, or do you feel bad for the abuse that you are witnessing? What happens behind closed doors in large-scale factory farming is far worse than leaving a dog out in the cold, or kicking a cat, or the sheer neglect of an animal. It is unimaginably worse, and yet it goes on every second of every day, and many of us unknowingly support that cruelty by creating a demand for animal food products with our purchases of meat, milk, and eggs, and with our purchases of leather, wool, and fur, when there are countless cruelty-free alternatives.

Take a minute to think of an act of cruelty toward animals that you witnessed—whether violence, neglect, or even killing. Think of it for a moment, even just to honor that individual who was abused. Let it linger and pinball inside your head and heart long enough to recognize what you're feeling in this present moment. Do you feel happy or sad? Do you feel helpless or mad? Do you care at all, or do you feel nothing?

The reason I've asked you to recall abuse to an animal that you've witnessed is because most of the abuse that happens (on factory farms and in slaughterhouses) is out of sight and out of mind for almost every-one. As a result, we never pause and take a moment to think about what that individual is going through before they end up at the grocery store or on our plates.

Again, just let your mind drift away for a minute or two, forgetting about the pages you're reading or what is coming next. Reflect on some act of cruelty that made you feel something, whatever those feelings were, knowing that it is okay to have an emotional reaction to animal cruelty, and to embrace your true feelings. What was that experience like for you? How did it really make you feel?

Now, take another minute to recall an act of kindness toward an animal that you witnessed. Either a dog or cat being rescued from danger, a sea turtle getting a net removed from her body and returned to the ocean, a baby calf that was on his way to slaughter but was given a second chance to frolic in the pasture of an animal sanctuary, or an injured bird that has been rehabilitated and can fly again.

What acts of kindness have you witnessed being directed toward domesticated, farmed, or wild animals? Think of particular moments and an isolated incident to reflect upon right now. Relive that moment of kindness in your head and in your heart. Really feel it again in the present to the best of your ability. Close your eyes if it helps you bring this memory back to life. How does it make you feel to see kindness being offered to the most innocent and vulnerable among us? Do you feel happy or sad? Do you feel helpless or mad? Do you care at all, or do you feel nothing? What was that experience like for you? If you felt moved in any way, particularly if you felt moments of happiness or peace, understand that by living a vegan lifestyle in a non-vegan world, you can experience those feelings all the time.

LEARN TO HONOR YOUR WHY

Small, consistent actions can help us develop habits and help reinforce our why. But by recognizing our why as a sacred thing and honoring it, we can further cement our commitment.

The most rewarding decision I've made in my life was becoming vegan on December 8, 1995. I celebrate my vegan anniversary every bit as much as I celebrate my birthday or other yearly milestones, and I know that many of you do, too. We're not alone on this vegan journey, even if at times it can feel isolating. Know that there are millions of other people, just like you, who care for animals just like you do, and that compassion can prevail if we come together, support one another, and collectively push the vegan movement forward.

But how do we find the inspiration to live a vegan life in a non-vegan world without giving up hope? Part of it involves acknowledging the sad reality of factory farming and deciding to take a personal stand against it, while not letting it keep us depressed. It means finding joy *because* you are vegan, and in knowing that you are making a difference in the lives of others every single day. So let the reality of animal suffering be your fuel to promote kindness and compassion, knowing that your actions as a vegan advocate directly contribute to a reduction in animal suffering. That is how to keep moving forward, despite all the sad realities present in contemporary society.

It's also crucial to find community, realize that we have the power to change the world with our purchasing choices (more on that later), and to make sure to take the time to celebrate all the victories we see in support of animals. When major car companies decide to move away from leather interiors, that is a win for animals. When clothing and fashion brands do away with fur, that is another win for animals. Regardless of their intentions, which are almost always driven by profits, when McDonald's and Burger King offer vegan options worldwide, and prominently promote them to their customers, that, too, is a win for animals. We have to see it that way; otherwise, being vegan in a non-vegan world can feel lonely, depressing, and uninspiring. That's no way to power a movement forward.

So what will you do today to celebrate the day you became vegan, reinforce your why, and contribute to a kinder tomorrow for animals?

THE RISE AND REACH OF THE NUTRITIONAL WHY

Vegans are one of the fastest growing communities in the world.

Like many social justice movements that are deeply committed to changing the world, there are meaningful ethical and moral reasons why people choose to leave animals off their plates.

But there are also many very practical reasons that appeal to a mainstream audience, including the trend of reducing/eliminating animal protein for desired health improvement. You read that correctly. With all the deeply rooted compassionate, environmental, spiritual, and save-the-planet reasons to eat plants in place of animals, most of us are driven to a plant-based diet for health reasons, research shows.

To differentiate "vegan" from "plant-based," veganism takes a moral stance against animal exploitation, whereas plant-based refers to one's diet or eating habit. Veganism, therefore, is not a diet (though it is often lumped into the "diet" category in grocery stores, in bookstores, online, and in conversation), but rather a philosophical way of living.

Why would people be drawn to a vegan lifestyle because of health reasons? At the time of this writing, the act of eating animals contributes to a greater number of lifestyle-related deaths, increased likelihood of early mortality, and more exorbitant health care costs than any other action we take.[17] Furthermore, consider that potentially deadly viruses are often connected by animal exploitation (swine flu, avian bird flu, etc.) and we arrive at another practical point in support of veganism.

But for now, the Standard American Diet (or Standard Western Diet) is our greatest health nemesis. For the first time in decades, the US life expectancy is declining, from an average age of 78 down to 76 today. The two-and-a-half-year drop in life expectancy from 2020 to 2021 was the largest two-year reduction in US life span since the 1920s, according to the Centers for Disease Control and Prevention (CDC). Michelle Williams, the dean of the Harvard T.H. Chan School of Public Health, explained a primary driver in the decline of US life expectancy when she said, "Where we are different than other high-income countries is that we emphasize rescue care, acute care at the expense of investing in, supporting, and enabling health promotion and disease prevention."[18]

Many people who have eaten a Western diet for years, with the majority of their caloric intake coming from animals and animal by-products, and have found themselves to be obese, diabetic, hypertensive, or on the verge of cancer or a cardiac event, have been drawn to a plant-based diet that is free of dietary cholesterol, loaded with fiber, vitamins, minerals, antioxidants, and phytonutrients, while also being low in calorie density and high in nutrient density. Once people are introduced to plant-based nutrition, they often discover a name commonly associated with it, which is "vegan," and explore more about what veganism entails. Eventually many of them get on board for the animals and environment.

Many, but not all. There are millions of people who eat a plant-based diet for health without moral or ethical concerns for animals and still continue to wear (and buy) leather and fur, and who might find joy in circuses, zoos, and rodeos. They only choose not to eat animals to keep their body fat or their cholesterol lower than they might otherwise be, or to reduce the risk of health concerns connected to eating animal fat and protein. That's the nutritional *why* for a lot of people who end up as "vegans."

But what about the rest of us?

The most compelling reason to be vegan, from a global perspective, is to help the survival of our planet by using fewer resources and contributing to lower amounts of greenhouse gas emission, methane production, overall pollution, and excessive land and water use.

That leads us to the most common reason that people come to a vegan lifestyle and *stay* vegan for the long haul: for ethical and moral whys, often grouped under the name of animal rights.

In fact, one could make the case that really the *only* true argument in favor of veganism is an ethical argument. After all, you could easily eat a 95 percent plant-based diet with 5 percent of calories coming from animals and still live a very long and healthy life with nearly all of the health and nutritional benefits of a fully plant-based diet.

While the preservation of our planet is still a complicated pursuit, with so many varying viewpoints from experts as to what planet Earth can and cannot withstand and for how much longer, the ethical stance that it is wrong to kill innocent animals, who are sentient beings like us, is the one that sticks for so many people, myself included.

A brief note on the particular language here: Many people adopt a *plant-based* diet for potential health improvements; after a doctor's recommendation; from a friend's suggestion; after reading a book, watching a documentary, or reading a news story; after hearing about it by word of mouth; or from numerous other sources. But the motivations aren't always the same. When you survey established *vegans* about their motivations for making the change, the clear answer is "for the animals." But if you survey *plant-based dieters* about their motivations behind their lifestyle, they will say it's "for their health." Here are a few examples to illustrate. A 2019 global survey for "Why People Go Vegan,"[19] conducted by VOMAD, with 12,814 participants from 97 countries, revealed that participants' main reasons for going vegan were the following:

- 68.1 percent for the animals
- 17.4 percent for health
- 9.7 percent for the environment
- 4.8 percent for other

Yet another survey, by Statista, showed the leading motivations that led people to take part in Veganuary (the world's largest and most popular vegan challenge program which takes place during the month of January every year) worldwide in 2022[20] were:

- 44 percent for animals
- 21 percent for personal health
- 19 percent for the environment
- 7 percent for a change/challenge/curiosity
- 5 percent for global health (pandemics)
- 2 percent for a friend/partner/family member
- 1 percent for other

In contrast, a 2021 Faunalytics study showed that a person's journey to going "vegetarian or vegan" was motivated by the following factors:[21]

- 42 percent for health
- 20 percent for animal protection
- 20 percent for other
- 18 percent for environmental concerns

This Faunalytics study had only 222 participants, all of whom were brand-new vegans, or in the process of transitioning to veganism or vegetarianism, but it is an interesting juxtaposition to the previous studies, nonetheless. Another survey, conducted by researchers at Yale, asked respondents questions about whether they were "willing to adopt plant-based diets," and all respondents rated their health as the top concern (above "how companies affect the environment," "global warming," and "protecting animals").[22]

When the wording is changed from motivations to become "vegan" to motivations for adopting "plant-based diets" or "going vegan or vegetarian," as you might suspect, the leading motivation tends to be for personal health, which has been determined through multiple independent surveys, including ones I have conducted. You get different survey results

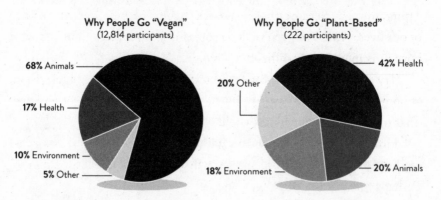

Motivations for Adopting a Vegan Lifestyle or Plant-Based Diet

Why People Go "Vegan"
(12,814 participants)

68% Animals
17% Health
10% Environment
5% Other

Why People Go "Plant-Based"
(222 participants)

42% Health
20% Other
18% Environment
20% Animals

based on how people identify. At the end of the day, what matters most to animals is a human's *actions*, not their motivations.

> At the end of the day, what matters most to animals is a human's *actions*, not their motivations.

WE'RE CONDITIONED TO BE NON-VEGAN

Most people eat meat because most people enjoy meat. Beyond questions of taste, cost, and convenience, there are cultural and culinary traditions, religious beliefs, societal pressures, habitual patterns, geographical influences, and many other factors wrapped up in our conscious or unconscious decision-making process of determining what's for dinner.

Associations with masculinity, power, and being "at the top of the food chain" are also contributors to our insatiable desire to eat animals. Individual and family economics, aggressive marketing by the animal agriculture industry, food deserts with limited access to fresh produce, and the conditioning we've had since we were born drive that behavior as well. For many of us, the foods available within the public school system shaped our views about food, and conditioned our palates to prefer eating animals, because those were the habits we built over the course of our lives. And when you've done something essentially since you were born, it is increasingly difficult to change.

Try going thirty days without watching a single minute of television, at home, at restaurants, at airports, or anywhere else you might find one. That might be easy for some people.

How about going thirty days without using the internet? No social media, no online searching, no access to Wi-Fi whatsoever for a month. Perhaps that is still doable for some.

How about not using your smartphone for thirty days? No calls, no texts, no photos, no use whatsoever. That's hard, right? Why?

Because you've become conditioned to use your phone, or the internet, or television, and your world revolves around those applications, just as your world revolves around the types of foods you have been eating your entire life. But many of those temptations are often a requirement for work—checking email, being on call, and needing devices to give us directions so we can navigate through life. We don't *need* animal foods for our jobs or to get us through the day, and those eating habits can be changed and improved from a health and environmental perspective by switching to plants.

It is here that moral and practical whys can meet with tremendous power.

So how hard would it be to go without eating animals for a month? It's a lot easier than you think, especially once you learn more about nutrition and which foods to consume in place of meat, milk, eggs, and other animal by-products.

At the end of the day, in order for a plant-based diet and vegan life-style to stick, you're going to have to enjoy the taste of the food you eat, or else you'll revert back to previous, comforting patterns. That's why it's not only important to understand why you're motivated to reduce animal suffering, but also understand and experience the vast range of flavors, textures, and satisfaction that come from plant-based foods. Whether it's traditional health food such as salads, smoothies, stir-fried vegetables, or burrito bowls, or plant-based versions of cheeseburgers, milkshakes, loaded fries, chicken sandwiches, or Buffalo wings, all of those and much more can be prepared without causing unnecessary animal suffering.

Nearly one hundred million people worldwide at present time have chosen to live a vegan lifestyle. It's an influential community that is impacting the supply and demand of foods offered around the world. This trend isn't going anywhere soon, and veganism is growing rapidly, for good reason. Living compassionately is rewarding. Living healthfully has numerous physical, emotional, and psychological benefits. Making a difference in the world is intrinsically fulfilling, and being part of a like-minded community enriches lives.

If one hundred million people can find their why and give up eating animals for much longer than thirty days, you can as well.

WHY IN ACTION: TONI OKAMOTO

Of the approximately one hundred million people who follow a plant-based diet or identify as vegan, I suspect there are thousands who were initially inspired to do so, or are motivated to continue eating plants, as a result of the influence of longtime vegan, and author of *Plant-Based on a Budget*, Toni Okamoto. Her book title is also the name of the brand she has built, which, through her website and social media platforms, shows readers how to affordably eat a healthy, plant-based diet. All the while, she supports her audience and provides them with tools to help them sustain long-term veganism, including recommended cooking supplies, books, apps, and other resources—and, of course, plenty of tasty recipes.

Toni has amassed an online audience of more than a million followers, giving her significant influence, particularly in the plant-based cooking community. She is also very clear about her own *why* to become, and stay, vegan.

"I spent many years of my life working at a farmed animal sanctuary and a vegan advocacy charity before pursuing Plant-Based on a Budget as my full-time career," she told me. "What drives me each day is a desire to help slash the number of animals used for food. Animals tend to be pretty bad off in any human society, and that's one reason why I'm so passionate about market choices that make it easier for people to do the right thing, while giving them the tools to help them succeed."

In addition to understanding our own *why* for our vegan lifestyle, and taking actions based on those driving forces, we also have to meet people where they are if we hope to grow this movement to perhaps hundreds of millions of vegans, or maybe someday, billions of people choosing to eat plants rather than animals.

"It's great to talk about animal protection and climate change," Toni added, "but we should remember what really motivates people's food choices. They want food that tastes great and that they can afford. That's the whole premise of my books and my social media posts: you can enjoy foods you love, and at food costs you're going to love, too. Through my social media platform, I reach hundreds of thousands of people each week with positive messages about plant-based eating. And every day I hear from people who've cut back or totally eliminated their animal consumption."

Toni's friend, colleague, podcast cohost, and coauthor of *The Friendly Vegan Cookbook*, Michelle Cehn, also has a platform of more than one million followers with her World of Vegan brand. Together, they make plant-based eating tasty, affordable, accessible, and fun, which does a great service for animals. If these two authors and podcast hosts reach millions of people with their compassionate message, imagine what the future of veganism could be mere years from now as more people embrace their own *whys* for leaning into a vegan lifestyle, including people of influence.

Animal exploitation is all around us, but the more aware of it that we become, the more compassionate choices we can make in the future. Most of us don't have a clue how cosmetics get made, or how body care products or medicines are tested on animals, or how animal bones, skin, and tendons are used to produce gelatin, which is found in common food products. Whether you're already aware of the inherent cruelty wrapped up in the production of many products we use regularly or you're learning about some of them for the first time, you can feel empowered knowing you have the ability to choose more compassionate items and contribute to less cruelty.

Doing so is often as simple as selecting a different item on the shelf in the store, or picking an alternative menu item at the restaurant, looking for a "cruelty-free" or "not tested on animals logo" on a package, or searching for a vegan certification symbol on any product. Over time, you'll automatically know which brands and which products are more aligned with your inner compassion as a result of taking those easy measures to investigate the level of cruelty associated with any purchase.

As Toni and Michelle are doing with food, we can close that gap between ourselves and the products we use by asking questions, learning from others, and questioning the status quo to create a greater demand for the types of products we will proudly support. When it comes to other forms of animal exploitation and abuse, many of us perhaps haven't been to a zoo, a rodeo, a bullfight, or a place like SeaWorld to observe animals stuck in captivity for their entire lives and tortured for our entertainment. But we can relate on some level to being stuck at home, stuck in our car in traffic, or stuck in an office, and how unpleasant that can be, even for mere hours, let alone an entire lifetime.

This is the first time in history that a movement has been started to liberate an oppressed group, when the oppressed group cannot speak for themselves and must rely on their oppressors to speak up for them in order for the movement to take hold. Some activists have described it as a "moral emergency," with a pressing necessity to speak for those who can't speak for themselves.

Consider that scenario for a moment. Unlike slavery, or the oppression of women, gay or transgender individuals, or any other oppressed human group, not only can animals not speak on their own behalf, but they must wait for their oppressors to decide to go against their own personal interests and speak up for them. This makes for an incredible uphill battle for an animal's quest for liberation. They are completely beholden to you and me to take action and to do something on their behalf.

Humans are inconsistent in our behavior toward other animals, and we label some as good, bad, scary, or those worthy of our consideration of not intentionally harming them. Why do many of us feel justified in killing cows but not dogs? Or are okay with eating chickens but not cats? How and where else do we draw the line? It's fine to eat tuna, but not whales? Salmon are on the menu, but we leave dolphins off because they perform tricks and appear to be more like us in their ability to communicate. We perceive horses as beautiful, and tend to treat them well with no desire to eat them, but sheep and goats don't get the same considerations, and we eat them. We step on spiders and ants without thinking twice about it, but give a pass to turtles, and we tend to view ladybugs as cute.

Of course, there are also legal influences of animal abuse, and social and real-world consequences to abusing particular animals, which guides some of our behavior. We get upset when people hunt lions and tigers, but not when they hunt deer and elk. We might even cry when seeing an image of a dead giraffe or elephant, shot by poachers or big game hunters, but we put the heads or skins of other animals we shot on the walls of our homes for all to see.

It seems rather obvious that every animal, regardless of species, has a desire to live a life free of fear, pain, and suffering as much as possible. No being wants to suffer. We all want the chance to live our whys.

As we move into the next chapter, looking at how we can put our privilege, resources, skills, and selves into better service, consider these ten steps to better understand your daily actions, to reduce animal suffering through new routines and habits, and to discover your personal why:

1. Ask yourself why you're vegan, and answer your question sincerely.
2. Evaluate your actions to see if they are in alignment with your why.
3. What measurable differences do you make in the world around you?
4. How can you spread veganism in your community?
5. What are the most common obstacles you see to embracing veganism among your friends and family?
6. Most people do particular things (such as eat animals) because other people do them, too, and they become normalized in our society. What actions will you do differently?

7. What thirty-day challenge can you incorporate into your lifestyle?

8. In what ways will you inspire others to consider veganism for themselves?

9. How does living a compassionate, vegan lifestyle enrich your life?

10. Why are nonhuman animals worthy of our consideration?

CHAPTER 3

IDENTIFYING YOUR RESOURCES

USE YOUR STRENGTHS TO HELP OTHERS

"Just being vegan is so useful in terms of society, because when you exercise that muscle of empathy towards a voiceless group, animals, it means that every time you sit down to eat a meal, you're forcing yourself to look beyond your own selfish wants, out to the bigger picture. And as the wider world emerges to you, you can see that it's something worth your attention and something connected to what you do."
—Kerry McCarthy, animal rights activist

As we discussed earlier, veganism is not about purity or perfection, regardless of whether purists or perfectionists try to convince you otherwise. Veganism is about reducing animal cruelty, and we do that through conscious efforts, whether it is food choices and/or our clothing, cosmetics, entertainment (animals in captivity), and other purchases we make every day.

If we continue to financially support the oppression and suffering of animals through our habits, behaviors, purchases, and desires for particular foods or clothing, we will continue to see animals suffer. But if we vote with our dollars, and put our financial and other efforts toward compassionate, cruelty-free foods, clothing, and entertainment, we send a message that we're not going to support exploitation. When enough people stand up and say, "No more," this is when change happens.

I've been vegan for so long that I remember when there were very few non-dairy milk options, primarily soy and rice milk, from merely a handful of brands. Fast-forward just a couple of decades later, and many mainstream grocery stores have about a 50/50 split of dairy and non-dairy beverage options in the "dairy" section.

Furthermore, the actual sales figures reveal a massive rise in non-dairy milks, cheeses, and other product sales, and a stark decline in animal-based dairy food sales.[23]

I've also been vegan long enough to recall when there were just a few brands offering alternatives to meat, and they weren't always inspiring, though their effort was greatly appreciated. But today, as a result of tens or even hundreds of millions of vegans, vegetarians, flexitarians, and vegan allies purchasing plant-based meat products over the years, meat alternatives are a multiple-billion–dollar industry that even the meat industry wants in on. While the world's largest food companies are jumping on board because of economics rather than compassion, the end result is the same: a reduction in animal cruelty and butchery, and an increase in popularity for more sustainable plant-based and alternative protein options.

We see that the influence of our money is powerful. But it's only a fraction of the power we really have at our disposal to wield as advocates.

You have so much more to offer others than just your financial resources. Though monetary donations and financial resources tend to dominate the mainstream effective altruism conversations, there are some strikingly impactful ways to help animals by using your skills, talents, resources, connections, and time. In this chapter, we'll explore some of the most effective approaches to reducing animal suffering while using resources that you very likely have at your fingertips, waiting to be deployed. These include leveraging your personal audience to benefit animals, speaking up and leading by positive example, and volunteering your time—none of which require an exact talent or skill set, such as writing effective articles, making persuasive videos that go viral, or creating your own business—though those could be part of your contribution.

I'll also walk you through some examples of approaches that I have taken, using effective vegan altruism as my guide to reducing animal suffering, without relying on financial donations to effective charities. As you'll see with many of my examples, these are actions that nearly all of us can take anytime to make a significant impact for animals.

BE A STRONG V

Consider the following categories and think of your own capabilities in these areas:

Skills

Talents

Resources

Other strengths

Network

Generosity

Volunteering

You can think of this list as STRONG V for "Strong Vegan." When we make use of our inner Strong Vegan capabilities, we can do amazing things for animals. What comes to mind when you think of yourself and your abilities in these areas? The next question to answer is: How can you use your strengths to help animals? I'll answer these questions for myself so you can get an idea of how to identify your own strengths and apply them to animal advocacy.

First, let's define STRONG V:

Skills: Abilities that you learned through practice, such as speaking a foreign language, cooking, and photography, as well as many job-related skills such as graphic design, computer programming, accounting, nursing, public speaking, and most things that we go to school to learn. Character traits, such as perseverance and grit, can be categorized as skills or talents, as some personal traits could be intrinsic, while others are learned.

Talents: Abilities you were born with and that come naturally to you, such as singing, athleticism, critical thinking, problem solving, communication, and creativity.

Resources: Things you have access to, such as information, money, technology, materials, tools, energy, time, and other physical and intellectual items.

Other strengths: Natural or learned abilities such as leadership, teamwork, resilience, social skills, time management, empathy, emotional intelligence, and active listening.

Network: Your connections, audience, friends, family, colleagues, customers, clients, mentors, and other associates that comprise your overall community.

Generosity: The ways in which you altruistically give of yourself to help others, in the form of financial contributions, donations of items with monetary value, physical products and intellectual property, and myriad other forms of giving, from emotional support to expressing gratitude.

Volunteering: The time you allocate solely for giving, without expecting anything in return, such as volunteering at an animal rescue, a sanctuary, a soup kitchen, or helping someone with a project, teaching someone a new skill, or championing a campaign that you believe in.

Leveraging your Strong Vegan capabilities is something you can do every day to help animals, but first, you have to identify those capabilities. It's not always easy, because it's a form of honestly evaluating your core skills and talents, the resources you have, and the time you give to others.

So be honest when you make your own list. Your unique set of capabilities will play a role in making the world a better place for others, and you need to know what assets you're working with. To help you in generating that list, I'll run through some examples for inspiration of how I effectively use my Strong Vegan capabilities to help animals.

WHEN VEGANISM COMES TO DINNER

Requesting vegan menu items at non-vegan establishments could have a more profound impact than you might initially suspect. Consider my dinner theater example. My wife and I are season ticket holders at a Broadway-style dinner theater performing arts center.

When my wife and I attended our first musical at the theater, we noticed that there wasn't even a single vegan menu item. We had to make substitutions and modify the singular vegetarian option just so we could enjoy our meal. The meals were often so low in calories, typically just an assortment of vegetables, that my wife would bring baked tofu in a plastic resealable container, stuffed in her purse, so we could have something more substantial and not be hungry throughout the four-hour production.

There are comment cards on the table at our venue, so each time we would go we would politely and constructively comment on the lack of vegan options, while also requesting vegan menu options for ourselves and for other patrons to enjoy. We also met with the theater manager in person, praising the theater, the venue, and the entertainment, while also requesting vegan options face-to-face, in addition to the comment cards. After attending just a couple of shows, we became season ticket holders. At that point, we got to know the theater manager a bit better because, after all, now we were committed and paid in advance for a whole year's worth of shows, and she spent more time talking with us.

By the time the next musical was onstage, a couple of months later, we showed up and, sure enough, there was a dedicated vegan entrée on the menu for three hundred people to choose from nightly. When we saw that, we were ecstatic, and we thanked the theater manager. That night, while she was doing her announcements just before the show started, she expressed to the audience the value of the comment cards and that they take the comments seriously. Then she looked over at me and my wife and said something along the lines of, "Because our season ticket holders over there, who are vegans, filled out a comment card requesting vegan options on the menu, we listened, and we now serve vegan options every night. That's how seriously we take your feedback."

Not only did they add a vegan entrée to the menu, but over the months, as we continued to provide feedback, the vegan entrée became more substantial, more appealing, and more popular. Furthermore, veganism was mentioned positively in front of a group of three hundred people, and perhaps the theater manager mentioned that same story other nights when we weren't there, reaching potentially thousands of people, letting them know that vegan food is available due to an increase in demand.

This positive result didn't cost us anything but our time and effort, which was minimal, since we were already season ticket holders, and it just took a few minutes to fill out a comment card and have brief conversations with the theater manager. Now, we get to enjoy a hearty vegan entrée every time we visit our northern Colorado dinner theater. We also invite friends and family, hoping that their selection of the vegan menu item will send a message that there is indeed a demand for it.

In this example, we used our communication skills, our writing, our friendliness, and our relationship-building characteristics to persuade the dinner theater to permanently add vegan items to their menu.

BECOMING A VEGAN
COACH OR MENTOR

Though having a vegan coach certainly isn't a requirement to thrive as a vegan, it could be helpful in myriad ways. Just like in many other areas of life, having a coach could be incredibly useful in your quest to get the most out of your experience. Many of us grew up with coaches in one form or another—often associated with sports, music, or art. Many of my closest friends today are coaches, and most of them are vegan coaches, primarily in the health and fitness industry. If you're already vegan, chances are you would be a great candidate to be a vegan coach, or receive mentorship from a vegan coach to learn how to become a coach yourself.

Becoming a vegan coach or mentor for another vegan or aspiring vegan doesn't cost you anything but your time and effort, but it could make a difference between that person leaving veganism behind or staying vegan for the long haul. Furthermore, you can make a good living as a vegan coach, as many of my colleagues have done and are currently doing. There are many different areas of coaching, from a general vegan lifestyle coach, to a vegan health and fitness coach, to a vegan business coach, to chefs, nutritionists, and other types of teachers and mentors who span the spectrum of expertise. Some vegans are experts in film-making, photography, finance, yoga, massage therapy, travel, business, event planning, and other areas, and regardless of your particular talent, skill, background, education, or interest, there is likely something that you can teach others that will help them stay on the vegan path.

I also want to make it clear that there is no shame in hiring a coach even if you're a seasoned vegan. As a vegan of nearly thirty years, I learn from vegan coaches, trainers, mentors, and experts all the time, and I seek out their services to help me in one area of life or another—including during the process of writing this book, which was supported by the help of multiple editors. Though I'm a former champion vegan athlete, and literally wrote the book on the subject (*The Plant-Based*

Athlete), I still, at times, seek out a vegan fitness coach to help me stay on track. Excelling at anything in life takes hard work, and having a supportive coach in your corner could prove to be highly impactful in your quest to master veganism or just to support you in an area of your practice where you're struggling.

If some of your strong characteristics are confidence, leadership, empathy, communication, enthusiasm, support, creativity, motivation, and inspiration, then your natural abilities could make you an outstanding coach, which is a way to contribute to growing the vegan movement while reducing animal suffering. There are plenty of vegan coaching certification programs, offered by many nonprofit organizations. You can earn a certificate in plant-based nutrition from Dr. T. Colin Campbell's online plant-based nutrition course from eCornell, Victoria Moran's Main Street Vegan Academy, John Oberg's social media advocacy courses, or Melanie Joy's effective vegan advocacy courses.

There are plenty of other places to look for certification, which is beneficial for credibility, safety, and furthering your knowledge base. But none of those certifications are even required to be a vegan coach. Perhaps you're already a certified personal trainer, a licensed nutritionist, a trained chef, or an expert or knowledgeable in other areas, and you happen to be an experienced vegan, too. That's enough to coach others along their vegan journey, and it could be a highly rewarding path to take as a career or as a side project.

VOLUNTEERING AND FUNDRAISING TO HELP RESCUED ANIMALS

We've already learned about the groundbreaking work that Farm Sanctuary has done to pave the way for thousands of animal sanctuaries to follow in their footsteps. Sanctuaries play an important role in giving people an opportunity to view animals differently, often for the first time, seeing cows as individuals, rather than burgers, and seeing pigs as intelligent and playful animals, rather than bacon. Any time you have the opportunity to meet your food while it's still alive can help influence your perspective about animals, and about food.

Animal sanctuaries often (essentially always) rely on fundraising and donations because they're not selling the animals to profit off them. Quite the contrary, they're actually investing lots of money into veterinary care, food, housing, and other resources for the duration of animals' lives, which, for some animals, could be ten to twenty years.

In order for animal sanctuaries to stay open, to continue to rescue animals, to provide care for them to live out their lives in peace, to keep up with veterinary support and large food bills, and to continue their education to the general public, they require lots of financial support. They also need to pay for their land, their staff, their equipment, and other overhead expenses. In addition to volunteering in various capacities, such as helping take care of animals, or performing farm chores, there are many ways that you can effectively use your skills, talents, and resources to help animal sanctuaries, animal shelters, and rescue operations raise funds.

Almost all animal sanctuaries offer the possibility to sponsor an animal with a monthly or yearly payment to directly support an individual animal that you'll know by name and have the opportunity to visit in person or to learn about on social media or via animal sanctuary websites. This is an effective way for sanctuaries to keep revenue coming in. If you have a business, your business could sponsor animals as well. Many people adopt turkeys around Thanksgiving, for example, even if they live thousands of miles away from a particular animal sanctuary, but want their donation to make a difference for a specific animal.

Sanctuaries also host events, which are effective in many ways, from fundraising, to getting hundreds or even thousands of people to their farm to raise awareness and inspire people to view animals as friends, not food. There are plenty of themed events, from formal galas, to Mother's and Father's Day events, to guest speaker series, to summer carnivals with rides and games. Those types of events help bring in important funds to keep sanctuaries operational, while also providing education and inspiration. All you have to do to help make a difference is pro-mote the events, attend some of them, and share photos and videos of your experiences.

One of the strategies that animal sanctuaries deploy is getting sup-port from wealthy donors and celebrities. Famous animal activists like Moby and Joaquin Phoenix have helped bring awareness and financial resources to the important work animal sanctuaries do. Some celebrities write seven-figure checks to animal sanctuaries and other animal charity groups. If that's not in your budget, don't worry; it's not in mine either, but there is still a lot we can do to help fundraise for animals.

My friends at The Vegan Gym (an online vegan personal train-ing company that you'll read about later on) recently hosted a pull-up challenge at the world's largest vegan festival, the Los Angeles Vegan Street Fair. For every pull-up completed by festivalgoers who partici-pated in the challenge, The Vegan Gym donated one dollar to Farm Sanctuary. Throughout the course of the day, festival attendees com-pleted a combined 3,557 pull-ups, raising more than $3,500 in a single day for Farm Sanctuary. Furthermore, that same group volunteered with a team of twenty vegan athletes at the Farm Sanctuary farm, doing work that included removing downed trees from flash floods in Southern California.

One of the ways that I personally support animal sanctuaries is by giving guest presentations at them, drawing a crowd that often ends up buying merchandise and donating to the sanctuary in one way or another. I also donate all my book sales after my presentation to the sanctuary. I sign books and ship them to animal sanctuaries or drop signed books off in person for sanctuaries that are within a driving distance from my house in northern Colorado. I donate other items as well, like vegan fitness-themed apparel, magazines, and vegan foods and sports supplements that can all be resold for profits by the sanctuaries. I also make cash donations and buy from the gift shop essentially every time I visit a sanctuary. I have quite the collection of sanctuary hats and T-shirts by now!

Aside from donating funds and raising awareness, which is primarily what we've touched on so far, there are also opportunities to volunteer and do some farm work to help the animal sanctuary staff, and the animals. Sanctuaries can always use volunteers to do everything from cleaning out animal stalls, to moving equipment around, to feeding and watering animals, to countless odd jobs that need to be completed on a daily basis. My friend and fellow vegan weight lifter Doug Tice volunteers his time and strength at Aimee's Farm Animal Sanctuary in the suburbs of Phoenix, Arizona.

If you're not inclined to do farm work, or don't live near an animal sanctuary, there are plenty of other ways to volunteer. You could run campaigns and raise money by seeking donations at your school, your place of work, and within your community. On your birthday, if you celebrate, in lieu of gifts, you can request that your family and friends make a donation to an animal charity in your name. You could create art of any kind to sell and donate the proceeds to an animal charity. You could volunteer your services for skills like web design, marketing, advertising, photography, videography, administration, and more, to help an animal charity save on their overhead costs. I'm sure you can think of plenty of ways to use your varied skills and talents to volunteer for animal charity organizations in ways that make an impactful difference.

In 2022, I attended an annual gala celebration at Luvin Arms Animal Sanctuary, which sits in the shadows of the majestic Rocky Mountains, about half an hour northwest of Denver. Knowing there would be a silent auction for attendees to bid on, leading up to the event, I recruited thousands of dollars' worth of donated products from numerous companies I work with. Indeed, those donated items, including apparel, sports nutrition products, vegan restaurant gift cards, and plenty of books, raised thousands of dollars for Luvin Arms. It didn't cost me anything to recruit those products, yet it yielded thousands of dollars in fundraising for the sanctuary. I simply used to my advantage my connections, my network, and my communication skills to arrange the donations, which was done in a matter of minutes, by sending emails to my contacts.

Not only was there a silent auction with bidding that lasted for a few hours, there was also a live auction with items to bid on such as weeklong vacations in rental houses in exotic places like beach towns in Mexico, which were donated by friends, family, and supporters of the animal sanctuary. Attendees can assume that they're going to be paying above retail value for nearly every auction item, knowing that the objective of the fundraising event is to raise as much money as possible in a single evening. But it's also a feel-good experience where you get to go home with something desirable while you make your winning auction bid. It's a win-win situation for all. Imagine going on your $5,000 trip to Mexico, knowing that you're not paying a major corporate hotel, but that 100 percent of your lodging expense went directly to helping rescued animals. The vacation is really just the bonus for many people, as you will likely find even more satisfaction in knowing that your donation is helping others.

Luvin Arms set the audacious goal of raising $200,000 over the course of just a few hours that evening. They ended up surpassing their goal because of the many resources that were donated to them for supporters like me, my wife, and two hundred other attendees to bid on. My wife and I walked away with a number of auction items we "won" by having the highest bid, knowing full well we likely paid way over retail price. By leveraging the collective skills, talents, resources, and connections of their community, Luvin Arms was able to have a lively auction with a professional auctioneer (who volunteered his time for the cause), and a professional audience of people who paid $150 per person to attend (knowing the ticket price was also part of the fundraising effort), ensuring that by the end of the night they raised nearly a quarter of a million dollars for their farm animal sanctuary. It was a collective effort, and each contribution counted.

Now, imagine if they had more auction items donated, or had increased the capacity of their audience by just 25 percent. That combination would likely raise an additional $100,000. It got me thinking about the following year's gala, and I decided to dedicate just a small fraction of my spare time to recruiting auction items over the course of months, rather than only spending a few weeks recruiting items as I had previously done. And sure enough, that effort at the 2023 Luvin Arms annual gala helped raise many thousands more dollars that went to lifesaving efforts to feed, house, and take care of rescued farmed animals. It helped Luvin Arms educate the general public all year long about the plight of farmed animals, leading to an increased awareness in veganism and an overall decrease in animal suffering. After having attended my first Luvin Arms gala, I recognized that, though my donations of $20 and $30 books are helpful, I could be substantially more effective by getting high ticket items donated, such as months of free vegan coaching from The Vegan Gym and other vegan coaching programs, worth potentially thousands of dollars, which is precisely what I focused on. Every auction item counts, but some provide a far greater return than others, and that's where I put my energy for the auction the following year, and that's the approach that I will take with each ensuing gala, holding aspirations of helping Luvin Arms (and other sanctuaries) raise perhaps more than a million dollars in a single evening.

Luvin Arms relied on their network of people like me, and in turn, I called upon my contacts and my community to donate valuable items to be auctioned off, and collectively, it helped spare animals from suffering. This is something anyone can do, since we all have our own networks and resources to draw from. You are probably better connected than you realize, and surely you know people who are business owners, company managers, skilled laborers, artists, or others who have access to products and services that you could recruit in ways that help animals. Consider using your own skills, talents, resources, and connections to contribute to fundraising efforts for animal charities in similar ways.

MORE FOOD FOR THOUGHT

Here are some additional ideas from friends in the vegan community to help inspire you:

The company Complement, cofounded by my friends Matt Frazier and Matt Tullman, partnered with One Tree Planted to plant a tree for every plant-based nutrition product they sold. They planted thousands of trees during this partnership. That not only helps us, and our planet, it provides a habitat for animals and insects, too.

More recently, Complement donated tens of thousands of plant-based meals to kids in need, through their initiative of donating one meal per product sold, with the audacious goal of donating more than one million plant-based meals to underserved youth communities. This introduces plant-based nutrition to children, while also sparing animals that might have otherwise been consumed as food.

Complement is just one company that embraces effective vegan altruism by giving back to help animals. They rely on their large community of subscribers, customers, and online followers to make this endeavor possible. They tap into their own altruistic motivations and apply skillful and persuasive writing to get this initiative off the ground. Through their connections they establish partnerships, and because of the size of their network, and their general favorability among their audience, they are able to produce impressive results. They know what their strengths are, and they lean into them to make a positive impact for animals and our planet.

Next Level Burger, a 100 percent organic vegan national burger chain, runs numerous campaigns all throughout the year to contribute to supporting sustainable food practices. During the holidays, for example, they have a vegan turkey sandwich called the Gobbler, which they offer for the entire month of November. For every Gobbler sold, they donate one to a local food pantry, providing plant-based meals for those in need. Since animal products are some of the cheapest and most heavily subsidized food sources, many people in need would otherwise be consuming low-grade fast food, such as chicken nuggets, wings, and burgers.

Next Level Burger is committed to giving back all year round with various themes advertised throughout the year, not just during the holidays. They also donate gift cards to animal charity fundraising events and host events at their restaurants that raise funds and awareness of large-scale animal production, while offering solutions such as eating plants instead of animals.

With their national presence, serving thousands of customers daily, Next Level Burger is able to call upon a variety of strengths including marketing, advertising, relationship-building, local partnerships, national media coverage, generosity, and their inherent altruism to give back in meaningful ways that serve their mission, while helping spare animals.

Holistic Holiday at Sea, founded by Sandy Pukel, puts on the longest-running vegan cruise, which is where I met my wife in 2011, and has donated hundreds of thousands of dollars to numerous charities that benefit humans and animals. During every cruise they sell raffle tickets for unique prizes, such as complimentary stays at wellness retreats, cookware, health consultations, food products, and much more, and they donate all proceeds from raffle ticket sales to worthy charities. They count on their connections to dozens of brands that donate products with tens of thousands of dollars' worth of raffle prizes per cruise. They also market the raffle prizes to their two thousand–person captive audience that is on board the vegan cruise for a week. Benefiting from their connections, their marketing skills, and their relationships and trust they've built between prize donors and raffle ticket buyers has enabled them to raise hundreds of thousands of dollars over the past twenty years for meaningful charities.

The Vegan Gym donates a percentage of their profits to animal sanctuaries. They also host their own fundraising events, as described earlier with their pull-up challenge, with the goal of giving to effective animal organizations. Altruistic giving is built into their company's culture and DNA and they actively look for ways to contribute in the most impactful ways. They call upon their physical strength attributes to perform work on the farm, as well as characteristics such as teamwork and effective time management to volunteer in meaningful ways and raise money efficiently. They also leave their imprint on social media in order to reach a large audience online, which helps their company grow, ensuring they will be able to give more to help others.

Fair Wind Big Island Ocean Guides is a family-owned sustainable boat tour company on the Big Island of Hawaii that started in the early 1970s. Today, they are one of the island's most popular excursion providers, guiding hundreds of guests per day, often selling out trips weeks in advance as one of the most popular and reputable companies operating in Kailua-Kona. They also focus on sustainability—their commitment to recycling, composting green waste, becoming sustainable tourism certified, providing an ocean-safe mineral-based sunscreen for guests, eliminating single-use items, and—you guessed it—a dedication to serving a fully plant-based menu on board. They focus on what they call "planet-friendly food," which includes locally grown food from their own farm, producing approximately one thousand vegan meals per day.

Their plant-based offerings took effect in the early 2020s, during the Covid-19 pandemic, when they realized they needed to take a stronger environmental stance, despite their other sustainability initiatives in place for over a decade.

Fair Wind uses their resources, including their own sustainable farm, to grow the food for many of their meals. That includes supplying the family members who bake the cookies and prepare meals for multiple boat trips daily, every day of the week. They rely on their strong reputation to carry out an industry-leading approach to conservation; their adoption of veganism as a company policy has only enhanced (not hindered) their business. Their connections and network help them thrive and navigate choppy waters, particularly with their approach to make plant-based foods not only the default option on board, but the only option.

The animal rights organization Vegan Outreach hosts a campaign called "Vegan Chef Challenge." Victor Flores is the campaign manager, and his goal is to get non-vegan restaurants in a given city to add vegan entrées to their menu for a month, while supporting all participating restaurants in the city all month long. The goal is to drive customers to try the participating vegan entrées, and to then vote on a winning vegan menu item, awarding a restaurant the title of Vegan Chef Challenge winner, which they could display proudly in their restaurant, bringing more awareness to vegan food. Throughout the month, Vegan Outreach promotes the participating restaurants and chefs via their website, social media, and other traditional media, landing them TV spots in some cases, like in Amarillo, Texas, where they had eight television features in a single month, promoting the Vegan Chef Challenge on local television news stations. Victor told me that about 60 percent of participating restaurants end up leaving their vegan entrées on their menus, which has a net positive impact on reducing animal suffering by providing more compassionate items, which in some cases could have replaced an animal-based menu item. Victor and Vegan Outreach use their network, their connections, their resources, and their time to visit restaurants in person, or reach out to them via phone or email to get them on board as participants in the Vegan Chef Challenge. As is often the case, it mostly takes time and effort to make a difference for animals, which is what Vegan Outreach has been doing for decades.

While meeting with the cofounder and president of Dharma Voices for Animals, Bob Isaacson, I hopped on a live video chat with a monk in Sri Lanka who was connected to members of the Sri Lankan parliament and responsible for preventing one hundred thousand monkeys from being deported to China to be used in animal experimentation labs. This was just another day in the office for the monk, who, during the time of our video chat, was busy spaying and neutering stray dogs and cats near a temple in Sri Lanka. The monk claimed to have had that profound level of impact and influence on those primates' lives simply as a result of his connection to members of his country's governing body. Sometimes all it takes is a connection to someone in a position of power to prevent unimaginable suffering.

I met a gentleman named Luis, who is a successful, professional website designer. He even has a YouTube channel with approximately four hundred thousand subscribers resulting from his talent and his ability to teach others how to build amazing websites. He told me that one of the ways he contributes to the vegan movement to reduce animal suffering is by offering his services to effective animal charities for free. This act of generosity likely saves animal organizations tens or hundreds of thousands of dollars per year in salaries they would have had to pay others. Those organizations can instead use those funds to directly help animals. It also means their websites will be of very high quality, likely leading to an increase in organic traffic and donations.

OUR COLLECTIVE STRENGTH AT WORK

As you can see, very few of the stories I just shared required a very particular set of skills or inherent talents. They just involved individuals speaking up, stepping up, and spending a small amount of time helping animals in powerful ways. These, I argue, are actions we can, and should, all take, in one form or another.

Of course, if you have particular capabilities, such as large financial resources, a massive audience, connections to highly influential people, or particular strengths like writing or videography, you could use those abilities to make significant contributions for animals. From donating to the most effective charities, to raising awareness about animal suffering to your audience, to writing articles for major publications, to creating content that has the potential to go viral, you, and your network, are more powerful than you probably realize.

Though the mainstream effective altruism community prioritizes financial donations and encourages us to give a percentage of our income to the most effective charities that reduce suffering (which I agree with), my approach with effective vegan altruism is to encourage us to look at *all* of our strengths and to recognize that we have so much more to offer than just our financial resources. Revisit the list of STRONG V capabilities from the beginning of the chapter to see what assets you can contribute to reducing animal suffering.

We've also seen that it is becoming more common for for-profit companies to engage in "altruistic" marketing campaigns, particularly in the vegan product industry, by donating a percentage of their proceeds to help animals, or by overtly championing campaigns to raise money directly for animal charities. If this truly becomes the norm, not just among vegan companies, but within all vegan personal brands (including yours and mine), we can collectively raise a lot of funds for animals.

In the next chapter, we'll explore how to most effectively use our financial resources to help the most animals, including learning which organizations we should be donating to for the best return on investment (animals spared per dollar spent).

CHAPTER 4

USING YOUR FINANCIAL POWER FOR GOOD

CHANGE YOU CAN BELIEVE IN

"Effective altruism is about asking, 'How can I make the biggest difference I can?' and using evidence and careful reasoning to try to find an answer. It takes a scientific approach to doing good. Just as science consists of the honest and impartial attempt to work out what's true, and a commitment to believe the truth whatever that turns out to be, effective altruism consists of the honest and impartial attempt to work out what's best for the world, and a commitment to do what's best whatever that turns out to be."

—William MacAskill, cofounder of the
effective altruism movement

As William MacAskill points out in *Doing Good Better*, "the benefits of ethical consumerism are often small compared to the good that well-targeted donations can do."

Case in point: Consider that after a full year of living a vegan lifestyle with all of your food and other purchases being made with cruelty-free intentions, you'll spare 105 to 365 animals. This range is due to the nature of your purchases, from the amount of food you buy to reach your daily calorie needs, to your non-food-related purchases, such as cosmetics and clothing, which can provide alleviation of animal suffering. But by donating a portion of your income to the most effective animal charities, the number of animals you would spare could be five, ten, twenty, or even one hundred times as many. For some donors, it could be thousands of times as many animals spared, based on the size of the financial donation. Of course, MacAskill recommends doing both, living compassionately while also donating generously.

Here's an example: If you're a fairly active person, consuming a typical American daily calorie intake of 3,750 calories per day, which is slightly greater than the national average per capita calorie intake for adults of 3,540, according to the United Nations, by living a vegan lifestyle, you'll spare a number of animals closer to the higher end of this scale, say about three hundred per year.[24] But, if in addition to living a vegan lifestyle, and sparing a few hundred animals, you also donate a thousand dollars to an effective organization, like Food for Life Global, which provides vegan meals to hungry children in the developing world for just fifty cents per meal, you could spare a thousand animals that might have been bred, slaughtered, and consumed if those vegan meals were not provided. With a yearly donation that comes out to less than one hundred dollars per month, you could spare three times the number of animals as you would by not donating to animal charities.

Furthermore, if you were to double or triple your yearly donation or donate to a variety of effective organizations that can spare an animal's life for less than fifty cents, you can see how you could have a net impact that is five or ten times greater than just living your day-to-day vegan life.

In addition to individual donors, conscious companies could donate tens of thousands of dollars, sparing tens of thousands of animals, which is hundreds of times more effective than an individual vegan who spares a few hundred animals per year. A typical vegan would need to live a vegan lifestyle for decades to come close to the impact that donating to the most effective animal charities can accomplish in reducing animal suffering. Therefore, donating a portion of your income, along with living a compassionate vegan lifestyle, is a winning combination that propels veganism forward and spares a larger number of animals from their typical factory-farmed fate. We need to work smarter, not harder, in the name of compassion for animals.

Many vegans feel that just by being vegan and promoting veganism within their communities, they are already "doing enough." I know I have felt that way throughout my life. "I'm already living a compassionate vegan lifestyle, talking about it, writing about it, encouraging others to become vegan, and now I am being asked to donate to animal charities, too?" Sound familiar?

Well, if we want to be impactful and help as many animals as possible, then we have to acknowledge that it's our donation dollars, not the foods we eat, that will make the bigger difference for animals. I have to admit that it took me a while to accept and embrace that reality.

Donating money doesn't always rise to the top of the animal suffering reduction priority list, often, perhaps, because—once we donate—we no longer feel like we have control of our resources the way we do when we spend on vegan food, but it should probably be at the top of our priority list given the evidence proving its effectiveness.

At the end of the day, money talks. Any cause worth fighting for will likely take financial resources if it is going to succeed. That's why it is so easy to see that a finite amount of money can go a long way outside of the United States and other affluent nations. If $100 USD can save a few hundred chickens in the USA, that same $100 might be able to save thousands of chickens, or even tens of thousands of chickens, outside of the US. In order to truly do the most good, we have to think globally.

But where do we start? Who should we be giving all this money to in the first place?

Enter Animal Charity Evaluators.

ANIMAL CHARITY EVALUATORS

Every year, Animal Charity Evaluators uses rigorous methods to analyze which organizations do the most to help animals. Their evaluations are detailed and thorough, taking into account factors such as the interventions each initiative uses, the outcomes they work toward, the countries in which their programs take place, and the groups of animals their program affects. They also review the charity's plans for expansion, their financial records—including revenue and expenditure projections—and evaluate the cost effectiveness of an organization's programs to help animals. Furthermore, they evaluate organizational leadership and culture, by surveying staff, volunteers, and managers. Additionally, they make projections about the need for additional funding for each organization, based on their current budgets, their plans, and their ability to carry out campaigns that have an efficient return on investment. They also look at areas that an organization prioritizes, such as corporate outreach, movement building, vegan outreach, supporting or conducting animal advocacy research, and organizational policies.

As you can tell by their name (Animal Charity Evaluators), and by their detailed and evidence-based approach, the whole purpose and function of ACE is to use data and evidence to conclude which organizations are the most effective for animals. This saves the rest of us a whole lot of time, effort, trial, and error. ACE was founded with effective altruism principles in mind, and MacAskill helped set up the organization to figure out how to best help animals, just as he had done with determining the best approaches to help reduce poverty among the poorest people on the planet. Therefore, I defer to ACE for their expertise, at least in the areas of determining which organizations to donate to. ACE's comprehensive reports of their top charities are dozens of pages long, making for an insightful review of animal organizations you've likely heard of, and others that you will be happy to learn about.

ACE offers calls to action to donate to the most effective organizations, including evaluating how much total revenue would be helpful for a given charity to carry out their ambitious plans to help animals. Not only have they rigorously evaluated thousands of animal charities worldwide, but upon determining the most effective charities to contribute to, they make a call to action, encouraging people to donate to award-winning organizations, giving more support to the charities doing the most good.

A decade after their founding, ACE has already helped raise tens of millions of dollars, which has spared hundreds of millions of animals, making them an effective altruism entity in and of themselves, even though their primary objective is to help raise money for the most effective organizations that they evaluate.

With this in mind, it stands to reason that donating to ACE directly would be an effective use of donation dollars, even though their work encourages donors to donate to the best organizations. What makes the effective altruism community unique is that many organizations support and promote one another because they embrace a shared goal of reducing suffering, and so long as that goal is being accomplished effectively, it is less relevant which particular *effective* organization that you donate to.

THE MOST EFFECTIVE ANIMAL CHARITIES OF 2022

Each year, ACE selects their top charities, followed by their standout charities, determined through an evaluation process they have been conducting since 2014, analyzing more than three thousand animal organizations during that period. Drum roll, please . . .

The Animal Charity Evaluators Top Charities of 2022 were Faunalytics, The Humane League, the Good Food Institute, and Wild Animal Initiative. You will read about most of the top animal charities from

2022 in this and upcoming chapters. Eleven charities made the next tier Standout Charity list, including Mercy For Animals, Compassion USA, and a whole host of international organizations with offices based in Turkey, Denmark, Sri Lanka, Vietnam, India, China, the Philippines, Indonesia, Thailand, and Brazil (all of which are listed later on). Additional organizations that were left off the Standout Charity list, but came in as honorable mentions, still doing amazing work for animals, and in the top 1 percent of effective animal organizations worldwide, included charities from Poland, Ukraine, Italy, Slovakia, Chile, Mexico, and the US.

As stated earlier in this chapter, and previously throughout the book, some of the most effective ways we can help animals are by supporting organizations outside of the United States, where the dollar goes so much further. This list of the most effective animal organizations supports that notion, as many of them have international offices and focus their work outside of the United States.

Let's take a look at one of the best animal charities in the world, learning why they earned top honors.

The Humane League

The Humane League, a global animal welfare organization that works to end the abuse of animals raised for food, claims that they can positively impact a chicken's life for as little as $1 per three chickens, or for about thirty-three cents per chicken. They are universally acknowledged to be one of the most effective animal organizations in the world. Not only were they a 2022 recipient of the Top Charity Award by ACE, but they have won the award every single year since ACE's founding in 2014. It comes as no surprise to me that The Humane League would be a perennial top animal charity because of their founder, Nick Cooney.

Cooney's obsession with results, not emotions or feelings, supported by a bottom-line approach that for-profit companies take to not only stay in business, but to grow, is at the foundation of what he calls "smart charity." It also comes as no surprise (to me) that Cooney cofounded the Good Food Institute (another ACE Top Animal Charity of 2022) and was executive vice president of Mercy For Animals (a previous ACE Top Charity, and current Standout Charity), and played a major role at Farm Sanctuary, the world's most influential animal sanctuary. He has since cofounded New Crop Capital, a venture capital trust that invests in plant-based cultured meat, dairy, and egg companies, and is currently a managing partner at Lever VC, an investment fund focused on alternative protein companies. Nick Cooney left The Humane League's board in 2018 and the organization continues to carry out campaigns to help animals, especially chickens, and maintains their status as a world leader in making animals' lives better.

I had the privilege of interviewing The Humane League president, Dr. Vicky Bond, about the effectiveness of The Humane League's advocacy for animals. The veterinarian turned animal charity organization president shared insights about their influence and impact, particularly on laying hens in the commercial egg industry and chickens reared for meat—which is where some of the greatest animal cruelty takes place, in some of the largest numbers (second only to fish and sea animals such as shrimp as far as total number of lives in the food industry).

"The majority of our current focus is on freeing laying hens from cages," Dr. Bond explained. "On factory farms, where the vast majority of the global egg supply comes from, eggs are produced by subjecting female chickens to unbelievable acts of cruelty. Birds are crammed together in filthy cages, where they have almost no ability to engage in natural behaviors or even spread their wings. Meanwhile, their bodies are pushed to produce as many eggs as possible: almost one a day. Compare that to a wild chicken, who would naturally lay close to twelve eggs and then sit on them until they hatch. On factory farms, their bodies have been genetically selected to keep laying six eggs per week until they are sent to slaughter. At the end of their abbreviated lives, they're destined to become cheap meat or pet food via a brutal process known as live-shackle slaughter.

"Via our corporate outreach and campaigns, we're able to directly measure our cage-free efforts and their impact based on the number of food companies that both commit to and implement our requests to source 100 percent cage-free eggs," Dr. Bond explained. "As a result, we're also able to estimate the number of hens who will never have to endure life in a cage. Thanks to our work through the Open Wing Alliance, alongside other organizations around the world, nearly 2,500 companies have announced cage-free commitments, and an estimated hundreds of millions of egg-laying hens in the US will finally be able to spread their wings and stand on solid ground.

"Founded by The Humane League in 2015, The Open Wing Alliance (OWA) is a global coalition of one hundred animal protection organizations in seventy-two countries, on six continents, united to end the abuse of chickens worldwide. They also do campaigning around broilers (chickens raised for meat) as they are raised and killed for food more than any other land animal, and have no laws protecting them in the US. In the US alone, nine billion chickens are raised and killed each year for food. Globally, the estimated number jumps to sixty-five billion chickens annually. And every moment of these chickens' six or seven weeks of life—from hatching to hanging upside down in the slaughter line—[is] full of abuse and suffering. To date, the OWA has secured higher welfare policies, like the Better Chicken Commitment, from 570 companies to protect chickens from having to experience the worst forms of abuse in the meat industry."

I have so much respect for the work The Humane League does to create real, measurable change, not just feel-good stories. They are impacting hundreds of millions of animal lives every single year, which is why they are routinely awarded as the best organization when it comes to helping the greatest number of animals—largely owing to the fact that their work focuses on chickens. When it comes to effective vegan altruism, Dr. Bond, like many at The Humane League, exemplifies the practice in action, leaving being a veterinarian to effectively use her skills, talents, and resources to help the most animals.

"From the moment I knew it was possible to be a veterinarian, I always aspired to a career centered on helping animals," she said. "I did eventually become a vet, but while learning about how animals were raised for food, I felt that to truly help animals would be to use my veterinary knowledge for institutional change: pressuring companies to improve how they treat the countless animals in their supply chain.

"Around the world, over seventy billion animals are suffering unimaginable conditions in factory farms. If I were to continue working with animals on farms, I would be treating a single animal at a time, minimizing my potential impact and not addressing suffering on a larger scale. But now, by getting even a single company to end cages for egg-laying hens, we help many millions of animals every year. That was my inspiration for going into this work—knowing the entire food system needed to change. And my past work as a vet gave me the expertise and credentials to make executives see the data and necessity of a kinder present and future."

Dr. Bond explained to me how The Humane League evaluates what actions will be most impactful by using their expertise to determine what they call their "theory of change," a map that outlines steps they take to achieve their mission to end the abuse of animals raised for food. This process involves establishing incremental (short-term, intermediate, and final) outcomes to ensure that they are effective in their efforts. Their emphasis on effectiveness steers their decisions and actions, which produce positive results for animals.

Like many of the most effective animal organizations in the world, The Humane League doesn't expect everyone to adopt a vegan lifestyle immediately or overnight. They encourage practical, incremental steps toward plant-based eating and vegan living because that approach is most effective for a sustained meat and dairy reduction.[25]

"Incorporating more plant-based staples—like beans, legumes, grains, and fresh or frozen produce—can be a simple and healthy way to cut down on meat and dairy, and at the same time, food spending," Dr. Bond said. "An Oxford study found that switching to a vegan, vegetarian, or flexitarian diet in countries like the US and Western Europe could reduce one's food bill by up to 33 percent—saving both money and lives by keeping animals off the plate."[26]

Dr. Bond brought up another elephant in the room: accessibility to plant-based alternatives. In many cases, cheap, fast food and convenience store snacks are the only viable and affordable options within walking distance or within a general short drive even in developed countries. The fast-food restaurant down the street and the gas station convenience store on the corner might be the only options that some can consistently reach, depending on their transportation limitations.

These regions, devoid of plant-based (and generally healthier) food options—commonly referred to as food deserts—describe places where fresh, healthy food isn't available within walking distance. Food deserts provide a substantial barrier to healthy plant-based eating, and they are awash in the US. I grew up near one, with 7-Eleven and Circle K as the only stores with groceries within walking distance. I was on a farm a few miles out of town, but for many of my schoolmates, and for literally hundreds of families in the same neighborhood, they had to walk for a mile or two before coming across a grocery store, even in a densely populated part of town.

The general public wants healthier food options, Dr. Bond said. "Surveys reliably show that the public in the US cares deeply about farm animals and wants them to be protected from suffering," she added. "A study by Walmart revealed that 77 percent of its shoppers were likely to increase their level of trust in a retailer whose policies improved the treatment of animals in their supply chain, and 66 percent were more likely to purchase their products. A 2020 ASPCA survey found that the vast majority (89 percent) of Americans are concerned about industrial animal agriculture, citing animal welfare, worker safety, or public health risks as a concern. The same survey found that about three-fourths of consumers (74 percent) think that the government should be supporting farmers transitioning to more plant-based options."

Some steps are being made, even in food deserts, to get more plants (and healthier food options) to consumers. Here are a couple of examples: In 2022, Beyond Meat partnered with PepsiCo to distribute Beyond Meat jerky to 56,000 locations within the US, including gas station convenience stores, and in the world's largest grocer, Walmart, among many other places, including all the leading grocery stores. It's not that vegan jerky will solve the food desert crisis, and it's not a substitute for fresh produce, but Beyond Meat's entry into nearly every convenience store in the nation could open up doors for other products from Beyond Meat, or from other plant-based companies to cut into the market share that the animal agriculture industry dominates, while creating more plant-based options for consumers. It also provides a cholesterol-free and lower fat option to a very popular snack that is consumed by millions of people who regularly eat animal-based jerky. Sometimes, one of the most important first steps is getting your foot in the door. Perhaps someday there will be plant-based hot dogs, sausages, and sandwiches available in every convenience store, replacing, or competing with, animal-based options.

Nearly every convenience store in the US now carries plant-based snack bars, protein bars, and cookies, from brands such as Clif Bar, Lärabar, Lenny & Larry's, and other emerging plant-based, or plant-forward brands. There are plant-based ready-to-drink protein drinks and smoothies available at most mainstream retailers now, too, including at gas station convenience stores (this is largely because these products are owned by parent companies such as Coca-Cola, PepsiCo, and Nestlé, which have relationships and earned shelf space at every major retail convenience and grocery store). Nuts, fruits, coconut water, sometimes non-dairy milks, and plenty of other plant-based foods, like chips, crackers, bread, and nut butters, are also available in convenience stores. But their prices are higher than at grocery stores, their selection is smaller, and this doesn't solve the issue of finding adequate options for breakfast, lunch, and dinner. Luckily, fast-food restaurants are increasingly offering plant-based options, which help provide somewhat healthier options for consumers, even in food deserts.

As a writer who spends a lot of time on the road, I have been impressed with particular gas station convenience stores that offer huge displays of bananas, and even freshly cut fruits, such as cups of watermelon, honeydew, and cantaloupe chunks. Those, in addition to the increase in general plant-based snacks, such as trail mixes, plant-based jerky, and non-dairy beverages, are signs of progress that many consumers are seeking.

If these plant-based options do indeed cut down on consumer spending on animal-based foods, then they are not only good for human health, but effective in reducing animal suffering. The Humane League understands this, and they understand celebrating incremental steps, from removing cages to offering more plant-based options, knowing that the road from the starting line to the finish line is often long, winding, and full of obstacles. As long as we continue moving forward along that bumpy road to a more compassionate future, we at least give ourselves a chance at someday making it to the finish line, which represents a brighter day for animals.

Dr. Bond personifies, and The Humane League exemplifies, what it means to be effective. Dr. Bond describes effectiveness for animals this way: "To be effective is to be excellent at what you do. At The Humane League, we focus on institutional change to decrease the suffering of animals raised for food. We are part of the larger movement, each doing our best work to make a difference for animals. The Humane League works by targeting the largest food companies using our tried and tested campaigns to impact millions of animals." Here are some examples she shared with me: "Over the years, we've taken on the largest food companies and had massive wins in both our policy acquisition and accountability work: General Mills. PepsiCo. Grupo Bimbo. Starbucks. Subway. Burger King. Chipotle. Pret A Manger. KFC. Pizza Hut. Taco Bell. Whole Foods. And the world's biggest institutional food providers—Sodexo, Aramark, and Compass Group—have all enacted animal welfare policies."

I believe The Humane League is right to focus on the big picture as a way to elicit the most change for animals. The more people are aware of the harms animals face in our broken food system, the more likely they are to lean into plant-based lifestyles over time, particularly with the rise of influential plant-based health documentaries (and books) that elicited a change in dietary patterns for millions of people.

Forks Over Knives is the most influential brand in that space, fol-. lowing their groundbreaking documentary (*Forks Over Knives*) about the relationship between diet and disease that debuted in 2011, followed by multiple bestselling books, including their main cookbook, *Forks Over Knives—The Cookbook*, which has sold more than one million copies. They also have their own cooking school, recipe app, bestselling magazine, and social media communities amassing more than five million followers. And their approach is a health-centered focus that, consequently, has been one of the most influential and effective methods for reducing animal suffering over the past couple of decades. I even refer to their massive influence on the mainstream public embracing a plant-based diet in my presentations and conversations as "The Forks Over Knives Effect." That's the power of reaching the masses, which is what The Humane League also embraces.

To recap, The Humane League focuses on helping the most abused animals (chickens), which are suffering in the greatest numbers, second only to fish and shrimp. They accomplish their results by working with thousands of companies to create institutional changes that impact hundreds of millions of animals, particularly chickens. They use their theory of change map, which focuses on short-term, intermediate, and final outcomes of effective outreach, by figuring out which efforts will impact the most animals. Dr. Bond's decision to leave the veterinary profession in order to create policy change within the world's top food companies is an example of her excellence and dedication to doing the most good. Dr. Bond and The Humane League are examples of effective vegan altruism, and I encourage you to join me in supporting their amazing work.

Consider visiting thehumaneleague.org to support their efforts for as little as a dollar (which can help three chickens live a better life). Though small donations still add up, when factoring processing fees and other overhead costs, it becomes clear that to be more effective one would create a more substantial monthly donation, such as $25 per month, or $100 per month, or by donating a percentage of your annual income to effective animal charities. The Humane League has estimated that it takes approximately $2.50 to spare one hen from a cage. You can also take action against animal cruelty through The Humane League's Fast Action Network on their website. Small online actions can help push their campaigns forward and create real change for millions of animals around the world.

CONSIDERING INTERNATIONAL ANIMAL CHARITIES

The truth is that our money goes further internationally. Contributing financially to help animals in the poorest parts of the world is something I hope many readers will contemplate quite seriously—myself included.

ACE recommends the Federation of Indian Animal Protection Organizations (FIAPO) and Fish Welfare Initiative (FWI), both based in India, as Standout Charities for international animal rights donations.

ACE also recommends Dharma Voices for Animals (DVA), the only international Buddhist animal rights organization in the world, which primarily has a presence in Sri Lanka, Thailand, Vietnam, Myanmar, and other locations where the US dollar can make a profound impact in stretching further than it would in the US, though they also work in the US, Germany, Finland, Australia, and other affluent nations.

Sinergia Animal, which works to improve farmed animal welfare standards, increase the availability of animal-free products, and strengthen animal advocacy, is another ACE Standout Charity operating in Indonesia, Colombia, Uruguay, Ecuador, and Peru, among other locations in the Global South.

Mercy For Animals, a former ACE Top Charity, and current Stand-out Charity, also conducts outreach in many international locations where the US dollar goes a long way, including India, Brazil, and Mexico. They also operate in the US and Canada.

Though ACE is the most well-known and comprehensive animal charity evaluator, they are just one such organization. Charity Navigator is another organization that evaluates the efficacy of charities, including nonprofit animal organizations. You likely have additional animal charities that you're aware of, from popular national organizations, to local organizations in your community. In the spirit of doing something rather than nothing, you can always choose to support one of those charities versus any we've covered here or that ACE recommends.

We all have biases. For many of us, one of our strongest biases is our proximity bias, which basically describes our preference to help particular animals close to us—in our towns, in our states, in our countries. We also often have preferences toward pets and domesticated animals, or exotic wild animals, such as rhinos, elephants, gorillas, and animals on the verge of extinction.

A lot of those leanings make perfect sense. But if we can at least try to remove our personal biases and look as objectively as possible, we can recognize that many of these international organizations working in Asia, Africa, and South and Central America are not only worthy of our support, but can do a whole lot more good with the resources we might give them.

But how *much* more good, exactly?

In *Doing Good Better*, William MacAskill speaks to how impactful it can be to use US dollars outside of the Western world to help animals. "If you're on the typical U.S. wage of $28,000 [in 2015 when his book was published] per year, the benefit you'd get from an additional $28,000 in income is the same as the benefit a poor Indian farmer would get from an additional $220," he wrote. "This gives us good theoretical reasons for thinking that the same amount of money can do one hundred times as much to benefit the very poorest people in the world as it can to benefit typical citizens of the United States. If you can earn as much as the typical American worker, then you are one hundred times as rich as the very poorest people in the world, which means additional income can do a hundred times as much to benefit the extreme poor as it can to benefit you or me."

Given this example comparing the income of the average American to a poor farmer in India, the same amount of money can also theoretically do one hundred times more good to enrich the lives of animals in India than it can in America. That is significant, and we expect a similar hundredfold financial impact for animals in numerous developing nations around the globe as well.

PLAN YOUR CONTRIBUTIONS IN A WAY THAT WORKS FOR YOU

I realize it can be exhausting to constantly be encouraged to give money, particularly if money is tight. Even if we know that donating to effective charities is more impactful than just being vegan and not donating to any organizations, I understand that, in today's economy, donating might not be an option for you right now.

If at some point it does become an option, I hope you will consider donating to the smart charities that make the greatest impact for animals. You will get introduced to other animal charities later in the book, as many aspects of effective altruism, for better or for worse, revolve around financial contributions.

I will be candid with you about my own contributions to effective organizations, my support for profit-driven vegan companies and products, and my support for individuals who I view as being effective change makers, reducing animal suffering. I've made good and bad contributions, and some really great ones. I've gone through phases where I deliberately "earn to give," by going out of my way to generate additional income, by taking on a second job, accepting an additional role in a company, or working on various side projects, so that I can give more away, supporting those who can benefit more from my contribution

than I would benefit by holding on to resources and not contributing them. I have always given—often too much, and sometimes not
enough, or to the wrong groups, and perhaps many of you can relate to
those experiences.

One of the most powerful and educational experiences I've gained
from writing this book has been learning more about how I can maximize my effectiveness—simply by changing my mindset and my priorities, and removing some of my biases in order make the biggest impact.
I admit that, as a result of writing this book, I have also been convinced
to support some organizations and not others, compelled to use my time
in some ways rather than others, and motivated to use my platforms in
more effective ways than others. This book has helped me grow as an
imperfect vegan trying like hell to help animals have better lives.

Oftentimes, we get caught up in "the warm glow effect" (a common term used to describe our own emotional feeling of doing good
regardless of the efficacy of our actions) of giving to the specific charities
that make us feel good. If we're able to set aside biases, and confidently
move forward with the most impactful approaches that help the largest
number of animals, we will be on the path of effective vegan altruism.
I encourage you to consider the full spectrum of organizations, companies, and individuals to support as you navigate through the many
amazing options for effective contributions in one capacity or another.

> If we're able to set aside biases, and confidently
> move forward with the most impactful approaches
> that help the largest number of animals, we will be
> on the path of effective vegan altruism. I encourage
> you to consider the full spectrum of organizations,
> companies, and individuals to support as you
> navigate through the many amazing options for
> effective contributions in one capacity or another.

Looking at the median US salary for full-time workers today, at approximately $45,000 USD per year, if you donated just 5 percent of your annual income to the most effective animal charities, it would amount to a $2,250 donation.[27] If you donated to The Humane League, which, as you recall, can spare three chickens per dollar, your donation would spare 6,750 animals from living a life of suffering. Compare that to the 105–365 animals you would spare each year by living a vegan life-style and not donating to effective animal charities.

If you donated 10 percent of your annual income to The Humane League, at the median US salary, you would spare 13,500 animals, or up to approximately 135 times more animals than being vegan alone. If you make closer to the "average" US annual salary of $55,000 per year, which is different from the median salary (factoring in the full sum of money earned divided by the number of workers), 5 percent of your income donated to smart charities would be $2,750, and 10 percent would be $5,500, which could spare 16,500 chickens if donated to The Humane League.

For my colleagues making $100,000 per year, donating 10 percent of your income ($10,000) to smart charities could spare thirty thousand lives, or approximately three hundred times more animals than being vegan alone. This, I hope, gives you plenty of food for thought when it comes to using your money for good.

Efficacy of Donating to Effective Animal Charities

Each vegan spares the lives of 365 animals per year

+ 5% of their median annual salary donated to an animal charity	=	7,115 animals* spared per year
+ 10% of their median annual salary donated to an animal charity	=	13,500 animals* spared per year
+ 5% of their average annual salary donated to an animal charity	=	8,250 animals* spared per year
+ 10% of their average annual salary donated to an animal charity	=	16,500 animals* spared per year

*Includes 365 animals spared each year by a typical vegan

One of the most helpful approaches is to make automatic recurring monthly donations because that keeps consistent revenue coming in for charities to anticipate, which helps them with their budget planning, but there are many approaches you can take. Another popular and effective strategy is to save a percentage of your monthly income in an account, just as you might transfer monthly income into a savings or investment account. Then, at the end of the year, when you're ready to make a lump sum donation, you can look for opportunities to have your donation doubled or tripled.

Nearly all of the major animal charities have wealthy donors who match donations up to a certain amount, typically in the hundreds of thousands of dollars. If you make a year-end donation of $2,000 during a donation-matching campaign, your donation could turn into $4,000 or $6,000. These donation-matching campaigns typically happen multiple times per year, especially on what is called "Giving Tuesday," the Tuesday after Thanksgiving, following Black Friday and Cyber Monday, and at the end of the calendar year when people are assessing their finances and making charitable donations before the New Year. You can learn about when these particular campaigns happen by subscribing to particular animal charity newsletters and by following them on social media. That's how I routinely hear about opportunities for my donations to be doubled or tripled.

Regardless of how you approach your own charitable giving, you can feel confident that as long as your donation is going to an effective organization, it is having a meaningful impact. Determine your preferred organizations to donate to, and initiate a monthly or yearly donation today to make the biggest impact on animals.

The animals can't thank you, nor should you be motivated by their gratitude, but please allow me to thank you for your heartfelt generosity to help the abused, neglected, exploited innocent individuals who share similar emotions that you and I experience. With deep gratitude, I appreciate your compassion for others.

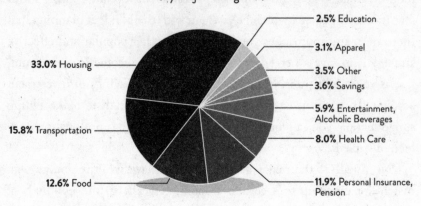

Share of US Household Consumer Expenditures
(By Major Categories)

2.5% Education

3.1% Apparel

3.5% Other

3.6% Savings

33.0% Housing

5.9% Entertainment, Alcoholic Beverages

8.0% Health Care

15.8% Transportation

12.6% Food

11.9% Personal Insurance, Pension

Here's a typical breakdown of household expenditures in the United States. Some spending categories are nonnegotiable, but can you make room in your budget by cutting down on unnecessary or occasional expenditures like new clothes, entertainment, and going out to eat? Of course, shifting where your food money goes from animal to plant sources makes a big difference already. I challenge you to look at your own budget and see how your spending measures up—and where you might make room for spending to help animals. Data source: USDA, Economic Research Service using data from the US Bureau of Labor Statistics, Consumer Expenditure Survey, 2016.

CHAPTER 5

VEGAN FOR GOOD

STAYING VEGAN FOR THE LONG HAUL

"Kaizen is an effective, enjoyable way to achieve a specific goal, but it also extends a more profound challenge: to meet life's constant demands for change by seeking out continual— but always small—improvement."
—Dr. Robert Maurer, author of *One Small Step Can Change Your Life: The Kaizen Way*

Earlier we talked briefly about how taking small, deliberate actions that add up over time can produce big results. The practice is instrumental in embarking on veganism in a way that prevents the practice from feeling overwhelming initially, finding and returning to your why, and staying vegan for the long haul.

The kaizen system is a popular Japanese strategy for improving habits, processes, and products by implementing small, incremental changes. Typically used by businesses, such as Toyota, which applied the kaizen system to become the world's leading car manufacturer, kaizen can be used by anyone looking to create efficient systems that produce desired results, from athletes, to parents, to students, to animal rights advocates. Kaizen has helped people overcome addiction, break bad habits, and create new, positive ones. It has also helped people stay committed to the changes they've made. It is a tried-and-true system of taking tiny steps that add up over time. Think *Atomic Habits*, before *Atomic Habits* was a thing.

Though the kaizen system is now synonymous with Japanese business organizations, and part of Japanese culture, kaizen actually got its start from the United States government. At a health conference in Tucson, Arizona, a couple of years ago, I heard Dr. Robert Maurer tell the story. Dr. Maurer wrote the national bestseller *One Small Step Can Change Your Life: The Kaizen Way*, translated into forty languages worldwide. In his short habit-change book, he explained the kaizen history:

Despite the foreign name, kaizen—small steps for continual improvement—was first applied systematically in Depression-era America. When France fell to Nazi Germany in 1940, American leaders realized how urgently the Allies needed shipments of our military equipment. They also were forced to acknowledge that American soldiers might soon be sent abroad as well, requiring their own tanks, weapons, and supplies. American manufacturers would need to step up the quality and quantity of their equipment production, and quickly. The challenge was intensified by the loss of many qualified factory supervisors to the American armed forces, which were busy making preparations for war.

To overcome these time and personnel constraints, the U.S. government created management courses called Training Within Industries (TWI) and offered them to corporations throughout America. One of these courses held the seeds of what would, in another time and place, become known as kaizen. Instead of encouraging radical, more innovative change to produce the demanded results, the TWI course exhorted managers toward what it called "continuous improvement."

This approach encouraged supervisors, managers, and workers to look for hundreds of small improvements to enhance their productivity, rather than an overhaul of an entire system. Small, deliberate improvements proved to pay off. Dr. Maurer continued,

This philosophy of small steps toward improvement was introduced to Japan after the war, when General Douglas MacArthur's occupation forces began to rebuild that devastated country. If you are familiar with Japan's corporate dominance in the late twentieth century, you may be surprised to hear that many of its postwar businesses were run poorly with slack management practices and low employee morale.

General MacArthur saw the need to improve Japanese efficiency and raise business standards. A thriving Japanese economy was in MacArthur's best interest, because a strong society could provide a bulwark against a possible threat from North Korea and keep his troops in steady supplies. He brought in the U.S. government's TWI specialists, including those who emphasized the importance of small, daily steps toward change. Japanese businesses—which rebuilt themselves on the bedrock of small steps—soon rocketed to unheard-of-levels of productivity. Small steps were so successful that the Japanese gave them a name of their own: kaizen.

Much as I did with effective altruism, turning the name into effective *vegan* altruism, I have also altered the kaizen way to give it my own name for the purpose of this book, as the *vegan kaizen system*. The purpose of this particular name and approach is to build up habits that are consistent with moral veganism to reduce recidivism from a plant-based diet or vegan lifestyle. Oftentimes, it is our habits, not our moral compass, that guide our behaviors, and the kaizen strategy of small steps leading to big results is something that animal rights activists, vegan advocates, and effective altruists could utilize to stay committed for the long haul.

Efficient processes are what many businesses run on, and though reducing animal suffering isn't a business in and of itself, we should look at our goal like it is a business endeavor. Many businesses achieve results and positively impact people and animals, and we can learn a lot from the systems they use to achieve such goals. The objective is not to try to tackle a problem that is too big or achieve a goal that is too grand. If we set out to end factory farming and replace all meat in grocery stores and restaurants with plants, we will fail miserably. But if we set a goal of impacting the life of one animal today, we can avoid the feelings of being overwhelmed with the monumental task of ending all factory farming by embracing a practical and achievable goal that we can build on.

> Efficient processes are what many businesses run on, and though reducing animal suffering isn't a business in and of itself, we should look at our goal like it is a business endeavor. Many businesses achieve results and positively impact people and animals, and we can learn a lot from the systems they use to achieve such goals.

This is the same approach actor Will Smith talked about in a 2002 interview with Charlie Rose, reflecting on an experience of building a brick wall when he was a child. When Smith was building a wall with his younger brother for his father's shop, as school-age kids, it took them a year and a half to complete it, by laying bricks after school. "You don't set out to build a wall," Smith said. "You don't say, 'I'm going to build the biggest, baddest, greatest wall that's ever been built.' You don't start there. You say, 'I'm going to lay this brick as perfectly as a brick can be laid' . . . you do that every single day, and soon you have a wall.' It's difficult to take the first step when you look [at] how big the task is. The task is never huge to me. It's always one brick."

It's the same approach to learning a new language, writing a book, building an airplane, a freeway, or a city, and it's the same approach to apply to animal activism to reduce animal suffering. Exchange Smith's words for a vegan or animal rights expression. "You don't set out to save every animal. You don't say, 'I'm going to save every animal on Earth from a life of misery.' You don't start there. You say, 'I'm going to reduce animal suffering today as effectively as I possibly can' . . . you do that every single day, and soon you've saved as many animals as possible." Finishing with a vegan version of Smith's punch line: "It's difficult to initiate action to start reducing animal suffering when you're confronted by the harsh reality of billions of innocent lives suffering every year. The quest is never daunting to me. It's always about reducing animal suffering as effectively as possible, which I can achieve through actions I take every single day."

Consider what happens when we ask someone to do thirty to sixty minutes of exercise per day to benefit their own health—it makes it unlikely that they will do it. The "ask" is just too big. If, instead, we ask someone to exercise for just one minute a day, or maybe for two minutes a day, that's something most people can manage. You are more likely to agree to exercise for two minutes per day than for an hour per day. Though two minutes of exercise might not be enough to help you achieve your fitness goals right away, it sets you on the path to future success. Think of all the small tasks we're often unwilling to do because they seem daunting: going for a walk, writing an online review to support a friend's company or product, practicing a foreign language, playing a musical instrument, taking the time to prepare some healthy plant-based meals, or numerous other scenarios you can think of in your own life.

Most of us can't be bothered to go for a walk, exercise for an hour a day, or complete similar tasks such as reading twenty pages a day, or meditating for five minutes a day. We just don't act in those ways anymore in today's short-attention-span era, and we're better off asking someone to read one page per day, meditate for thirty seconds per day, or call or text a single friend once per week. If the goal is too large, we'll be intimidated from the start and will be unlikely to complete the tasks required to achieve the goal. If the goal is small, such as tiny, consistent steps, we can find success on a daily basis, and the goal can be expanded, whether it's walking, writing, exercising, reading, or keeping in touch with friends and loved ones.

KAIZEN GOES VEGAN

Kaizen applies to veganism in many ways, from why and how we embrace veganism, to how we promote and present the vegan lifestyle and philosophy to others, to how we can use small, empowering steps to stay vegan.

Kaizen is about more than just helping businesses produce more efficient results and greater profits. It extends beyond weight loss goals and overcoming addictions. Kaizen speaks to more than relationship struggles, stress, anxiety, and managing financial decisions and time management. At its core, kaizen is about habit changing, consistency, and progress, and the kaizen principles can be applied to nearly every area of life, to bring more peace and serenity to any pursuit.

One particular helpful aspect of kaizen that relates well to veganism is being open to receiving and applying feedback from others. We often think we know what is best, including believing we know the best ways to reduce animal suffering, but if we remain open to feedback, and to new ideas, we can learn how to be even more effective. That, of course, is the pursuit of this book: learning from effective vegan advocates from all over the world and sharing their strategies for change.

When I spent ten years working for what would become the number one plant-based sports nutrition company in the world, Vega, they weren't always at the top. They started small and climbed to the top of the industry because Vega's founder, Charles Chang, much like Toyota, constantly sought out suggestions, and remained open to feedback from employees and contractors who worked for him. Charles built a company culture based on team input, gathering many different perspectives from individuals from lots of unique backgrounds. The idea is that everyone brings value and experience, and when their ideas are shared, and listened to, and when many of them are applied, greater success can be experienced.

Whether a for-profit company, a nonprofit organization, or even an individual entity, such as an online influencer or YouTuber, we all have the opportunity to learn and grow by listening to our community. I believe this is especially important in the animal rights community, where every decision carries a lot of weight, because it has the opportunity to save lives and reduce animal suffering. Listening to feedback from those intimately involved in a process toward achieving a goal can be invaluable.

To clarify, this is much different than the concept of "the customer is always right." Customer feedback is often based on customer wants, not on what drives a company forward. We all want improvements to nearly every product we've ever used, but that feedback is not necessarily always helpful for a company, brand, or organization that has a commitment to fulfilling their mission. For example, just because a paying customer on Southwest Airlines (SWA) asks the flight attendant for a sandwich, and even if they start a whole movement to get their friends and family to campaign to have SWA offer in-flight sandwiches, rather than just peanuts or pretzels, it does not influence SWA's decision about what to offer their customers. That is because they have already identified what their company DNA is, which is built around cheap flights, friendly service, and no frills. So complain all you want, but you're not getting anything but peanuts.

However, if an SWA employee notices that passengers aren't paying attention to safety briefings before the flight, they might make suggestions and recommendations based on their observations, and those suggestions could be put into practice. On a recent SWA flight I took from Seattle to Denver, the flight attendant, about to go over the safety briefing, said on the speaker, "Did anyone lose this?" which caused everyone to immediately look up, and then he continued, "Now that I have your attention, we'll go over a short safety briefing of this plane." There will be times when customers have input that is adopted and applied to company or organization policy, but most kaizen-style suggestions for improved processes will likely come from within an organization, since team members tend to care more about company effectiveness than customers, who are more concerned about satisfaction with a product or service.

Sometimes we have to step back from our all-or-nothing, go-big-or-go-home, and audacious expectations, which are common mindsets in America, to slow down and be more effective at whatever we are doing. Kaizen steps can also be making small donations to effective organizations, as we covered in the last chapter. You can always increase your donations, investments, and support over time. It might not make financial sense for you to eat at a vegan restaurant every day of the week, but maybe you start by supporting a vegan restaurant once per month, and then work up to once per week if that fits into your plan (and budget).

THE POWER OF HABITS AND BUILDING NEW PRACTICES

Habits are everything. It comes as no surprise to many of us that *Atomic Habits* is the bestselling book in the world over the past half decade, with well over twelve million copies sold over just the past few years. Though it is, in the opinion of many, seemingly aimed at a beginner audience in the areas of developing habits, such as flossing your teeth or putting your shoes on, the book sells like crazy by sharing information that most of us already know. Habits are so important to us that we often jump at constant reminders in easy-to-understand strategies and tips.

Small steps, taken consistently, do indeed compound over time to produce meaningful results. The vegan kaizen system is results-driven, based on the validity of incremental, continual steps of forward progress, and has the potential to impact a lot of animals if applied in effective ways.

One of those ways, of course, is through building new habits—whether donating to the best organizations on a monthly basis, volunteering on a weekly basis, or giving, supporting, or otherwise contributing to causes you care about. It all starts with the routines and habits that you develop and follow on a regular basis.

One way to start any new habit is to weigh out the options between what it will mean to you if you start a new habit versus what it will mean to you if you don't start a new habit. Sometimes that internal conversation is all you need to answer the question "Is it worth it?" Of course, that question has multiple meanings behind it. Is it worth it to start something new, or is it worth it to stay where you are, and not pursue any particular new habit? What will it mean to you to not even try? Those are also questions worth contemplating as you decide your future endeavors.

There is no question that habit change is hard; in fact, it's likely one of the hardest things there is to do. Sticking with a current routine is one of the easiest things in the world, and that makes it even harder to disrupt your current routine and add to it, alter it, or ultimately do something completely different.

As a species, humans tend to look forward to the future. We say, "Someday, I'd like to do this." Or, "One day I want to experience that." Yet we repeatedly don't get past the starting blocks. Either the goal just seems out of reach or unrealistic, or the comfort of where we are now feels more satisfying than the risk of the unknown, which could include hard work, setbacks, and ultimately failure.

> There is no question that habit change is hard; in fact, it's likely one of the hardest things there is to do.

Failing to even try at all is the only surefire way to fail. I'm not going to sit here and say that it's easy to embark on a new journey, to summon the courage to actually create new daily habits, or to be consistent in such a way that it produces results, but I can say with confidence that the pursuit is often worth it, regardless of the outcome. I can't tell you how many of my goals and dreams didn't work out for me, but I found the pursuit to be the rewarding part of the journey. That's where the joy is—in the pursuit, not just in the end result. In fact, sometimes the end result, even if it lands in your favor, is underwhelming in comparison to the journey it took you to get there.

When it comes to building new habits, creating changes that stick, and helping others find the motivation to pursue their own meaningful goals, turn back to your *why*. Let it guide you and reinforce your conviction in the face of change that may be hard, even when broken down into small steps. When embarking on a new habit, I often turn my attention to some of the world's most successful vegan coaches, drawing on their expertise and looking at how they applied the vegan kaizen system to produce remarkable results for themselves, and for their clients.

BUILDING STAYING STRENGTH: THE VEGAN GYM

Perhaps the most successful vegan fitness coaching company in the world is aptly named The Vegan Gym, cofounded by brothers Leif and Anders Arnesen. By all reasonable accounts, The Vegan Gym shouldn't even be here, but not only are they here, The Vegan Gym is a thriving business that has the goal of helping one million vegans get into the best shape of their lives. They believe that the more healthy and fit vegans there are in the world, the faster veganism will spread. They are determined to inspire change, spread compassion, and challenge the status quo.

But when the two brothers founded the online vegan personal training company in 2017, and launched their coaching program, The Vegan Superhero Academy, in 2018, business was slow, and Leif and Anders were the only coaches, training a small number of clients. Leading up to the Covid-19 pandemic, they considered getting part-time jobs to support their business in the early, building phase. Then, business really picked up and has been growing steadily ever since. Today, they have a staff of more than twenty, and have coached more than two thousand vegans in their quest to someday help one million vegans build their bodies with a plant-based diet.

Though they initially had big, lofty goals, the reality set in that, for their company to grow, they would need to slow down and apply the vegan kaizen system of taking small, deliberate steps, even if at times it was painfully slow. By hiring their own business coaches, and learning strategies to attract more clients, they followed their newfound principles, gained more clients, and found themselves in a position to hire another trainer to work for them. As they continued to attract new clients, they added more trainers, and eventually, just months after business really picked up, Leif and Anders were no longer training clients directly, and they would use their unique sets of skills and talents to run the business—hiring more people, building new systems, and applying kaizen techniques all along the way.

What was once on the verge of collapse became a million-dollar brand a year later and a multimillion-dollar brand by the following year. While I don't get hung up on the financial figures, their growth *is* impressive, and as we've learned throughout the book, and will continue to learn, the more financial resources available, the more good we can do. As their company grew, so did the impact they had on animals, furthering their success toward their larger mission—which is being achieved by taking small, deliberate actions.

The Vegan Gym pays their team well, and their team works hard, buying into The Vegan Gym's mission of having the greatest impact by growing as much as possible. The Vegan Gym supports many other vegan companies, brands, and individuals, including me, when they ordered a copy of my previous book for every single one of their clients attending their annual Vegan Superhero Academy Retreat, invited me to be the keynote speaker multiple years running, and said "yes" every time I asked them to promote one of my projects. They donate to numerous charities. Their ads, which feature strong, fit vegans in images and videos, require thousands of dollars to produce—and then The Vegan Gym spends hundreds of thousands more to promote those ads to ensure they get seen by millions of people, including many non-vegans who are able to see a side of veganism they are perhaps getting exposed to for the first time. That, of course, is a form of effective advocacy in its own right.

To this day, they take small, deliberate, incremental steps to continue to pursue their "lofty" goal of helping one million vegans, but they know it starts with helping one person at a time, which turns into dozens, then hundreds, then thousands, and eventually millions. They are under no illusions that they will provide one-on-one coaching for one million vegans, which is why they also created a podcast, a YouTube channel, an apparel brand, and a website with a free nutrition course, articles, videos, and other resources to help millions of vegans thrive.

"Every vegan we help initiates a ripple effect in their personal lives, impacting other people," Leif said. "I have heard hundreds of stories of our clients inspiring their friends, family members, and coworkers to reduce or eliminate the animal products on their plates. About 15 percent of our clients were veg-curious meat-eaters who wanted to transition to a healthier, more compassionate lifestyle with nutritional guidance from plant-based nutrition experts. We have now worked with over three hundred meat-eaters to help them become healthy, fit vegans (70 percent female, 29 percent male, and 1 percent other).

"Every vegan we help initiates a ripple effect in their personal lives, impacting other people. I have heard hundreds of stories of our clients inspiring their friends, family members, and coworkers to reduce or eliminate the animal products on their plates."

"According to Harish Sethu, a data scientist and author of the *Counting Animals* blog, the average American consumes about twenty-five land animals per year—twenty-three chickens raised for meat, a third of a pig, a tenth of a cow, and about three-quarters of a turkey (plus a small amount of duck and other species). Add in aquatic animals—an estimated twelve fish and 137 shellfish (mainly shrimp)—and the number skyrockets up to roughly 174 animals. So, with us helping *just three hundred clients* to become healthy, fit vegans for the rest of their lives, it directly saves (spares) *2.4 million animals* [based on calculations using average life expectancy]. Additionally, the ripple effect of their inspirational physical and mental transformations have already touched the lives of thousands of people in just the past few years."

STAYING VEGAN IN A NON-VEGAN WORLD

The good we continue to do as vegans only grows, compounds, and inspires if we can find a way to remain vegan, which is challenging in our world.

In my view, one of the most important roles that The Vegan Gym and the other coaches in the vegan movement play is the role of reducing recidivism from veganism. Unfortunately, most people who become vegan will go back to eating animals at some point in their lives.

Since that harsh and painful reality exists, we have to acknowledge those who prolong veganism and plant-based diets among their communities, which is precisely what vegan coaches do. The Vegan Gym only works with clients who will adhere to a purely plant-based diet. That doesn't mean they only train vegans. What it means is that when someone comes to them seeking mentorship and coaching, that individual agrees to follow a purely plant-based diet, whether they identify as *vegan* or not when they enroll in the coaching program. This is a nonnegotiable for The Vegan Gym, even if it means turning away as many as 35 percent of potential clients who request their services. That's right, The Vegan

Gym leaves potentially hundreds of thousands of dollars on the table because they are unwilling to compromise by enabling people to eat animal products while in their coaching program. Sure, some clients might secretly deviate from the purely plant-based nutrition program, especially if they are new to veganism, but with a coach in their corner, they will be fully supported and encouraged to stay on track, while being provided with all the resources they need to do so, which leads to the cultivation of new, potentially long-lasting positive habits. With more than a dozen certified personal trainers on staff, along with registered dietitians and a physician, every single meal plan provided for their thousands of clients is dietitian approved, meaning it should help clients sustain their plant-based diets with that level of tailored precision.

None of us can predict whether The Vegan Gym clients (or any of us vegans) will indeed remain vegan for the rest of their lives, and it's unfortunately statistically unlikely due to recidivism rates of nearly 90 percent. But by having proper coaching in plant-based nutrition and fitness, with accountability partners, coaches, and team support, it does appear that those who go through The Vegan Superhero Academy are more likely to stay vegan longer than someone who does not have the habit-changing guidance and accountability support that The Vegan Superhero Academy provides.

Take Mikey, for example. Mikey joined The Vegan Superhero Academy at the lowest time in his life, debating whether he even deserved to keep living. As an omnivore addicted to fast food and with low self-esteem, he weighed 257 pounds at the height of five feet, five inches, with 42 percent body fat. Nearly half of his body weight was fat. He was on a downward spiral, and doctors told him he could die if he didn't make a change. Mikey spent most of his life being overweight, inactive, and eating fast food every single day, often multiple times per day, getting to the place where tying his shoes was a challenge to do without cramping. Even casual daily activities that many of us take for granted, like going for a long walk, were not options for Mikey.

Embarrassed by his body, he showered in the dark, avoided being in photos so he wouldn't have to see himself, wore baggy clothes, and hated the person he saw in the mirror every day. As fate would have it, he stumbled upon The Vegan Gym online, inquired, and then enrolled in The Vegan Superhero Academy coaching program. He embraced veganism, trusted his coach, and in less than nine months, he lost more than one hundred pounds, dropped his body fat percentage by half, gained confidence, learned to love himself, and transformed into a totally new person. Today, he is climbing mountains, doing ninety-minute gym workouts, and has a bubbly, outgoing personality that is in stark contrast to the person he was before. Furthermore, Mikey has become a leader in The Vegan Gym community with a transformation success story that others strive to achieve for themselves, viewing Mikey as an inspirational role model. Perhaps, most notably, Mikey is happy. Rather than dreading each day, he looks forward to every new day, and moves closer to achieving more milestones, new achievements, and greater happiness.

Mikey's newfound dedication to veganism is so strong that he created an online persona, the Flabulous Vegan, got a vegan tattoo, and now speaks out in support of ethical veganism and animal rights. He even did something that he previously thought would be impossible: Mikey entered a bodybuilding competition in November 2023, in the transformation category, sharing his incredible physical transformation success with a live audience. And he won the show! He earned first-place honors in his category and quite literally transformed from a morbidly obese omnivore to a champion vegan bodybuilder. Mikey effectively demonstrated the results of the power of consuming a plant-based diet, supported by a nurturing team of coaches, helping him become the happiest, healthiest, and best version of himself.

Is Mikey less likely to leave the vegan movement to become another statistic on the graph of vegan recidivism because of the support he received from The Vegan Gym? I believe so.

Another way that The Vegan Gym directly reduces vegan recidivism is through their annual Vegan Superhero Retreat, which attracts their online coaching clients from around the world. Approximately 150 clients gather for nearly a week in the Pocono Mountains on a 350-acre campground with all the amenities you would expect, which doubles as America's premier youth weight-loss summer camp facility. The Vegan Gym rents out the entire campground for a week every summer, which includes a full day of setup and cleanup. During the five days of in-person interactions, clients share meals together, engage in team-building and team-bonding games and sports in small and large groups, while listening to lectures, watching cooking demonstrations, and participating in everything from kayaking to zip lining to roasting vegan marshmallows around the campfire, building community, strengthening vegan resolve, and feeling more confident in their vegan lifestyles. With his newfound confidence, Mikey was one of the most outgoing participants at the 2023 Vegan Superhero Retreat, which was also the catalyst for his decision to commit to another two years of coaching. (All that happened *before* he won the bodybuilding competition, by the way.)

Since more than two thousand people have gone through their one-on-one coaching program, with thousands more likely to go through in just the next couple of years, it would be an interesting experiment to do a follow-up survey with hundreds of past clients years down the road to see how many of them are still vegan, as well as learn any other data that can be collected, such as how many people each former client influenced to go vegan as well. That data could then be compared to general levels of vegan recidivism to determine if indeed having plant-based nutrition, fitness, and lifestyle coaching extends the time that someone identifies as vegan.

It would also be interesting to see how many people who became vegan at the start of The Vegan Superhero Academy (those three hundred of the two thousand clients who were brand new to veganism, like Mikey) are still vegan years down the road at the time of the follow-up survey. That data could impact Leif's projection of 2.4 million potential animals spared, revealing fewer total animals spared if some people cease being vegan. In practice, if stories like Mikey's inspire thousands of others to embark on a vegan journey, then those numbers of animals spared could also significantly go up because of The Vegan Gym's net positive impact from word of mouth.

"The exciting part is that we are just getting started," Leif said. "I feel like we are on step two of a one-hundred-step journey. Our team will continue working hard to multiply our impact and ultimately touch the lives of millions of people, which will save tens of millions of animals."

Perhaps it is easier to view altruism within nonprofit organizations than it is through for-profit businesses. Partly, I suspect this is due to our own biases toward profit-seeking companies being naturally less altruistic than their nonprofit, animal-saving counterparts. We've certainly explored a variety of both for-profit and nonprofit entities throughout the book thus far, but I would be remiss not to mention my own perspective when evaluating The Vegan Gym and the other vegan coaches mentioned in these pages. I personally know all of the vegan coaches profiled in this book, as longtime friends and colleagues, and I can say with confidence that effective vegan altruism is at the core of every single one of their for-profit businesses. They were all animal rights and vegan advocates *before* they started their for-profit businesses, and, in fact, it is *because* they are vegan for the animals that they decided to create businesses that would help others become vegan, and stay vegan, therefore increasing their impact on reducing animal suffering by helping vegans, well, stay vegan.

"Saving animals is the foundation of our team's mission. Everything our team works on, from building nutrition programs for clients, to publishing vegan nutrition and fitness content, to working on our company's accounting records to ensure our business is healthy, profitable, and built for long-term survival, ultimately helps animals," Leif added. "But we are always looking for new ways to help more animals."

Doubling down on their effective vegan altruism, Leif shines light on the vast potential for vegan business success in a non-vegan world. He sets boundaries and has his own nonnegotiables about what his business will or will not support, regardless of peer pressure or changing trends.

"We only hire vegans, and we only work with vegans," he said. "A few years ago, a business coach we hired asked us to consider expanding our target demographic to include vegetarians and people who just occasionally eat meat but didn't want to become fully vegan. He said we were likely capping our growth potential by exclusively working with vegans (this includes people who are ready and willing to go fully vegan on day one of our program with our nutrition guidance). We said we didn't care and weren't willing to give clients animal products in their nutrition plans, no matter what. We have also never hired a non-vegan. Standing firm for what we believe in is far more important than boosting profits. And the irony is that our unwavering morals are what have allowed us to grow at 180 percent per year (this is our compounded annual growth rate over the past three years)."

I don't know about you, but I love a good, wholesome vegan success story, which makes me proud to support The Vegan Gym in ways that I am able to through my own platforms, including with this book.

For full transparency, in the summer of 2023, The Vegan Gym hired me as a consultant to help amplify their brand after collaborating with me on various campaigns for years. Knowing that we had a shared vision to create the greatest impact for animals, complementing our skills, talents, and strengths, I agreed to work with them to fulfill their mission of helping one million vegans get into the best shape of their lives. It appears that we are well on our way to accomplishing that. As part of my role, I managed the launch of Leif's book, *Get Lean with Plants*, which became a bestseller in multiple categories.

In true kaizen fashion, Leif's perspective on effectively influencing others starts with small steps. This has been his experience, starting from scratch, just like the rest of us, describing his journey from being a new vegan to managing perhaps the largest vegan online coaching business in the world: "I think the most effective way to promote veganism depends on two main factors: 1) the form of vegan advocacy that most resonates with you and aligns with your talents, and 2) your ability to understand your audience and tailor your message to align with what matters to them," he explained. "Take me, for example. I went vegan after being diagnosed with cancer, and then I transformed my body from a 'skinny fat' vegan to a vegan athlete. I have since inspired a handful of people in my personal life to go vegan. Not surprisingly, my favorite form of vegan advocacy is inspiring people through vegan health and fitness. I love helping vegans improve their health and fitness to serve as a shining example of what it means to be a healthy, fit vegan. But I also tailor my vegan message to my audience.

"One of the people I inspired to go vegan was my sister, Elke. I knew she cared more about saving the environment than achieving a certain level of health and fitness, so I encouraged her to watch the environmental documentary *Cowspiracy*, and I continued speaking with her about the environmental impact of our food system. A few months later, she went vegan. As another example, Ed Winters (known online as Earthling Ed) is an extraordinary speaker. He has inspired millions of people to go vegan or strengthen their vegan resilience through his writing, debates, and speeches. His vegan advocacy approach is effective because it's aligned with his talents, and he takes the time to understand his audience. He cares, and it shows. I think we need all forms of vegan advocacy to speak to the world. Some people will resonate more with Earthling Ed's message than mine. And vice versa. Every conversation helps. Every voice matters."

That is the vegan kaizen system in action, helping each of us take one small step that can change our lives.

Remember that taking small steps, even tiny actions, can lead to our biggest and best results over time because they don't overwhelm us or cause heightened stress or fear of failing or succeeding, and they don't tend to elicit general anxiety, since the steps seem so manageable and insignificant. As Dr. Mauer said in *One Small Step Can Change Your*

Life: The Kaizen Way: "Kaizen offers the possibility that through small acts of kindness, and even small moments of compassion and curiosity, we can change ourselves—and, eventually, humanity. What more important task does this life hold than to draw out the possibility in each moment?"

Ponder that question for a moment before we move into exploring how to most effectively use our personal platforms to take veganism mainstream.

CHAPTER 6

LEADING BY EXAMPLE

WHAT ACTIONS MAKE THE MOST DIFFERENCE?

"Showing people what it means to be an effective vegan athlete is really the heart and soul of our advocacy work. People don't like to be approached and berated about what habits they should change. When you intrigue them with your own lifestyle, leading by positive example, they come to you. And people are much more likely to make a change when they believe it was their own idea."

—Dani Taylor, cofounder of Vegan Proteins, cofounder of PlantBuilt, and comanager of Vegan Strong

When it comes to effectively promoting the vegan lifestyle, it seems that nothing is more powerful than leading by example. This can come in many forms, from how we carry ourselves to how we communicate about veganism. Leading by positive example is precisely why I was inspired to become vegan in the first place (from the positive example my older sister set), and why I chose a career as a vegan athlete, knowing how favorably people respond to examples that are set forth, particularly in sports. Growing up on a farm, raising animals that we would eventually sell at an auction to be turned into food, my sister, Tanya, rejected the idea that she had to break the fundamental trust that was built between her and the animals she raised, and she became a vegetarian at the age of ten in 1988, and eventually vegan at age fifteen.

I followed her lead but questioned whether I could achieve my health and fitness goals, which included building a strong, muscular body, without the inclusion of animal protein, since we all believed growing up that "milk does a body good." Tanya eased my concerns, helped me navigate my new vegan lifestyle when the internet was something most of us didn't have at home in the mid-1990s, and I did indeed achieve my health and fitness goals while following a vegan lifestyle. That enabled me to inspire millions of people to do the same over the next few decades, and if it weren't for Tanya's inherent compassion for the animals she raised, and then for all animals, particularly farmed animals, I don't know if I would have become the vegan athlete, author, and influential person I have become today. Her influence, therefore, is highly significant on reducing animal suffering, and I credit her for the impact that I have been able to have on others.

We all know we can have a profound impact on others, especially in our platform-rich age. This is true within veganism, too. Yes, many of us are inspired by the act of compassion, and the altruistic nature of reducing animal suffering, which is admirable, but when you actually talk to people and ask them why they became vegan, there is usually a catalyst of individual or collective personal influence that persuaded their decision. These are influences such as books, documentaries, and speeches by authors, producers, entertainers, podcasters, YouTubers, and other influential people, including athletes, chefs, doctors, musicians, and others who inspire us through the positive examples they set.

FAUNALYTICS AND THE
PATH TOWARD IMPACT

A huge part of forward progress for veganism is learning and understanding what methods are most effective in promoting veganism and in attracting others to reduce their impact on animal suffering. The answers to the question "What forms of animal advocacy are most effective?" might not be what you suspect.

Faunalytics, one of Animal Charity Evaluators' top charities that we mentioned in chapter four, conducts research and shares knowledge to help advocates help animals effectively. They also provide the world's biggest library of research about animal issues and animal advocacy. With more than four thousand articles and research summaries, their website is one you could get lost in for months—one might say they are *the reference* for effective examples of, well, leading by example.

One of those resources is their original 2022 study: *Planting Seeds: The Impact of Diet and Different Animal Advocacy Tactics.*[28] This particular study looks at the relative effectiveness of different advocacy tactics, and how successful each is in the short and long term. The study evaluated sixteen types of animal advocacy—disruptive protests, social media posts, educational workshops, showing graphic footage of animal abuse, celebrity influence, and vegan challenges, among others—and involved more than two thousand participants. The objective was to learn which approaches caused non-vegan study participants to not only decide to change their eating habits, but which approaches led to new behaviors, documented over a twenty-week period.

Their findings revealed good and bad news for vegan advocates of all types. Though some of their results were surprising to me, many of their results were ones I anticipated, particularly because I had already conducted dozens of interviews for this book before coming across this study. As a writer and published author in the vegan movement, I was pleased to see that books were one of the biggest drivers leading to a reduction in animal consumption. News articles and social media posts proved to be the most effective at changing people's behavior to eat fewer animals. The efficacy of social media posts was surprising to me because of the echo chambers we often find ourselves in within niche communities. On the other hand, disruptive protests, such as throwing red paint on people wearing fur, entering stores and businesses, causing an active disruption with a protest by shouting or chanting with a megaphone, occupying space, confronting consumers or store owners, and the like, not only produced no positive benefit to animals, but actually provoked anger and caused participants to eat more animals.

This study made clear that disruptive and non-disruptive protests are not beneficial for animals, regardless of how empowered we feel for "making a difference" and "standing up for animals." It simply doesn't work, and it often turns people away from veganism, causing them to contribute to even more animal suffering. It truly is a scenario where our own personal egos, convinced that we're making a difference, get in the way of actual progress. What's also difficult is criticizing fellow animal activists who "have their hearts in the right place," even if they aren't all that effective. And what's perhaps worse is that these activists think they are being effective, largely because of feedback from peers celebrating their boldness and willingness to take action. Many even brag about the number of times they have been arrested because it is a badge of honor as an activist. But the evidence suggests they're not effective, and actually contribute to *more* animals suffering due to creating an aversion to veganism. That's a tough pill for many vegan advocates to swallow, but if our goal is effectiveness, we must be open to realizing that what we're doing might not be the best approach, while actively taking the time to learn what is truly effective. The biggest issue here is the contrast between *believing* we are being impactful and actually *being* impactful, which requires that we set our egos aside and look at the data in order to best help animals, not help ourselves feel like we're making a difference.

Before I go any further, I will be clear that the results shared above were just from one particular study on the efficacy of animal advocacy. There will be plenty of anecdotal stories of disruptive and non-disruptive protests that changed hearts and minds and actions of non-vegans. Perhaps you have some of those personal experiences. The point of sharing this study is to show that, despite our own personal perspectives, observations, and biases, there are survey results from an audience we're trying to reach (non-vegans) that show very clearly that some of *our* favorite forms of activism that *we* think are effective might not be quite so impactful after all. I've been there. I've held signs, passed out literature, and protested circuses dating back nearly thirty years. I've marched in the streets of Los Angeles with hundreds of other animal rights activists. I've participated in national animal rights day demonstrations. I've volunteered with Anonymous for the Voiceless. I've been part of numerous PETA demonstrations, particularly in my younger years. And I have attended many animal rights conferences, and I know the feeling of a group mentality when hundreds of passionate people are fighting for the same cause.

Holding signs, shouting, heckling, confronting people, blocking access, throwing red paint on fur clothes, and other demonstrations might be empowering for us, but do little to help animals, whereas educational classes and workshops, and vegan challenges like the thirty-day vegan challenge Veganuary, do much more to inspire people to reduce their contributions to animal suffering. Using our skills, talents, resources, and time to write letters to newspapers, to write magazine and website articles, and to create a positive return on investment by reaching a massive mainstream audience with positivity, according to this Faunalytics study, does the most good to elicit a change in behavior.

Here are some direct quotes from the Faunalytics study that were a wake-up call for me and others, along with the organization's recommendations:

1. The results of this project primarily support the use of two forms of advocacy: social media posts and news articles. Social media posts and news articles effectively reduced self-reported animal product consumption in meat-avoiders and had no harmful effects on meat-eaters. They are also easier to implement and are lower cost than many other strategies, so we unconditionally recommend their use. If it would decrease costs, organizations could also consider targeting posts toward reducetarians and vegetarians rather than trying to persuade a general audience.

2. We also recommend forms of animal advocacy that were described as behavior-changing by people in Study 1 and that have been supported by causal evidence in other experiments: classroom education and meat-free challenges. 58 percent and 63 percent of our participants who had experienced these forms of advocacy reported reduced animal product consumption, respectively, and other research supports this claim.

3. We weakly recommend forms of advocacy that positively impacted meat-eaters' intentions or beliefs, but had no impact on behavior: graphic videos, leaflets, non-graphic videos, and celebrities. Our experiment did not find any impact of these forms of advocacy on behaviors, which is a substantial downside. However, if they can be made cost-effectively, swaying meat-eaters' intentions or beliefs may also be useful, in that it moves them one step closer to behavior change. The impact of these advocacy types on meat-eaters' intentions and beliefs varied so there is not sufficient space to cover them fairly here.

4. We recommend caution around the use of advocacy types that have not been supported by experimental data: educational information about animal welfare labels, documentaries, and billboards. The limited experimental research to date suggests that these advocacy types don't impact people's behaviors, with some evidence suggesting a positive impact on intentions only for documentaries and educational information. But we encourage additional experimental research for these three advocacy types since our caution is based on limited research.

5. The limited evidence from our two studies suggests that protests aren't helpful, and may in some cases cause harm. While it's important to note that our two studies don't provide definitive proof of protests' ineffectiveness by any means (and we don't know of any other experimental research looking at them), our experiment found that disruptive protests increased meat-eaters' self-reported consumption of animal products, while both disruptive and non-disruptive protests resulted in fewer petition signatures for animal welfare reforms in meat-avoiders. The accumulated evidence to date—which is minimal and would benefit from further study—leads us to believe that their impact is neutral at best, negative at worst.

6. Advocates can ensure that their advocacy materials of any type are as impactful as possible by testing how people respond to them. Specifically, advocates should strive to make their materials informative, engaging, and clear about the behavior change they suggest, as all of these characteristics were linked to taking a diet pledge and supporting welfare improvements. At the same time, advocates should aim to minimize perceptions of their materials as misleading, condescending, and angering, as these responses made people less willing to engage in pro-animal behavior.

7. Strong evidence about the impact of different advocacy types is still very limited, so more research is needed before making major changes to campaign or funding strategies. Throughout the report, we have placed more weight on evidence of behavior change versus intentions or beliefs, but we recommend that advocates and funders continue to support and study advocacy types that positively impact intentions or beliefs, and continue to study all kinds of advocacy, even those that appeared to have negative implications in this research. Behavior change occurs in stages, so advocacy types that only influenced beliefs

Advocacy Tactics Most Effective to Help Farmed Animals

Exposure: Percent of respondents who recalled seeing this type of advocacy.
Effectiveness: Percent of respondents who self-reported that experiencing advocacy caused them to reduce animal product consumption.

Ad or Billboard	Celebrity	Labeling (Info About Welfare)	Leaflet	News Article	Peer-to-Peer Outreach	Book	Classroom Education
35% Exposure 25% Effective	35% Exposure 25% Effective	55% Exposure 35% Effective	15% Exposure 43% Effective	55% Exposure 38% Effective	85% Exposure 32% Effective	10% Exposure 72% Effective	5% Exposure 60% Effective
Labeling (Vegan, Plant-Based)	Protest (Disruptive)	Protest (Non-Disruptive)	Social Media or Blog Post	Video (Graphic)	Video (Non-Graphic)	Documentary	Meat-Free Challenge
85% Exposure 25% Effective	15% Exposure 25% Effective	20% Exposure 38% Effective	55% Exposure 40% Effective	35% Exposure 40% Effective	40% Exposure 38% Effective	15% Exposure 55% Effective	15% Exposure 62% Effective

Lower Effectiveness, Range of Exposure   Average Effectiveness, Average Exposure   High Effectiveness, Low Exposure

Adapted from Faunalytics.

or intentions may still play a role in a long line of steps toward behavior change. And while we have strived to provide usable recommendations about all the advocacy types we considered, bear in mind that every study has its limitations, and no single report should ever be taken as definitive proof of impact.

THE POWER OF STORY: EARTHLING ED

Throughout the writing of this book, I interviewed dozens of vegan experts, and asked them a variety of questions about the effectiveness of promoting veganism and about impactful ways of reducing animal suffering. The name that came up more than all others combined was none other than Ed Winters, affectionately known online as Earthling Ed. Ed is the author of the books *This Is Vegan Propaganda* and *How to Argue With a Meat Eater (And Win Every Time)*. He is widely known as one of the greatest representatives of the movement, with some of the strongest arguments for veganism, and is considered one of the movement's most skillful and knowledgeable debaters.

It was a news story that inspired Ed to become vegan in the first place. His friend had brought up the idea of not eating animals as pizza toppings, which Ed thought was a bizarre perspective to have since he had spent his life enjoying eating meat, particularly chicken and bacon, but shortly after that first consideration of animals as anything other than food, he had a moment of awakening. It was a BBC news story about a truck carrying seven thousand chickens that crashed in the UK, killing more than 1,500 chickens on impact, while leaving hundreds more suffering with broken bones, broken wings, and even torn flesh hanging from their faces.

Ed was concerned for the well-being of the chickens. For the first time he evaluated his own emotions, feeling bad for the chickens who were suffering, barely alive, and for many who had died in the horrific truck crash, while also recognizing that he had, at the time, dead chickens in his refrigerator. Feeling a sense of sadness and guilt, he asked himself, "Are my taste buds more important than the life of an animal?" And, "How do I morally justify taking the life of an animal if it is unnecessary?"

Ultimately, those and other questions led to Ed becoming vegan, and emerging as one of the most prominent vegan activists today and a true testament of leading by example. In addition to his popular lectures, his wildly popular books, and his worldwide tours, Ed has also opened up multiple vegan restaurants, cofounded a nonprofit organization, cofounded an animal sanctuary, created a podcast, and produced an award-winning documentary. And at the time of this writing, Ed is just twenty-nine years old. Clearly, the news story that Ed saw on the BBC led to millions of animals being spared as a by-product of the influence that story had on Ed's actions. That's just one example of the power of news stories, and of digital and written content.

Leading by example could include starting our own business, becoming an online influencer, running for political office, creating a media company, becoming healthy and fit, or anything else where we have direct influence on those around us. Typically, the larger our audience, the greater potential influence we will have. Being aware of this for many years, I've made leading by positive example the cornerstone of my effective vegan advocacy as a writer, a speaker, and a champion athlete.

BECOMING POLITICAL TO HELP THE LARGEST NUMBER OF ANIMALS

Josh Balk might not have the name recognition that someone like "Earthling" Ed Winters has, and, in fact, his social media presence barely exists, yet he is arguably one of the world's most influential people in the history of the animal rights movement, directly improving the lives of billions of animals. Allow me to explain. Though he spent decades working for the largest animal protection organization in the world, the Humane Society of the United States (HSUS), sparing hundreds of millions of animals, his greatest accomplishment for the reduction of animal suffering occurred when he and his team achieved something that had never been done in our lifetime. Josh led the groundbreaking 2018 California Proposition 12 ballot campaign. It was the biggest legislative battle against agribusiness in US history, fighting for the banning of the production and sale of eggs, pork, and veal from caged animals in the world's fifth largest economy, the state of California. After a year of campaigning, including debating agribusiness on television, radio, and to newspaper editorial boards, raising and spending $13 million on advertising, and organizing a massive grassroots effort with thousands of volunteers, the law was passed with 63 percent of the vote.

California Proposition 12 became the strongest law ever enacted for farmed animals in the world, both with the highest animal welfare standard and reach of impact, owing to California's massive population and strength of economy. In subsequent years, Josh led campaigns that successfully passed cage-free egg laws in Oregon, Washington, Michigan, Colorado, Utah, Nevada, Arizona, Rhode Island, and Massachusetts.

Josh pointed out to me that "the number of people living in states with laws banning the sale of eggs from caged chickens would be larger than 92 percent of countries in the world."

In 2023, the US pork industry challenged California Proposition 12, and it went all the way up to the Supreme Court of the United States, where Josh defended the law, watching it be upheld with a vote of 5–4.

What led Josh to do this type of animal advocacy on a larger scale than nearly anyone in history were three guiding principles that steered his efforts to make the greatest impact for animals. He shared with me, "There are so many ways animals suffer inside factory farms that trying to solve every issue immediately will likely lead to no changes at all. In my mind, success requires focus. So I look to follow this formula: 1) Which animals by numbers are suffering the most? 2) Which animals have the greatest intensity of suffering? 3) What causes of suffering are we most likely going to defeat? This has led much of my work to focus on eliminating the caging of egg-laying chickens and mother pigs." His answer to these important questions: "The two most effective ways in which we can accomplish this is through passing laws and enacting (and enforcing) corporate commitments."

How do we do that?

"Aside from passing laws, we also have to wage—and win—corporate campaigns, getting the largest food companies to enact policies to stop using eggs and pork from caged animals. While I was at the Humane Society of the United States, I led a team that got virtually every major food company—including McDonald's, Burger King, Kroger, Costco, IHOP, and more—to make these commitments. Though making a commitment is one thing, getting a company to follow through is much harder. That's why I cofounded and am the CEO of The Accountability Board, which owns shares in every major publicly traded food company in the US, and increasingly throughout the world. As shareholders, we can engage companies to the highest levels and put pressure on their board of directors and executives. I've found this type of high-profile, and high-pressure legal action to be the most effective route to keep companies on track with their promises. And since these companies are global by nature, the policies we garner and enforce will have a global reach. As an example, if we get McDonald's to go cage-free globally, *including in China*, we'll be able to shift Chinese egg producers to cage-free in a political environment we'd be unable to do so by legislation."

THE POWER AND INFLUENCE OF POLITICS AND LEGISLATION CHANGE

Josh shared some of the results of his recent work to impact the greatest number of animals that suffer in the most egregious ways. "This collective work with legislative and corporate campaigning has pushed the US egg industry to be nearly 40 percent cage-free and the pork industry to now reach more than 40 percent gestation crate-free (or at least with housing systems where pigs are out of cages for the majority of their lives). When I started this work, the percentages were at nearly zero."

We can't just point out the problems. We must also provide solutions. That's where Josh has been innovative once again, carving out campaigns and accomplishing wins for farmed animals that had never been achieved before. In conjunction with banning eggs from caged hens, he also cofounded the world's leading vegan egg company with his best friend, Josh Tetrick. "When I cofounded Eat Just, a major motivation was to help ordinary people—not folks who were already vegan—to eat plant-based eggs. Now, the company's JUST Egg product—if considered an 'egg' company—would be one of the most popular egg brands in the country. And it's been so successful because everyday omnivores are giving it a try and continue buying it. And why did so many of them try it to begin with? Because the vegan in their life gave them a bottle, and now they're hooked!"

Josh is not the only vegan focused on creating political change. Former US presidential candidate Dennis Kucinich (2004 and 2008) has been vegan for decades and ran on platforms of sustainability. More contemporary examples include 2020 US presidential candidate Cory

Booker, an outspoken vegan advocate, using his platform while the senator of New Jersey to encourage plant-based eating and vegan living. New York City mayor Eric Adams has successfully enacted policies for meals in city hospitals to be plant-based by default, and he authored a book on plant-based eating and preventing and reversing common degenerative diseases associated with following a Standard American Diet. Colorado governor Jared Polis had an all-vegan wedding and is married to vegan and animal rights advocate, and First Gentleman, Marlon Reis. Reis's influence on Governor Polis likely resulted in Polis declaring March 20 a meat-free holiday in Colorado, honoring the "MeatOut Day" campaign started by the Farm Animal Rights Movement (FARM) in 1985, which takes place around the world every March, when observers leave animals off their plates. Arizona representative Dr. Amish Shah has passed the strongest legislation helping animals in the state's history, and at the time of this writing, he is running for a seat within the US House of Representatives.

Other political changes are happening all around us, within the United States and outside of the US borders, as more people like you and me are voting for the future we wish to see, speaking up for the voiceless, and standing up for basic rights that every sentient being deserves to experience.

LEADING BY EXAMPLE: VEGAN STRONG

Following more than fifteen years of running my own brand, Vegan Bodybuilding & Fitness, I joined Vegan Strong, a brand created by the sustainability-focused marketing agency Effect Partners, to make my greatest contributions to amplifying veganism and reducing animal suffering. As a not-for-profit organization determined to show the world that plants have all the protein we need, Vegan Strong consists of a team of champion vegan athletes who personify what it means to be a strong vegan. The objective of Vegan Strong is to lead by positive example, exhibiting, speaking, and touring at the largest fitness expos in America, distributing thousands of plant-based products, coupons, recipe booklets, and other materials to a mainstream, predominantly non-vegan, fitness audience.

The Vegan Strong team travels from fitness expo to fitness expo, to up to ten events per year, speaking onstage, performing cooking demonstrations, passing out plant-based products and literature, and leading by positive example among the most engaged fitness audiences in the world. The average fitness convention in America attracts about 25,000 enthusiasts over a one- or two-day fitness weekend. The outlier is the Arnold Sports Festival, named after bodybuilding icon Arnold Schwarzenegger, which is a three-day expo that brings a quarter million fans to the convention center in Columbus, Ohio, every spring. It is a sight to behold, and I have been there many times, including meeting Arnold on my twenty-first birthday in 2001. I still have the Polaroid photo, and have seen him many times since then, primarily at his world-renowned fitness festival, which is like nothing else on Earth. Vegan Strong has had a booth presence at the Arnold Sports Festival numerous times over the years, influencing the most dedicated fitness fans from around the globe.

The goal of the Vegan Strong team's presence at these shows, which attract a 99 percent non-vegan audience, is to show the mainstream fitness community that they can achieve their health and fitness goals by following an exclusively plant-based diet. Vegan Strong distributes plant-based foods, beverages, sports supplements, and information such as lists of high protein plant-based foods and plenty of high protein plant-based recipes, to a community that is hungry for knowledge and sports nutrition products. Vegan Strong also engages in conversations, answers questions about plant-based nutrition and veganism, sells donated plant-based products as a means of fundraising, sells books from champion vegan athletes on topics such as building muscle and burning fat on a plant-based diet, and offers free products to a range of fitness enthusiasts, professionals, and even the occasional fitness celebrity or icon.

We officially debuted Vegan Strong within the fitness community at the 2019 Arnold Sports Festival. Arnold himself walked right by our booth, with a security team of at least twenty officers creating a bubble around him. Our booth was so popular that we ran out of products to pass out on day two of the three-day expo. From that day on, we recruited even more product sponsors and donors to meet the demand. As we fully embraced Vegan Strong as a team of athletes who are committed to leading by example and promoting and distributing plant-based products at the largest fitness expos in America, we developed our Vegan Strong Method.

The Vegan Strong Method has the following principles and objectives:

- Lead by positive example as vegan athletes
- Distribute thousands of plant-based products, coupons, and pieces of literature per outreach event
- Help others replace animal-based foods with plant-based foods in their nutrition programs
- Provide education, inspiration, and support to those we engage with
- Teach others how to create new habits that reduce animal suffering
- Learn from our audience and improve our practices over time
- Calculate and evaluate the impact of our actions

The Vegan Strong Method strives to get plant-based products into the hands, homes, and mouths of fitness enthusiasts by the masses. Throughout the process of providing plant-based products to fitness fans, we support numerous companies and brands. This provides an opportunity for multiple entities to benefit—the animals, the recipients of the products, and the companies providing the products for us to distribute for them. We also understand that others can apply The Vegan Strong Method outside of the fitness industry, too, through leading by example and with the distribution of plant-based products and information.

As described earlier, the mainstream fitness expos where Vegan Strong exhibits draw audiences of around 25,000 for most shows, though at least three of the shows we attend draw crowds of more than 50,000 attendees—at expos in Los Angeles (the LA Fit Expo), Las Vegas (the Olympia Expo), and Columbus (the Arnold Sports Festival). In addition to all of the conversations we have, products we distribute, items we sell, coupons and booklets we pass out, and presentations we give, our booth, with its large-lettered, colorful "Vegan Strong" banner and the slogan "Plants Have All the Protein You Need," is seen by tens of thousands of people. I often see a light bulb going off in people's heads, which reflects in their eyes, when they stroll by the booth, look up, and see "Vegan Strong" and contemplate it for a moment, as if to think, "I didn't realize that was possible . . ." Many fitness fans are compelled to stop to talk to us, even if they had no initial intention of doing so, because of the juxtaposition posed by our tagline that plants have all the protein you need, which contrasts the mainstream fitness narrative about what to eat to build muscle.

Those are fun observations. Even more fun, and rewarding, is when people, including champion bodybuilders, come up to our booth with genuine interest and questions and walk away with answers, resources, information, and free plant-based products that they can try. When a team of champion vegan bodybuilders, powerlifters, personal trainers, fitness models, authors, and coaches display in physical form that we can build our bodies on a plant-based diet, that is, in itself, an effective form of advocacy for animals.

We're often one of only a few vegan exhibitors at these major fitness expos, and we're there to challenge the status quo and general perception of vegans, which is still not commonly associated with muscle mass and athletic performance. Furthermore, our team has a lot of vegan longevity, which surprises our audience. When they learn that our key ambassadors at the booth have all been vegan for ten to thirty years, with three of us for more than twenty years, respectively, they are immediately forced to recognize the reality in front of them that long-term veganism exists, and that every single one of us has been a champion in our sport as vegan athletes.

It should be stated before I go any further that fitness enthusiasts eat far more animals than typical omnivores. Mainstream bodybuilders, powerlifters, gym-goers, and athletes of all types often go out of their way to consume as much animal protein as possible—often in the form of eating as much chicken, beef, and fish; consuming as many eggs; and drinking as much dairy-based protein as they can. Most mainstream athletes serious enough to attend a fitness expo equate animal protein consumption with increased muscle mass and strength. For example, it's common for large male bodybuilders to eat five chicken breasts, dozens of egg whites, and drink half a dozen whey protein drinks all in a single day, along with many other animal foods, such as fish and animal by-products, including cheese and butter. Furthermore, dedicated athletes burn and eat more calories than the average person, which results in consuming far more animals per person than non-athletes. That's why Vegan Strong targets some of the world's largest consumers of animals.

On average, the typical serious mainstream fitness enthusiast who attends a major fitness expo eats about three times more animals than the typical meat-eating citizen in any developed country. And since so much of their consumption involves chickens, fish, eggs, and dairy, the extent of the animal suffering associated with their diet is even more considerable, which makes them prime targets to introduce plant-based products to. If they even just *reduce* their animal consumption as a result of our influence, that would be a win for animals, but if they could be effectively persuaded by our example to switch to a plant-based diet, their impact would be seismic.

Vegan Strong intentionally recruits plant-based products and coupons to distribute that match the fitness audience's interests, such as protein powders, protein bars, sports nutrition products, pre- and post-workout supplements, and plant-based meat, dairy, egg, and jerky alternatives. By introducing these options, we have the opportunity to cut into a very heavy meat-and-animal-food-based diet by replacing animals with plants in meal plans for serious and casual athletes and fitness fans across the country. This initiation into plant-based nutrition, and plant-based *sports* nutrition, is itself a powerful form of vegan advocacy, and something that remains the foundation of Vegan Strong's efforts to change the way that athletes fuel their performance.

The act of omnivores purchasing plant-based products in direct replacement of animal-based options provides support for the growth of the plant-based movement. Beyond that, bodybuilders and fitness enthusiasts are really into sports nutrition, and they prioritize their health and athletic performance, continuously and eagerly seeking new products, methods, and approaches to building their bodies. If we can get the most enthusiastic athletes among us on board with plant-based nutrition, the future is bright for animals.

Just one or two exhibitor experiences at fitness expos could replace tens of thousands of whey and casein protein drinks with pea, rice, hemp, and other plant-based proteins, and replace eggs and meat with plant-based alternatives, having a direct impact on tens of thousands of animals. Those figures are based on the volume of our product distribution, even if the consumer never buys another plant-based product in their life. If we're able to swap out animals and replace them with plants in even a single meal for these fitness enthusiasts, it means, even just for that particular meal, animals are no longer needed in the food supply chain, as a result of our Vegan Strong team distributing plant-based foods to a targeted audience.

Furthermore, there are people attending these events who are already leaning toward veganism, and they are often the most enthusiastic visitors to our Vegan Strong booth. Those individuals who are on the fence about veganism often end up embracing veganism after spending time with our collection of champion vegan athletes, having their questions answered and getting the inspiration they need to take the next step. One of the more rewarding aspects of our Vegan Strong tour, for me personally, is having conversations with people who have a sincere interest in becoming vegan and just need some support and guidance to fully embrace veganism.

I don't want to get hung up on the words "vegan" or "veganism," though I have been using them liberally here, because ultimately, these are plant-based diet steps people are taking, rather than embracing a completely new philosophy toward rejecting unnecessary animal suffering. So I should pause here, as I noticed myself using the word "vegan" a lot in these scenarios. Though some people are in fact gravitating toward a vegan lifestyle, it would be more accurate to say that these fitness enthusiasts are adopting more of a plant-based diet, which is still significant in reducing animal suffering—and is how we measure our effectiveness.

So what net impact does Vegan Strong have on animals by exhibiting at these fitness expos year after year? To accurately measure our impact, we're going to make some very conservative but plausible estimations, based on years of observations and experiences. This is Vegan Strong's influence, as I measure it:

Since we distribute between five and fifteen thousand plant-based products, coupons, and booklets per fitness expo, depending on the size of the event, we'll create some estimations based on the lowest numbers, determining that approximately five thousand people come by our booth at a given event. We exhibit at five to ten fitness expos per year, depending on a variety of factors, including our budget, the dates and locations of particular events, including some that overlap, and, of course, how Covid-19 impacted our tours from 2020–2022, which saw a decline in attendance and a reduction in total events, while some organizations paused before committing to organizing a massive expo in a large convention center during uncertain times.

Being conservative again, let's go with the lowest end here, and assume we exhibit at five events per year (for the record, during any "normal" year not impacted by Covid-19, we have never exhibited at fewer than seven expos in a calendar year). We want to be as accurate as we can about our impact, without projecting or making assumptions that land in our favor and create a false sense of impact, so we're going to remain reserved and say that we engage with five thousand people at five events per year. So that will be our starting point, for a total of 25,000 people that we distribute plant-based products, coupons, and literature to. This gets a bit more nuanced, because nearly everyone who comes by our booth gets more than one sample, say three or four samples on average, of a variety of different products. There are also paying customers who buy our Vegan Strong Bundle, which consists of full-size products that have dozens of servings respectively, along with an additional ten or more servings of complimentary products that go along with the full-size products in a Vegan Strong–branded tote bag. Therefore, hundreds out of the five thousand attendees who come by our booth leave with fifty to one hundred servings of plant-based foods, beverages, or supplements, while most walk away with just three or four total servings.

Even trickier yet is that we distribute thousands of coupons, including "free product" coupons, meaning there are thousands more "potential" meals or "servings" that attendees will consume in the future. That's significant, as is the influence of our full-color recipe and information booklet, which no doubt inspires some people to try plant-based recipes. Let's be judicious and assume that none of the thousands of coupons will be redeemed in stores and that our booklets will have no influence. We'll just create more averages on the very low end, assuming the typical person that comes by our booth walks away with five servings of plant-based foods, beverages, or sports supplements (since some get one sample, and others receive or purchase one hundred samples or "servings," such as from full-size tubs of protein powder). Some of the same attendees also come back on the second day of a two-day expo for even more samples, raising their individual total.

Since we know that we cater to a 99 percent non-vegan audience, which we gauge from conversations we have with attendees, and which matches general demographics within American society, particularly for this type of expo, we can safely assume that nearly all of these five servings of plant-based nutrition products would have been animal derived. Instead, lucky festivalgoers receive totally free nutrition bars, jerky, protein powders, nut butters, pea protein puffs, and sports supplement samples like branched-chain amino acid (BCAA) packets, with the opportunity to purchase some at 75 percent off the suggested retail price. We are universally known for having "the best deal at the show," because we are selling donated products at a low price point, on purpose, to entice people to invest into the plant-based diet and vegan lifestyle, whereas most other exhibitors are looking to profit off consumers. So now we are looking at 5,000 people per show, consuming 25,000 plant-based products, over the course of 5 shows per year, which would be 125,000 plant-based meals, snacks, supplements, or "servings" that would have otherwise been derived from animals. This, of course, does not include the fact that we give educational lectures and cooking demonstrations at some of these events, and makes the assumption that none of our printed materials from our coupons to recipe booklets, or our books and other resources at our booth, or from our conversations with show attendees, had any impact on future food choices among those who stop by our Vegan Strong booth.

Even with all of these careful estimations, we can measure our yearly impact and conclude that, each year, Vegan Strong directly displaced 125,000 meals that would have come from animals, and replaced them with plants. Since many meals people eat consist of multiple animals in a single sitting, such as a burger with beef (cows), dairy (different cows, which also leads to veal calves), bacon (pigs), and egg (chickens, which also impacts chicks) from the meats, toppings, and sauces of a single burger, we can plausibly conclude that by replacing 125,000 meals that would have been animal-based with plants, we're at least preventing nearly 125,000 animals from being killed for food each year. Surely, there are more calories in a burger than in a single serving of plant-based protein powder or vegan jerky, so this could be analyzed further into how many "calories" were replaced, rather than meals, but since we're already being very conservative, we likely don't need to be more nuanced into individual calories to make our point. Also, many of the products are a direct one-for-one replacement, such as a plant-based protein drink in place of an animal-based protein drink, a plant-based burger in place of an animal-based burger, and so on.

It's also true that a single cow would create many burgers for numerous meals for different people; so, theoretically, every burger consumed is not the result of a different animal's slaughter. A single dairy cow could produce many whey and casein protein drinks as well, so it might not always be a one-to-one ratio of each animal-based meal resulting in another animal's slaughter, and we're aware of those figures, as presented numerous times already in estimated animals consumed per capita per year. That's another reason why we're being conservative and not factoring in many of the other influences that would typically tip the scale in the favor of our positive net impact, such as all of our printed and digital content, our marketing and advertising, or even our actual conversations that take place for eight hours per day for multiple days per most expos, all year long.

Of course, if we wanted to get more nuanced, we would have to admit that of those 25,000 individuals we interacted with throughout the year, some of them, even just 1 percent of them, are likely to purchase a plant-based product instead of an animal-based product in the future, because of the plant-based samples or full-size products they received from our Vegan Strong booth or from their overall interactions with us. Even at just 1 percent of 25,000 individuals, that is 250 people who would likely make a repeat purchase of plant-based foods, beverages, or sports nutrition products, which would have otherwise come from animals. Furthermore, if they make that purchase just four times per year, that would be another 1,000 animals spared per year, on top of the 125,000 we're already sparing due to a lack of demand, as a result of omnivores getting a certain amount of calories (five servings, we determined) of plant-based foods, per individual, per year. Since Vegan Strong has been touring for the better part of five years, at approximately five expos per year, that means Vegan Strong has had a direct impact on sparing 625,000 animal lives.

We're also assuming our online presence of more than 25,000 social media followers and 5,000 newsletter subscribers made zero net impact on any omnivore's food choices. There's something else we didn't factor in either. We did not calculate what the numbers would look like if some people decided to become vegan after meeting our Vegan Strong team, nor did we factor in the influence that an individual Vegan Strong team member had beyond their interactions at each show. We have multiple Vegan Strong team members who have more than 100,000 social media followers on a single platform, others who are authors of multiple books, and those who are podcast hosts, coaches, gym owners, and trainers with more than one million social media followers combined. Imagine all of that net impact we're not calculating because it's too speculative, and we want to know our *real* impact. Here's another way to evaluate it:

Since we know that each vegan spares approximately 105–365 animals per year—on the higher end in Western societies—according to various estimates, and we know that our dedicated fitness audience consumes up to three times the national average of calories from animals, even if just a handful of the 25,000 people we engaged with become vegan, too, that would result in thousands more animals spared per year, for potentially tens of thousands of additional animals spared over a five-year period. We also didn't factor in the possibility of people of influence becoming vegan after meeting us, such as gym owners, trainers, coaches, dietitians, celebrities, podcasters, YouTubers, and others, and the net impact they could have on their audiences. That could lead to many more thousands of animals spared.

We also did not consider the far more likely outcome that some people, of the tens of thousands we meet, will simply choose plant-based meals over animal-based meals every once in a while, because of our Vegan Strong influence. It is highly likely that some people will be inspired to eat more plants, and when given the opportunity at a restaurant, or at home, will choose a plant-based option instead of eating animals, at least on occasion. And that could add up to many tens or hundreds of thousands of animals spared, in addition to the hundreds of thousands of animals spared that we already calculated. But we didn't want to make any assumptions, and we chose to stick with the lowest level of figures that we could, based on hard facts that we know, such as how many plant-based products we distributed to a 99 percent mainstream non-vegan audience.

Therefore, we'll settle for 625,000 animals spared over a five-year period, directly as a result of Vegan Strong's fitness expo tour. That's not nearly as many animals spared, saved, or impacted as when we as a vegan community collectively supported the Beyond Meat tacos at Del Taco, or the Beyond Orange Chicken at Panda Express, or the Impossible Whopper at Burger King, which served millions of plant-based meals to omnivores, but we are pleased with the impact we made on more than half a million animals, knowing internally that the actual figure could be twice that size. We also take pride in knowing that we successfully supported dozens of plant-based companies along the way, who likely retained customers after our initial introduction to them, helping them grow and expand.

What could the future look like? There's a whole world of possibilities out there. Imagine if some of the 125,000 individuals we met incorporated plant-based meals for their entire families, even just once or twice per month. We could be looking at tens of millions of meals switched from animals to plants, over just a five-year period. That should be enough encouragement to inspire many of us to follow The Vegan Strong Method. The question, then, becomes, how can you apply The Vegan Strong Method into your own animal advocacy? Remember, it all comes back to leading by positive example and getting plant-based products into the hands, homes, and mouths of omnivores, introducing them to products that could become staples in their households.

Though I have taken on many new projects, and I support lots of brands and companies, my support for Vegan Strong is still, well, strong. I'm still out on tour with Vegan Strong at a few events per year, accomplishing what we set out to do more than half a decade ago. I encourage you to apply The Vegan Strong Method to your lives, too. We all have friends or family that we can share plant-based products, foods, and beverages with, but it goes much further than that. It's the example we set, the resources we share, the ideas we introduce to others, and the way we replace animals on menus and meal plans with plants that matters most for animals. The Vegan Strong Method is just one approach of the many shared in this book. If these ideas have resonated with you, I encourage you to visit VeganStrong.com to see how you can support Vegan Strong's ongoing work to change the way the mainstream public views veganism. If you're curious to know which companies we recruited to donate products to Vegan Strong, you can visit VeganStrong.com/sponsors for a complete list. There is no guarantee that any given company on that list will support your endeavors, too, but if you mention that you were referred to them by me or by Vegan Strong, it just might help give you the inside connections you need to start accumulating your own supply of products and coupons to distribute to your community, with the mission of replacing animal-based foods with plant-based meals. That's where your STRONG V characteristics meet Vegan Strong. Use your connections and lead by positive example.

We've seen some ways that leading by example can drastically reduce animal suffering. Now, let's look at the power that technological advances, from non-meat protein development to social media, are having on accelerating the reduction of animal suffering.

CHAPTER 7

THE POWER OF TECHNOLOGY IN REDUCING ANIMAL SUFFERING

IT'S IN THE PALM OF YOUR HAND

"Utilizing social media is a highly influential way of maximizing impact for animals. It's where everyone is, and therefore is where we can influence massive amounts of people to create a better world for animals."

—John Oberg, animal rights activist

The vegan future, or a future of greatly reduced animal suffering, at least, that I and other advocates throughout this book have talked about, starts with the seeds we plant now to take root in the future.

Perhaps a slight variation of the *Field of Dreams* quote is apropos—"If you build it, *they* will come."

By following the most effective paths for change, committing to our why, identifying our strengths and resources to contribute toward this movement, using our financial power, leading by example to draw people to veganism, and utilizing technology and innovation in alternative proteins, we can achieve our goal of reducing animal suffering around the world.

We appear to be on the cusp of a breakthrough in technology that will help us achieve our goal of a vegan future faster than any other method we have experienced to date. That, of course, is the role that cultivated meat technology and other alternative protein technologies, such as precision fermentation, will play in the direct influence on the foods we will have access to in the not-too-distant future.

THE GOOD WORK OF THE GOOD FOOD INSTITUTE

One of the organizations obsessed with getting the taste, price, and convenience of alternative proteins on par with animal-based foods is the Good Food Institute (GFI). They are also one of the Animal Charity Evaluators' Top Charities helping animals. GFI might be the most impactful organization, globally, helping animals, particularly because of their involvement in alternative proteins and their influence on the future of food consumption. With arguably the most upside of any organization related to helping animals, since they are growing at such a rapid pace, and because they are involved with the science and technology of the ever-changing alternative protein landscape, they have become a global voice for the future of animal-free food (or reduced-cruelty food).

GFI is an international network of organizations developing the road map for a sustainable, secure, and just protein supply. They identify the most effective solutions, mobilize resources and talent, and empower partners across the food system to make alternative proteins accessible, affordable, and delicious. The GFI website has a database of an astonishing 1,300 alternative protein manufacturers and brands worldwide. That's how many companies (today) are working on solving our current protein crisis, helping to reduce animal suffering by keeping animals out of the protein supply chain. GFI is the most comprehensive organization working toward a better future for animals. They have hundreds of full-time staff members, operate with tens of millions of dollars annually, and they are deeply involved with the science, technology, and politics of creating a more sustainable future. They even work directly with multiple foreign governments, which are investing millions of dollars into alternative protein technology in places like Israel and Brazil. They are impactful, influential, and highly effective in numerous areas of policy and systemic change. GFI produces comprehensive reports, such as their Plant-Based State of the Industry Report, which for 2022, was 111 detailed pages long—nearly an entire book recapping just one small facet of their involvement in food sustainability.

In GFI's Plant-Based State of the Industry Report for 2022, they revealed that, in the United States, plant-based meat, egg, and dairy companies raised $1.2 billion in investment funds, bringing their totals to $7.8 billion invested into those plant-based food and beverage categories. Plant-based product sales surpassed $8 billion in 2022 alone, up 7 percent from the previous year, with global plant-based product sales surpassing $28 billion.[29]

I had the opportunity to interview GFI founder and president Bruce Friedrich about the role that GFI plays in reducing animal suffering. I have been well aware of GFI's global impact, and their focus on innovation, which will lead the way into the future, particularly in the alternative protein space, with cultivated meat, and an interview with Bruce is something I was looking forward to for a long time. Taking animals out of the food production system is a goal that GFI works tirelessly on, but also works very strategically on, ensuring that when the time comes for mass adoption of alternative proteins, producers, governments, retailers, and consumers alike will be ready to embrace the future.

US Retail Plant-Based Food Sales in 2022

	Dollar Sales	1-yr. Dollar Growth	3-yr. Dollar Growth	Dollar Share	Unit Sales	1-yr. Unit Growth	Unit Share	Household Penetration	Repeat Rate
Total Plant-Based Foods	$8.0 Billion	7%	44%	1.4%	1.9 Billion	-3%	1.2%	60%	80%
Plant-Based Meat	$1.4 Billion	-1%	43%	1.3%	255 Million	-8%	1.7%	18%	63%
Plant-Based Milk	$2.8 Billion	9%	36%	15.3%	749 Million	-2%	14.7%	41%	76%

Adapted from GFI.

"We want to feed ten billion people by 2050; we want to slash the climate impact of meat production; we want to eliminate antibiotics from the food supply; we want to slash pandemic risk; and we want to remove tens of billions of land animals and trillions of sea animals from the global food chain, with all of the massive external costs and animal suffering that go along with that," Bruce said.

My conversation with Bruce was fascinating, and I learned even more than I had anticipated, which further reinforces my appreciation for the incredible work GFI is doing. Bruce doesn't sugarcoat the harsh reality that we face as individuals who care about the well-being of animals and our planet, and shared some sobering statistics that are difficult to write because they are so alarming. Bruce informed me that there have been eleven peer-reviewed articles (thus far) reporting on how much animal agriculture there will be in 2050. Estimates range from a potential 62 to 242 percent global increase.

Bruce made the same observation that Better Meat Co. founder and president Paul Shapiro made (who you'll hear from later), that US meat consumption is higher, per capita, than it has ever been, and that our progress to mitigate animal suffering is only working to a small degree right now. But he has hope for the future.

"The guiding observation of GFI is that what we have been doing has been working up to a point—advocating dietary change is critically important—but it doesn't seem like it has been meaningfully decreasing the number of animals slaughtered," Bruce said. "But the theory of change for GFI is analogous to the theory of change of renewable energy and electric vehicles. Energy production and consumption as well as miles driven will go up through 2050. The challenge is not to change human nature, as that will be impossible. The challenge is to shift the world from fossil fuels to renewable energy. We can think about animal agriculture in the same way. If we make plant-based meat that is indistinguishable except that it doesn't have antibiotic and other drug residues, and is far less likely to have bacterial contamination, we can simply change the way meat is made instead of changing human nature.

"There is certainly some degree to which our work so far has reduced animal cruelty, but the long-term value comes when plant-based and cultivated meat actually tastes the same or better, and costs the same or less. The real displacement, the complete and total elimination of fossil fuels, gas vehicles, and industrial animal agriculture, only comes when you eliminate the green premium. And that means you need renewable energy, electric vehicles, and alternative proteins to compete in the marketplace. We are focused on the science, policy, and industry ecosystems that we are building to reach maximum displacement."

Continuing with our renewable energy and electric vehicle analogy, Bruce shared, "We [GFI] are the people behind the scenes, trying to make it so renewables go from a couple of percent to a hundred percent, so that electric vehicles go from a couple percent to a hundred percent, and the way you do that is you build the scientific ecosystem which brings down prices and increases convenience. So renewables, electric vehicles, and alternative proteins need to compete for everybody, not just the early adopters, not just the people who are willing to be inconvenienced and pay more. So, we're not the people trying to sell you Beyond, Boca, and Impossible burgers, when those things cost twice as much, or the chicken and fish versions that cost far more relative to conventional. We're the people trying to make it so that meat is made from plants, or cultivated from cells, and that is simply how meat is made. The private sector—Beyond and Impossible—can sell you Beyond and Impossible burgers. We want to create lots more Beyond Meats and Impossible Foods, but all of them need to be focused not on competing with one another, but on competing with the products of industrial animal agriculture."

Bruce's organization doubled down on their focus in science and technology, which does not extend to marketing any products to the general public. He reiterated that it is not GFI's job to sell vegan products to consumers, and that it is solely up to those entities (like Beyond Meat and Impossible Foods) to convince the general public to buy their products at premium prices. With such low levels of adoption of plant-based and alternative proteins today, due to the green premium of higher costs and tastes that are not on par with conventional meat products, much work needs to be done. Bruce added, "Our global battle cry is that governments should be putting $10.1 billion into this endeavor. And then, at the industry level, we're focused on convincing the really big food and meat companies to see alternative proteins as the future, and to put significant resources into their own plant-based and cell agriculture endeavors."

Naturally, I brought up the barriers that keep the general population from adopting a plant-based diet or vegan lifestyle on any sizable scale—taste, cost, and convenience—and Bruce replied optimistically considering how massive these barriers are. "I think once the plant-based products and cell agriculture compete on price and taste, they will win," he said.

What he is referring to is that there really isn't a psychological barrier, such as people being intimidated by alternative proteins, or that people are grossed out by the unfamiliar (such as cultivated meat), but that, put as simply as possible, people will, en masse, embrace plant-based and cultivated meat as soon as they reach price and taste parity. I hope he's right. It's also what GFI is banking on for our future. If it seems like there is an ongoing theme here, that is because there is a "single-minded focus" GFI has on creating price and taste parity for alternative proteins, which they're counting on, and investing heavily into, for the future of animal welfare and of humanity.

In the summer of 2023, cultivated meat was approved for sale in the United States by the USDA and became available in two restaurants a few weeks later. In San Francisco and Washington, DC (who knows, by time of publication, perhaps additional cities), you can find meat on menus that was made from animal cells without requiring animal slaughter. That's how fast technology can move. It seems like it was only a few years ago that plant-based meat started to get some serious attention from mainstream consumers, and now alternative proteins are a reality in America, too. That bodes well for a more compassionate future for animals, and it is only just the beginning. Technological advancements, particularly in food production, will be one of the most effective ways to reduce animal suffering, on the largest scale that we have perhaps ever seen in human history.

Wrapping up my interview with Bruce, he left me with some closing words: "We want consumer choice to dictate what people eat, and our focus is on making plant-based and cultivated meat win in the marketplace." At the end of the day, consumer preferences will drive supply and demand and will ultimately determine the fate of billions of animals. GFI is counting on food technology to make the decision to choose a more compassionate menu item an easy choice for consumers to make.

There is a desperate and immediate need to change our food system *now*, not just in the *future*, and I am determined to play a role in that, as I hope that you are, too. Focusing on science, technology, and politics is what *GFI* does, not what *I* do, and likely not what *you* do either. So it doesn't benefit animals for me to sit back and wait for mass adoption of alternative proteins, renewable energy, and electric cars in 2050. What we *can* do is donate to GFI now, so they can meet their goals as soon as possible.

HOW OUR GROWING UNDERSTANDING OF SOCIAL CONTAGION THEORIES CAN HELP ANIMALS

Nearly everyone who uses social media wants to accumulate followers. That's the currency that fuels our online economy. The more followers we acquire, the greater influence we will likely have, which results in more revenue we can generate to fund our agendas, like reducing animal suffering. Social media influence can even lead to celebrity status, which we've seen for decades. Celebrity status can lead to significant influence, and using influential status for positive change can be a great thing.

In today's society, we could quite literally see a single tweet from a major celebrity influence more people to become vegan than an entire vegan organization might be able to accomplish over a multi-year period—depending on the magnitude, significance, and total compounding impact of the social media reach of the particular celebrity. One documentary, with enough big names in it, reaching a wide enough audience, could have a greater impact on a particular outcome for animals than an organized group of activists could accomplish after years of exhausting work. That takes nothing away from the dedicated, hardworking vegan activists who tirelessly toil and labor to create local, global, and systemic changes, but it speaks to the reality of the power of celebrity and media influence in the world we're living in today.

If we have the goal, as many of us do, to create the most compassionate world around us, we're therefore more likely to achieve that through celebrity influence, or mainstream media influence, along with a foundation of grassroots campaigns than we are at a small grassroots level by itself without celebrity endorsement.

I'm the first to support grassroots activists and speak to the great work they have accomplished, and I've been involved in grassroots activism and outreach for my entire adult life, dating back to my early teenage years as a passionate new vegan in the mid-'90s. To this day, grassroots efforts are the foundation of the work I do as a writer, athlete, touring speaker, networker, collaborator, and vegan advocate. But grassroots efforts alone don't create rapid change. Look at how the world reacted when Lionel Messi finally brought a World Cup trophy back to Argentina in 2022. His celebratory post became the most popular Instagram post of all time. When celebrities, politicians, or people of significant influence release new books, they frequently become bestsellers. It's the celebrities and truly influential people, not most of us, who dominate the television and online-streaming airways, and who often control narratives on radio and other broadcasting platforms.

Though grassroots campaigns will always be the foundation of many movements, including the vegan movement, it won't always be what advances a movement the fastest or has the greatest overall impact by itself, particularly in an ever-changing social media climate. If you had a project you were trying to promote to reach as many people as possible, would you rather have a bunch of people with clipboards spending months gathering signatures and passing out flyers in small towns, or have a celebrity in your industry promote your project to twenty million followers in a single day?

> Though grassroots campaigns will always be the foundation of many movements, including the vegan movement, it won't always be what advances a movement the fastest or has the greatest overall impact by itself, particularly in an ever-changing social media climate.

But does reaching large numbers of people from celebrity influence lead to people taking action? As we saw last chapter in the Faunalytics study, not always. It usually needs some help.

In a 2023 *Hidden Brain* podcast hosted by Shankar Vedantam, titled "The Snowball Effect," Shankar's guest, author of *Change: How to Make Big Things Happen*, Damon Centola, a professor of engineering and applied sciences at the University of Pennsylvania, shared many examples, based on evidence, explaining what actually powers a movement forward. Whether it's the growth of social media platforms, like X, formerly known as Twitter, or the growth of social movements, like Black Lives Matter, or how the Ice Bucket Challenge to raise money and awareness of ALS took off, Dr. Centola explains what really leads to behavior change.

Dr. Centola explained the role of simple and complex contagions with regard to getting an idea to spread, while also describing weak and strong ties, which define relationships we have with one another. There is a general understanding that things spread from social contact—from viruses, to germs, to information, to ideas—but sometimes these transmissions are given too much credit as the thing that causes a movement to take hold. In essence, weak ties and simple contagions are often credited for the advancement of ideas and movements, when it is actually strong ties and complex contagions doing the work, sometimes dressed in simple contagion's clothing. Basically, what Dr. Centola is suggesting is that grassroots communities and engaged community members build up a movement that influencers and celebrities then adopt at a later time, helping them reach a tipping point, and the influencers or celebrities are often given credit for that achievement. This is despite the fact that it was actually built on the backs of strong, resilient communities that pushed an idea forward.

For example, Twitter's (now X) rise in popularity was initially credited to Oprah Winfrey, when Twitter cofounder Evan Williams was on her show in the early days of Twitter, but it was really the passionate tech users by the millions, especially in Silicon Valley, who built the foundation of Twitter's success. Oprah gave them their tipping point with mainstream adoption of the new technology.

Social change is a contagion process. Simple contagions occur when someone shares an idea that is already somewhat familiar to others, such as the ALS Ice Bucket Challenge, for example. One person shares it with another, word spreads, people are infected by the idea, and soon most people are familiar with the Ice Bucket Challenge and it goes "viral." On the other hand, complex contagions are harder for us to wrap our heads around and accept right away.

With complex contagions, we have to be convinced, and often accept certain costs, such as the social costs of adopting a vegan lifestyle. Joining a protest march, for instance, has risks involved and uncertainty, even if someone we know tells us about it. Complex contagions are also more closely related to creating social change because they often come from people in our network, rather than a simple contagion, which, per an example used in the podcast, is getting people to share cat videos online, which usually come from strangers in random posts we see on the internet and decide to share with our network.

Within complex contagions, such as social movements and causes, we often wait to see how our peer group responds to current events, such as watching to see whether our Facebook friends will change their profile photos to represent support for gay marriage, Black Lives Matter, the Ukraine war, or other noteworthy topics. Rarely are we the first to take a public stand on an important issue without waiting for social reinforcement from our peers before deciding how to act.

We need strong ties to support complex contagions, meaning that the grassroots activists, the communities of advocates, and our strong social groups that have shared visions are the foundations that help a movement take hold. There is also a "celebrity myth" regarding complex contagions that they are somehow early adopters. In reality, celebrities wait to see what their fans think of a current event or controversial idea before they actually take a stand on a given issue. Celebrities are rarely early adopters, but they help a movement achieve a critical point, as we saw with Oprah and Twitter. Regardless of when celebrities throw their support behind veganism, it helps reach a tipping point, which we have seen in many examples throughout our lives.

It's not just celebrities. Anyone who has access to major media outlets and the ability to reach the masses has real influence to create actual change. As a vegan for more than a quarter of a century, I have watched this unfold for decades. In recent years, I've had a front-row seat, seeing friends grow their platforms from no followers to millions of followers, while observing the influence (and opportunities) that comes with it. Many of us, including lots of you reading this book, have helped lay the foundation of the current animal rights and vegan movements, but if we don't have influencer and celebrity support, the road to reaching a tipping point is so much longer, which results in unfathomable amounts of animal suffering while we wait for our simple contagion moments. Therefore, we should use whatever connections we have to help expedite the process of raising awareness of veganism, even if we personally don't find influencers or celebrities to be particularly altruistic or endearing.

Some examples of celebrity influence to promote veganism and support animals include famous musicians Billie Eilish and Lizzo promoting veganism to their massive audiences of hundreds of millions combined. Greta Thunberg uses her platform of tens of millions to address vegan issues related to climate change, and the queen of social media, Kim Kardashian (along with many other celebrities), promotes vegan products to a massive audience of more than half a billion followers. Of course, looking at a complex contagion, Joaquin Phoenix is the quintessential celebrity that has been a voice for the voiceless for nearly his entire life.

LEVERAGING SOCIAL MEDIA TO HELP ANIMALS

So what if you're not an Academy Award–winning actor, a major musician, a massive celebrity, or if you're not all that well connected or famous, and only have a modest social media following? How do you make the greatest impact around you? According to datareportal.com, 4.76 billion people (59.4 percent of the total global population), especially in the developed world, use at least one social media platform to engage with the rest of the world, or at least engage within their community.

Social media is just as big a part of today's society as television or movies ever were, if not far more relevant, and engaged with by more people. Most distinctly, social media allows for two-way or multi-way communication, whereas television and movies are simply there for us to consume. Since social media is here to stay, and will be dominant in our society moving forward, let's learn how to purpose it to help animals. Over the following pages you will read stories and examples of how to benefit animals by strategically using social media, from some of the world's most influential vegan content creators.

Using social media and other forms of media to be a voice for the voiceless could just be one of the most empowering feelings you can experience, because you're literally saving lives and making a difference in the world. It's hard to know how to get started with content creation, but like anything else, there's a course for that—in fact, there are many such courses on that topic.

In the areas of creating content to help animals, activist John Oberg has you covered. His courses, which I have taken, are aptly named: Mastering Social Media to Change the World, Mastering Twitter to Change the World, and Mastering Instagram to Change the World, which you can find on johnoberg.org/courses.

What if I told you that you could make a living, even a full-time career, by promoting veganism on TikTok, Instagram, Facebook, Twitter/X, and YouTube—literally getting paid to help animals? Would you be interested?

If this were a classroom full of aspiring vegan activists, I imagine every hand being raised right now. Who wouldn't want to earn a full-time living by using fun and engaging social media platforms to help prevent animal suffering and save animal lives?

Today, vegan activists who have made social media vegan advocacy their careers, earning a full-time living posting on Twitter/X and Instagram, and uploading YouTube videos, also often get invited to give presentations about their vegan advocacy at many conferences and festivals around the world, living a rewarding, enriching, and altruistic life. So long as they reach some non-vegans with their message, or empower current vegans to keep going strong, surely they are making an impact for animals, even if at times it can be difficult to see.

John Oberg has what many vegan advocates would consider to be a "dream job." He uses Twitter/X and Instagram to help animals and has made a career out of doing so. As a result of his popularity on such platforms, he has also earned opportunities to speak on the topic of using social media to help animals all over the world, from Europe to South America. He even developed his own social media courses, helping others follow in his footsteps.

John is the first to recognize that it is fundamentally more challenging to quantify the net impact on animals that social media influence has, since views, impressions, likes, shares, and comments don't directly correlate with X number of meals changed from animals to plants. That doesn't mean the data isn't there—it's just harder to interpret. Even if some of John's posts go viral, with hundreds of thousands or millions of views, how do we know what percentage of viewers are non-vegan? Furthermore, how do we determine how the viral post impacted them and altered their eating habits or purchasing decisions? John has ways to measure his influence, such as reading the comments, engaging with people, and learning whether viewers are vegan or not, and finding out how they were influenced by the content he shared. John explained his interpretation of his social media impact this way:

"I measure the impact of my work to reduce suffering based on the number of individuals I reach through my social media advocacy," he said. "This data is provided by the social media platforms. Raising awareness about the ways in which animals suffer is the first step in inspiring compassion and reducing animal suffering. I determine which posts do the most good for animals based on the response I get from my audience—particularly how many people engage with a given post, how many people see the post, and how many people verbally express that the post impacted them. I put a great amount of weight on posts that highlight animals that suffer in greater numbers, such as chickens and fish."

John's dedication to helping share the plight of animals abused in the highest numbers is inspiring, especially since fish and chickens are not viewed as favorably as other animals—though they suffer in greater numbers, and often in more horrific ways. I have seen John's online content for years and have also spent years sharing it to attempt to widen its reach.

John believes that if people knew how animals were abused in order to become their food, that many, many more people would embrace veganism, or a plant-based diet. That is what he aims to communicate through his well-thought-out campaigns to increase the visibility of animal cruelty, particularly in our food system.

"Raising awareness about the ways in which farm animals are exploited from birth to death is one of the most effective ways to inspire compassion in others," he said. "Most people love animals, yet most people also don't know the extent to which animals suffer at the hands of industries that abuse animals. It's our job as animal advocates to make people aware of these realities. Social media allows us to do that exponentially more than almost any other way, and at very little cost."

It's true that nearly all of the major social media websites and apps are free to use, it only costs us our time in order to spread a message worth sharing, and John encourages us to do exactly that. If we have the time, and the platforms, we should use them for good. As a personal experiment of sorts, inspired by John's example, and after spending time with John in person and listening to one of his lectures at an animal rights conference while still editing this book, I decided to get more engaged in using social media.

I have long had a love/hate relationship with social media, which I'm sure many of you can relate to, but I embraced my largest online platform, my Vegan Bodybuilding & Fitness Facebook page, and used it to share ideas about animal suffering, while initiating many conversations about animal rights and veganism. To my complete and utter surprise, following two decades of using social media, and having essentially zero posts go "viral," I got to a point where my posts were organically reaching more than one million people per day based on the analytics data that Facebook provides. In fact, in a single week, I reached more than twenty million viewers. And over a twenty-eight-day period, I reached more than fifty million people with my various vegan-related photos and posts, which led to more than one million people engaging with my content. I also gained more than ten thousand new followers to my page in just a couple of months, pushing it toward a quarter of a million followers. I primarily posted what I called "vegan memes, meals, and muscle," along with vegan fitness transformation photos, and they strongly resonated with audiences. In fact, at least five of my posts reached more than five million people, with one particular meaningful post about how the dairy industry separates mother cows from their babies in order to sell their babies' milk, which reached more than fifteen million readers in less than a week. That post was so popular that I used the same and similar images a couple of months later and reached another ten million viewers with just three posts about the dairy industry, while gaining thousands of new followers to my page. I saw John again at a conference about ending factory farming in the fall of 2023 and was able to share my experiences with him. By this point, I had reached more than 70 million people over a 90-day period, and I thanked John for leading by example. By enthusiastically sharing my results with attendees at the conference, it inspired others to feel empowered to leverage their social media platforms in strategic ways to reduce factory farming too.

My "keys to success" included posting clever vegan memes I found online that I suspected would be "liked" and "shared" a lot based on how they performed on other pages, controversial content that resulted in thousands of people sharing their opinions, while making my posts spread like wildfire, and posting regularly (often every two to four hours, perhaps six times per day) to discover which posts would stick and gain traction. This approach, when followed consistently, had my Facebook page reaching a wider audience than many television shows, movies, and celebrities are able to reach, and thus, at the time of this writing, I'm still following this same formula to get millions of people talking

Performance ℹ

Followers: 245,174

Last 28 days

Reach	Content published
53.9M +383%	**139** +3%
from previous 28 days	from previous 28 days

Interactions	Net followers
1.5M +352%	**10.0K** +340%
from previous 28 days	from previous 28 days

Looking at the analytics of my Vegan Bodybuilding & Fitness Facebook page, I found that more than 53 million people were reached in only four weeks—and I am not an online celebrity.

about veganism, hoping that some positive outcomes will come from this increase in awareness. Social media influencers like John encouraged me to keep sharing content, even if up until my breakthrough I hadn't created any viral content before. And it seems to be the way the system works that once you break through, those viral posts keep coming and coming, which amplifies a message of compassion by bringing more people into the conversation. Importantly, it really doesn't take a lot of time to post multiple times per day, either. I have folders on my phone for "memes," and "favorite" images, as well as folders for "vegan food," and "influencers," so when I'm looking to make a particular post, I just explore one of my folders, and in less than a minute select an image, take a moment to decide what to say about the image, and then post it. I don't curate any content or post anything fancy. I don't schedule or plan it in advance. I just post in the present moment and wait to see what happens. My goal is to get people thinking about their own relationship to animal suffering, while providing food for thought for them to consider more compassionate choices.

The Importance of Quality Followers

When it comes to social media, it's not just about the number of follow-ers; it's the quality of followers that matters most. As serial entrepreneur Gary Vaynerchuk said many years ago, if you only had two followers, and they were Oprah Winfrey and Barack Obama, you'd be in pretty good shape. So it's not all about the follower count, but the quality of your audience. Both are helpful, though, as oftentimes the quantity of your audience will award you opportunities, such as landing a major book deal or a TED Talk, creating a platform to reach an even greater audience.

In recent years, I watched a colleague who has millions of social media followers land on the *New York Times* Best Seller list with her plant-based cookbook in 2022, which then awarded her an opportunity to be on *Good Morning America*, *Rachael Ray*, and many other popular television and online broadcasting platforms to share her message, reach-ing millions more people outside of social media. She amassed her own following, largely with a vegan kaizen approach of taking small steps, creating daily videos, for years, growing a following that was significant enough to land a book deal. Then, because of the success of her book, she was able to land media opportunities, which increased her overall reach and enhanced her activism.

Today, she has grown her audience to more than seven million social media followers, landed another book deal, and has spent numerous weeks on the *New York Times* Best Seller list. In her case, her social media following built her success, and as a result, her success has had a significant impact on reducing animal suffering. Her books are avail-able in Walmart, Target, and Barnes & Noble, and reach a mainstream audience, in addition to online sales through Amazon, where her book is regularly one of the top five hundred bestselling books in the world. She sold more than one hundred thousand hardcover copies in ten months, making her book the bestselling plant-based book of 2022. I am referring to Carleigh Bodrug's *PlantYou* cookbook and her PlantYou brand that has taken the internet by storm.

As one of the vegans (who is not a mainstream celebrity) with the largest online social media platforms, I asked Carleigh about her impact on animals with her newfound super influencer status.

"It feels like there are a million reasons to go vegan, but actually making the switch can feel very daunting, especially if you've grown up on a meat and potatoes diet," she said. "As a vegan food blog, at PlantYou, we try to bridge the gap between the desire to eat more plant-based food and actually putting it into action. Our goal is to help as many people as possible transition to a plant-based or plant-predominant lifestyle, by providing practical and delicious recipes, meal plans, and tips. Over the years, we've been very fortunate to garner an audience of over seven million people between my various social media channels. After polling my followers on multiple occasions, I know that the majority do not identify as vegan. With this in mind, I try to appeal to the masses to work plant-based meals into their weekly routine where they wouldn't otherwise. It's hard to measure the impact of this, but I can confidently say, through blog metrics and the sale of my cookbook, that millions have enjoyed more plant-based meals through our work, in turn saving the lives of thousands of animals."

Carleigh understands that it doesn't necessarily matter *why* someone eats more plants and fewer animals, but it's the fact that they *do* that ultimately matters—especially if people will adhere to a plant-based diet for a long period of time, having it become part of their identity and lifestyle. Carleigh doesn't believe that there is one single action that will do the most good for our fellow animals, and she echoed my position throughout this book that we don't need a few people practicing veganism perfectly—but rather, we need millions of people on board to "eradicate factory farming and look at broader solutions to help animals and the environment."

Carleigh recognizes her own strengths, and her system works, so she continues to promote it for the betterment of the world. "I personally lean into my strengths as a short video content creator and recipe developer," she said. "By creating short video content effectively, I know I can reach millions of people with delicious and simple plant-based recipes, and hopefully inspire them to dig deeper into the lifestyle. For someone else, say a doctor, their energy might be better spent educating our population on the health benefits of a plant-based lifestyle. Similarly, an animal activist who exposes the atrocities inside factory farms will appeal to another crowd of people who need that emotional appeal to go vegan."

Carleigh's commitment has awarded her many opportunities to create change for herself and in the lives of others, but she also has the self-awareness to recognize that veganism doesn't come easily for many people. Veganism has a low adoption rate as it is, representing just a few percent of the global population, at most; so removing additional barriers is paramount if the vegan "movement" is going to progress.

"It's very important to acknowledge that veganism and plant-based food in general is historically rooted in many cultures, including African, Indian, Asian, Indigenous cuisine, and more," she said. "It's critical that we make sure veganism has diverse representation in media, advertisements, and social campaigns from a variety of cultures and voices. Many of these authentic recipes rely on healthy and affordable plant-based staples like legumes, whole grains, veggies, fruits, nuts, and seeds, demonstrating the accessibility and richness of vegan food that further appeals to a wide population. Additionally, providing educational resources on the foundation of a balanced plant-based lifestyle in school systems, and in community programs, takes this one step further."

Carleigh is undoubtedly a powerful voice in the plant-based and vegan communities, leading by positive example, with overflowing enthusiasm, sharing with me on one occasion that her (gratitude) cup "overpours."

I know this all sounds great for those who have been fortunate enough to make it big, but if you're not famous, or a popular influencer, how do you get started? As the aforementioned Gary Vaynerchuk also says, everyone starts with zero followers. Regardless of the platform you use, you started with zero followers and you grew from there. You also don't have to have a major audience for your content to go viral. Sometimes a post, a photo, or a video resonates with an audience and *just spreads*.

THE REACH OF OUR TECHNOLOGICAL TIMES BEYOND SOCIAL MEDIA

Social media is not the only answer to saving the world, though. What if you spent your time writing opinion pieces or articles about animal rights or other similar topics for major newspapers across the country or around the world? What if you wrote magazine articles and submitted them for publication? What if you wrote thoughtful blogs and made them available for popular websites to use as a guest contributor piece? What if you spent more time reading about how to be an effective vegan advocate or took courses on the subject and then applied those practices outside of social media? Anything that reaches beyond the boundaries of your usual community is worth pursuing.

I'm reminded of the great philosopher and animal rights activist Peter Singer, who challenges us to do the most good. Is spending eight hours per day on social media having the same impact as if you were spending eight hours per day writing opinion or informative articles that will be submitted to newspapers? Would writing a book for eight hours per day be a better use than either of those options, in the case you hit it big with your book, since it would be potentially promoted on social media and in major newspapers, reaching a bunch of additional platforms beyond social media? Or is that too big of a gamble because there are a lot of unknowns, whereas sharing on social media provides instant results, with the potential to go viral? Would starting a podcast be a better use of time, or perhaps volunteering for an educational nonprofit? What about becoming a guest contributor for popular websites, submitting articles with some sort of vegan-leaning message that could end up being read by millions of readers for free online? What about going to school to become a registered dietitian, personal trainer, or a physician, giving you authority and credibility with the potential to create institutional change? Or what about taking courses and earning certifications to land a high-paying job so you can "earn to give" in order to contribute significant financial resources to the most effective animal charities?

What's the best use of time when factoring so many options? We could perhaps use some effective altruism principles to answer those questions, and philosophers like William MacAskill and Peter Singer would likely come to a logical conclusion after debating the topic at hand, but ultimately, of those options listed earlier, and countless others, it will come down to what your preferences are, and where your enjoyment lies. That's where you'll likely find the most effective use of your time to help animals.

While it seems like there is no clear choice as to what is the best use of time, universally speaking—without factoring in your own unique character traits compared to others—you can still use various systems of analysis to measure the impact of your time spent on varying efforts. One of those approaches is to determine how many animals you impact per hour worked, or some other unit of measurement that is associated with time and effort invested. As it turns out, according to the study we saw last chapter, the use of social media is an effective way to not only get non-vegans thinking about veganism, but it also effectively gets non-vegans to *take action* supporting veganism. The study showed a direct reduction in animal consumption among those non-vegans who were impacted by vegan messages on social media. So stop scrolling, and start posting! The data suggests that social media is just one of the effective approaches to bring more people into the vegan community. Here's another hint: celebrities, generally speaking within the vegan movement, aren't all that effective in eliciting change, after all. I look forward to sharing some of the other survey results with you later in the book.

Clearly, social media can be impactful when the most effective people use it for good. Just as writing, filmmaking, photography, storytelling, and other areas of bringing attention to helping animals can be effectual if the right people are doing it. Those exact activities could otherwise be ineffective if not performed by those who have a talent or passion for it. That appears to be a theme shared by many members of the vegan movement—that we should become aware of our strengths and weaknesses, and deploy our talents and skills effectively—not just following our passions, but following our effective capabilities, to elicit change. Auditing your own actions will help you determine how to get the greatest return on investment for your time spent helping animals, so revisit the STRONG V characteristics from chapter three to hone in on your strengths and put them to use for good.

CHAPTER 8

THE VEGAN CAREER

CONSCIOUS CAPITALISM FOR BETTER BUSINESS

"You have to build something so irresistible that people can't help but to knock on your door and throw money at you. You need to keep your eyes on the prize and focus on the consumer. Focus on what you're selling. Focus on the community. And then all of the people will be lined up at your feet trying to give you money."

—Pinky Cole, Founder and CEO of Slutty Vegan, a $100 million value vegan brand

We just learned about one of the "dream jobs" in the quest to reduce animal suffering, which is using social media to make a living helping animals. But there is another "dream job" in this movement, which is starting your own vegan business or organization. That's what we'll explore here, learning from those who have done exactly that, and also considering whether starting your own operation and following your passions is really the most effective way to be a vegan advocate.

Here are some questions to get you thinking about the process: Is there a need for the products or services you plan to offer? What problems does your solution solve? Who will consume your products or your information? How will you create assets and content that an audience will resonate with? What's your mission and purpose behind the business or organization you want to create? Who's your competition and how does your approach differentiate from what already exists in the market? In what ways can you improve upon existing products or services? What's unique about your approach? How will you ensure that your business or organization will become profitable, sustainable, and influential? Do you want to be in charge of hiring, firing, and managing people? Are you prepared to create a work schedule that will almost certainly require significantly more time invested than the standard forty hours per week for the typical full-time American worker? Are you willing to fund your endeavor or take on investments, partnerships, and loans to afford to get your project off the ground? Are there examples of successful businesses or organizations that provide a proof of concept showing that your endeavor has a chance at success, too? What will happen if you succeed? What will happen if you fail? These, and many other questions, should be at the forefront before you take your first step forward as a business or organization founder. There are also some fundamental questions to answer before you ultimately take your next steps.

Is there really a need for you to create your own business, or should you apply to join a current organization and bring your skills, talents, and strengths to an existing entity? That is perhaps the most important question to answer. Your answer will likely be determined by a desire to be self-employed or be an employee or contractor working for someone else. That is a common determining factor, one that separates entrepreneurs from traditional workers. Answer those questions, and others that are unique to you and your current situation—such as, how will your partner, children, or other people or pets be impacted by your decision?

Then come up with any additional questions that will guide your decision and create a plan as to whether you will start your own business or organization or use your strengths to join an existing entity.

BUSINESS START-UP FOOD FOR THOUGHT

Most new start-ups are unlikely to succeed long-term, but that doesn't mean that they can't succeed. It simply needs to be stated up front that most start-up businesses and organizations are destined for failure. And when I say "most," I'm actually referring to about a 90 percent fail rate. That's correct. Nine out of every ten new businesses will fail.

Approximately 10 percent will fail within the first year, and about half of all businesses won't make it past five years. Then, it gets worse after that, with about 75 percent of all businesses, across all industries, not making it more than fifteen years, according to data from the United States Bureau of Labor Statistics.

Furthermore, first-time business start-up founders have a success rate of only 18 percent, meaning that 82 percent of all other first-time business founders will fail. So don't get too excited and run out the door to open your first business bank account. The odds are dramatically stacked against you. Sparing some of the other details, including typical start-up costs (thousands of dollars) and other obstacles, which you can (and should) read up on if you indeed plan on starting your own business, there is another perspective to consider.

If you can find an established nonprofit organization or for-profit company that resonates with you, it could be more effective to use your skills, talents, passion, and enthusiasm to support the organizations of your choice that are already fully operational and successful. This is different advice than would have been offered twenty or thirty years ago when creating your own business had a higher success rate and there was a greater need for innovation and new products and services. There were fewer organizations and companies back then, and there was a greater demand for new products and services. Think about it. The internet was just emerging a few decades ago. Before the advent of the World Wide Web, there were many traditional businesses, especially brick-and-mortar stores, and there was a high demand for such establishments during times of urban growth with a booming population. It was almost as if businesses "couldn't fail" some decades ago, because there was so much expansion happening that they were always in demand, with enough customers to keep their businesses going. And in some cases, they were the only game in town, so to speak, such as local newspapers, grocery stores, appliance stores, gas stations, and auto repair shops. We relied heavily on these businesses, and many of them succeeded for decades, even generations. Then along came the internet and it changed the game—and not in a bad way; it just restructured what it meant to start a new business. Now, all of a sudden, there were millions of new job opportunities within the tech and internet industries, and we adapted to the biggest game changer in business since perhaps the Industrial Revolution.

Fast-forward to today, and basically every single one of us who uses social media has our own personal brand, whether we realize it or not. Our image is our brand. Our reputation is our brand. Our online activity is our brand. That's the reality of the world we live in. Whether our personal brand is a registered business, a certified nonprofit organization, or our own audience that we created, we have to acknowledge that we all represent our own brands. This is true for authors, photographers, content creators, speakers, consultants, and for stay-at-home moms and dads. We all have brands, but that doesn't mean we need to turn them into a business. Sure, we can sell crafts, self-published books, nutrition products, tools and equipment, services of any type, and we can buy, sell, and trade comic books and sports cards online, for example, all because of our personal brands. A side project or hobby is far different from a full-on business or organization.

In 2022, I attended the Denver VegFest (vegan festival) since I live just an hour away. I had been a speaker and exhibitor in previous years, but this time around I was just there as an attendee to network and get to know my local vegan community, as a recent transplant to Colorado. I was most interested in listening to the speakers. One particular panel was especially fascinating. It consisted of five farm animal sanctuary founders or directors. An attendee in the audience posed a question for the panelists, asking for advice about starting her own animal sanctuary, as she expressed a passion for it and that it had been a dream for years to open her own farmed animal sanctuary. Every single one of the animal sanctuary representatives, from five different sanctuaries, advised against starting her own animal rescue. Their reasons often overlapped, with themes such as constantly fundraising, never having any days off, not getting enough sleep, receiving constant phone calls from people wanting to drop off unwanted animals, and the emotional trauma that is involved in running a farm sanctuary operation, which includes witnessing the deaths of many animals once they reach their natural life span or who die prematurely from a condition related to their rescue.

Not a single farm animal sanctuary founder or director gave any indication that the woman, who had a passion for rescuing animals, should start her own animal sanctuary. It was not about the risk of competition within the same geographical area, worrying about donors splitting their money among even more sanctuaries, but it simply had to do with the fact that 90 percent of animal sanctuary start-ups are also likely to fail, like any other business or organization start-up, and that most people don't know what they're getting into. Those who have lived animal sanctuary life, 24/7, for years, shared stories of missing their families, not being able to travel for holidays, dealing with extreme weather conditions and the impact that has on their animal residents, and the tremendous burden that is the ongoing need for fundraising. Farm animal sanctuary owners don't just rescue, house, and take care of animals. Their main job is to raise money—constantly. And it becomes exhausting. Ultimately, what the panelists suggested is what I'm also suggesting that you at least consider, which is finding an established animal sanctuary and volunteering for a while to see if you enjoy it. Then, perhaps, apply for a job at an animal sanctuary for at least a year or so before ever deciding if that is something you would actually want to pursue full time. Furthermore, if your goal is to rescue, save, and spare animals from suffering, one of the most effective things you can do is donate money to the most efficacious animal charities, including donating directly to your preferred animal sanctuary.

In 2023, I met Juliana Castaneda Turner, the founder of Juliana's Animal Sanctuary, which sits at ten thousand feet elevation in Colombia. Though I am surrounded by animal sanctuaries where I live in Colorado, I wanted to see if Juliana shared some of the same recommendations as my local animal sanctuary founders regarding starting one's own animal sanctuary.

I also wanted to know her story.

Juliana became a vegetarian at the age of five, when she realized that burgers didn't grow on trees, but were the by-product of killing cows. At age eleven, she had a vision of owning a large piece of land for rescued animals and started saving money to turn her dream into a reality. By the age of twenty-three, with the money she had saved for more than a decade, and with help from a friend, and a loan from a bank, her animal sanctuary dream was indeed realized.

That was nearly twenty years ago.

"It's crucial that people understand the characteristics of a real sanctuary," she said. "A true sanctuary never purchases animals for any reason, even under the guise of rescue. When we buy an animal from a farmer, even with the intention of saving their life, we're essentially telling the farmer that the animal is an object with a price. Moreover, this inadvertently supports the industry. The money spent will enable them to acquire two more animals, so it is not saving, but is hurting more animals. It's important to acknowledge that we can't save all animals by taking them to our sanctuaries. Equally significant is the understanding that not even all the sanctuaries worldwide can rescue every animal. Consequently, we should refrain from overpopulating sanctuaries with animals that we can't adequately care for or accommodate. A hallmark of a genuine sanctuary is its emphasis on educational programs, as education is our core mission."

Juliana continued, "Animals are here to communicate the truth to the world and express their needs. Our role is to facilitate this communication and help people reconnect with their empathy. If a sanctuary lacks an educational program, the impact on animals is limited. The real heroes are the public, and our role is to educate them about the farm industry and help them to go vegan. In Colombia, with our sanctuary, we have four robust educational programs, with our school initiative 'Animal Club' being the most significant. Through this program, children learn about the reality animals face. We educate them on how to share this reality with the world, and many of them become volunteers themselves. Sanctuaries often receive less economical support compared to other animal charities. This is because people often misunderstand our work, assuming we only rescue animals. In reality, a sanctuary is much more than that; it's an educational hub for veganism. Ultimately, we are the only ones truly *saving* lives. The labor is arduous, demanding our time, our mental health, and our physical well-being. This is why there are so few genuine farm sanctuaries worldwide."

When asked if she would recommend that others start their own animal sanctuaries, she didn't hold back. "I strongly recommend that if you have the money and time, start by volunteering for a year at a sanctuary to face the reality, and then consider that decision. For those who have the resources to start, there are numerous sanctuaries worldwide that need more support. Let's join forces, support each other, and grow together. Many individuals begin sanctuaries driven by their emotions but end up failing miserably. This is often because they believe that running a sanctuary is like what we see on social media—beautiful videos, photos, and interactions with animals. However, there's so much more to it than that. If someone genuinely wants to help animals, I encourage them to support those who are already doing good work, and help them establish more educational programs. But if someone really wants to do it, volunteer for a year first, face the reality, and follow the Global

Federation of Animal Sanctuaries and The Open Sanctuary Project for support and guidance."

I realize that this might not be the message you wanted to hear when you were pumped up and excited to learn about how to create your own vegan career, such as starting an animal sanctuary.

But there's a second part to this story, and there are plenty of compassionate companies and organizations that have been successful, including many of my friends and colleagues within the vegan community.

First, though, let's address an elephant in the room. Should you follow your passion when determining what direction to go in for your career?

MAKE REAL CHANGE HAPPEN BY NOT FOLLOWING YOUR PASSION

I wrestled with this topic for a few months while writing this book. I had literally signed "Follow your passion and make it happen!" in thousands of copies of books I had previously published over the years, and that same message has been in my email signature for over a decade—until now. I was the guy giving motivational talks on tour about how you should follow your passion to get the most out of life. I was a sincere believer in discovering your passion and working like hell to turn your passion into a career to create a truly meaningful life. I surrounded myself with others who were self-starters, driven, and hardworking like I was, and I subscribed to the "follow your passion" mantra with no reservations. Until I read the three primary books that inspired me to write this book, *The Most Good You Can Do* (Singer, 2015), *Doing Good Better* (MacAskill, 2015), and *How to Be Great at Doing Good* (Cooney, 2015), and all three of those texts adamantly advised readers to *not* follow your passion. In fact, when discussing these topics, they had bold headlines saying, "Don't Follow Your Passion," and, "Following Your Passion Is a Bad Idea."

This was surprising to me. I had dedicated my life to following my passion and working incredibly hard to make it happen. It seemed to be working for me. I had wanted to be a writer since I was eight years old, and here I was as a *New York Times* bestselling author. I had also wanted to be an athlete when I grew up, and I became a champion runner and a champion bodybuilder, and built a career around my vegan bodybuilding reputation. Following my passion worked for me. I was relatively happy, relatively successful, and essentially every day I woke up, I got to do what I enjoyed doing. So what's wrong with following your passion? Shouldn't everyone have the opportunity to see their passions realized with a little hard work and self-belief?

Then I realized, in a way that I perhaps hadn't fully understood before, that I am the 1 percent. I always knew that I came from a place of privilege, as a white male, born in America, raised by college-educated parents, in one of the most desirable cities in the country. I was aware of the head start that I got in life, and I was, and am, eternally grateful for it. It also gave me a sense of responsibility to make the most of my fortunate circumstances, and to give back as much as possible, which ultimately led me to becoming an effective altruist, before I ever knew that there was a term for my approach to life. I am one of the few people who actually experienced a childhood dream come true by following my passion, dedicating my life to achieving specific goals, and seeing those goals and dreams realized in front of me. For 99 percent of us, that just doesn't happen. William MacAskill explained why that is the case when he argued:

Taken literally, the idea of following your passion is terrible advice. Finding a career that's the right 'fit' for you is crucial to finding a career, but believing you must find some preordained 'passion' and then pursue jobs that match it is all wrong. Ask yourself, is following your passion a good way to achieve personal satisfaction in the job you love? Should you pick a career by identifying your greatest interest, finding jobs that 'match' that interest and pursuing them no matter what? On the basis of evidence, the answer seems to be no. First and most simply, most people don't have passions that fit the world of work. In one study of Canadian college students, it was found that 84 percent of students had passions, and 90 percent of these involved sports, music, and art. But looking at census data, we can see that only 3 percent of jobs are in sports, music, and art industries. Even if only half the students followed their passion, the majority would fail to secure a job. In these cases, 'doing what you're passionate about' can be actively harmful.[30]

Those statistics and that singular perspective had me rethinking the thousands of books that I signed for readers over the years with this exact inscription: "Follow your passion and make it happen!"

MacAskill goes on to hammer home additional points that are in direct conflict with following your passion, such as the reality that your passions change. I would agree, and argue that most of us have likely replaced some of our childhood passions with current passions, and that your passions today are likely different than they were a mere five, ten, or fifteen years ago. They might even be different than they were a few months ago. Furthermore, many people don't have specific passions in life, making this concept of following their passion a moot point.

I don't regret the past, nor can I change it, but these perspectives from MacAskill and others in the effective altruism movement have me questioning my mindset moving forward. In MacAskill's eye-opening and perspective shifting argument against chasing your passion, he also argues that the "best predictors of job satisfaction are features of the job itself, rather than facts about personal passion." MacAskill encourages us to take a different route, which he describes this way:

"Instead of trying to figure out which career to pursue based on whatever you happen to be most interested in today, you should start looking for work with certain important features. If you find that, passion will follow . . . Research shows that the most consistent predictor of job satisfaction is engaging work, which can be broken down into five factors (this is known in psychology as the job characteristics theory):

1. Independence—To what extent do you have control over how you go about your work?

2. Sense of completion—To what extent does the job involve completing a whole piece of work so that your contribution to the end product is easily visible, rather than being merely a small part of a much larger product?

3. Variety—To what extent does the job require you to perform a range of different activities, using different skills and talents?

4. Feedback from the job—How easy is it to know whether you're performing well or badly?

5. Contribution—To what extent does your work 'make a difference,' as defined by positive contributions to the well-being of other people?

One of my early passions was to make my vegan bodybuilding lifestyle my full-time career. I created a website in 2003, at age twenty-three, and produced a basic apparel line with my brand logo and slogan on it. I built a large online community over the years with thousands of active members, and landed speaking engagements around the globe. My role as one of the few notable vegan bodybuilders in the world helped me secure a full-time job as a spokesperson, sales representative, and national tour manager for Vega, one of the largest plant-based nutrition companies in the world at the time. Though I was living my passion, bodybuilding eventually became a burden for me, as an expectation, directly associated with my image, and as something that I "had" to do to maintain my reputation. There were times when I hated working out in the gym because I felt like I was required to do so in order to maintain my image, and it weighed heavily on me, especially as my interests changed.

My "dream job" with Vega soon became more challenging, reporting to numerous managers, and having to create and maintain spreadsheets, which I despised. I had to take on tasks that were no longer interesting to me and perform jobs that no longer served my goals, and after a while, my passion turned into resentment and burnout in bodybuilding and my full-time job. Both passions and job positions still afforded me many meaningful opportunities, including pursuing other passions, which included world travel, and I found bodybuilding and my role with Vega to be fulfilling, even if my flame for those endeavors eventually burned out.

Attempting to run my own business as a wannabe entrepreneur proved to be not so fruitful or financially sustainable, largely due to my altruistic nature, which focused on giving products away and doing jobs for free in order to contribute to a cause, rather than focusing on profiting off others. My Vega job was much more profitable than my own personal brand (which wasn't a real business, but a money-losing hobby at best), and it opened up doors for me to pursue some new passions like writing. After a full decade working for Vega, positioning myself to chase my next passion in this ever-evolving pursuit of happiness, I embraced a full-time writing career, publishing one book after another, which led to speaking, touring, and signing books throughout the world.

After publishing a few books, and looking for my next passion yet again, I stumbled upon an opportunity for a new full-time position as the director of a nonprofit organization specializing in promoting the vegan fitness lifestyle at the largest fitness expos in America, which you read about earlier. I cofounded the Vegan Strong fitness expo tour and managed the Vegan Strong brand, assembling a team of vegan athletes to exhibit, speak, and teach the vegan fitness lifestyle at consumer shows, trade shows, and industry professional shows, as well as online through seminars and via professional videos and social media. After cofounding Vegan Strong in 2018, I spent years passionately leading a team of champion vegan athletes on a quest to show the mainstream fitness community that plants have all the protein we need, which we successfully did for years. It's what we continue to do today, to the tune of distributing more than 125,000 plant-based product samples and coupons to mainstream fitness expo attendees every year, replacing what would have likely been close to 125,000 animal-based meals, since more than 90 percent of our show attendees are non-vegans.

My role as the director of Vegan Strong was passion-filled for years, but about five years into it, it really started to run its course for me, because what looked amazing on paper, and for outsiders looking in, turned into basically full-time fundraising, constantly asking for money, and other forms of donations, every week of the year, just to keep our organization going. Yes, I was touring incredible places with amazing friends, and engaging with fans and signing books, and most importantly making a measurable impact for animals by replacing tens of thousands of animal-based meals with plant-based meals every year as a result of our tour. But the burden of essentially begging for money, donations, and support, uncertain year after year if we could even continue, became too great of a burden for me to carry, and once again, I decided to look for my next passion.

Ultimately, I learned that rather than following my passion, I needed to find a good fit, where I could add value, feel valued, and do meaningful work without the ongoing stress of continuously seeking donations and working around the clock as a marketing machine trying to attract enough eyeballs to make my work feel like it was worthwhile. One of the biggest epiphanies for me was realizing that I needed to embrace more hobbies so I could separate work from pleasure, even if in an ideal world those might intersect often. Therefore, rather than my passions burning out, which happened every time I pursued my passion as a "career," I got to keep my passions as hobbies to engage in on the weekends, in the evenings, or when I separated work from leisure time. This decision, while completing the writing of this book, was one of the most impactful choices I've made to have a truly positive work-life balance. I have a regular job now that might not be passion-filled, though it is still within the vegan industry, but it affords me the opportunity to earn an income doing work centered around what I'm naturally good at, while being an important part of a team that I am able to contribute to and feeling like a valued member of the workforce community. This creates room for my hobbies to take center stage when I'm not working, rather than feeling like I need to be "working every moment of the day" and living a life with very few hobbies, which was my previous reality. MacAskill's arguments for not following your passion rang true for me once I put it to the test to experience for myself and realized the life-changing truth behind his words in ways that impacted my life for the better.

Nick Cooney dedicates a few pages of his book *How to Be Great at Doing Good* to criticizing the idea of following your passion with his own take-home messages that might shift your way of thinking, as it did for me. One of Cooney's statements resonated with me particularly, in ways I hadn't anticipated. In addressing the role of doing meaningful charity work for worthy causes, contemplating following your passion within the nonprofit sector, Cooney expressed the following: "If our main goal in doing charity work is to obtain personal enjoyment by supporting a good cause that interests us, then yes, following our passion could be a good idea. But if our main goal in doing charity work is to make the world a better place, then we should do the work that will accomplish the most good. Odds are that the charity work that will accomplish the most good is not the charity work that we initially feel most passionate about." And here's the part that got me: "As with so much standard charity advice, the idea that we should follow our passion is a self-serving maxim that wraps itself in the cloak of altruism. What it really tells us is that our own enjoyment should come first and that we should follow that enjoyment where it takes us. How much we actually help the world is secondary in importance."

That hit me hard. All these years of focusing on my passion, striving to live a fulfilled and meaningful life, were self-serving, rather than taking a step back and recognizing where my skills, talents, resources, connections, and strengths could better serve the world around me. I hadn't thought of this perspective previously, and it immediately altered my behavior and, subsequently, my actions and my mission. I realized that I have so much to offer the world beyond my own hopes, dreams, and goals, and that by leveraging my strengths to help others, I discovered new, inherent passions that have been ignited because I know I'm bringing more joy to those I am serving. Perhaps this will be a moment of awakening for you, too. With so many in need of help and support, is following our passions even a considerate thing to do in the grand scheme of things? I guess it depends on the altruistic nature of it. Cooney offers up some final thoughts on the topic: "The good news is that, for many of us, we'll eventually become passionate about whatever type of charity work we choose to do, even if we don't feel that way at the start. When we become deeply involved with something positive, we tend to become enthusiastic about it. Knowing how much good our charity work is doing for the world makes it all the more likely that, when we lead with our brains, our hearts will follow."

Though for 99 percent of us, following our passion, at least when it comes to determining our career, is bad advice, it does work out from time to time. More likely, though, as Cooney suggested, for those of us who are following our passions that don't lead to a fulfilling career, "that's what hobbies are for." If following your passion hasn't been working for you, you're not alone—in fact, you're in the vast majority, and as numerous experts suggest, it's perhaps best to separate your work from your passions and keep your passions as hobbies, like sports (and now book writing) are for me.

For those of you who are determined to create a vegan business or personal brand, there are plenty of role models to look up to. For every successful vegan product, company, brand, and organization, there are teams of individuals who were committed to making their dreams happen, often for altruistic reasons of reducing animal suffering and improving the world. Let's take a look at some case studies.

FOOD FOR LIFE GLOBAL

Food for Life Global (ffl.org) provides more than one million vegan meals to hungry children in the developing world every single day, for only fifty cents per meal. I met Food For Life Global co-founder, Paul Rodney Turner, while attending the Animal and Vegan Advocacy Summit, the world's leading animal rights conference.

Like many highly impactful vegan organizations, Food for Life Global started with humble beginnings. Food for Life Global is a modern-day revival of the ancient Indian culture of hospitality. Since the beginning of recorded time, the sharing of food has been a fundamental part of the civilized world, and in India, such hospitality was based on the understanding of the equality of all beings. In 1974, an elderly Indian swami, Srila Prabhupada, shocked and saddened upon seeing a group of village children fighting with street dogs over scraps of food, told his yoga students: "No one within ten miles of a temple should go hungry . . . I want you to immediately begin serving food." Hearkening to the swami's plea, his followers around the world were inspired to expand that original effort into a global network of free food kitchens, cafés, vans, and mobile services, establishing daily delivery routes in many large cities around the world. To date, Food for Life Global has a network of 250 affiliates that have served over eight billion vegan meals, at a current rate of over one million meals per day.

Beyond providing plant-based meals to hungry children in countries like Ukraine, Kenya, Uganda, India, and in Paul's current home country of Colombia, Food for Life Global has responded to some of the greatest natural disasters in modern history, including the great Asian tsunami of 2004, when fifty volunteers from around the world converged on Sri Lanka and India and provided more than 350,000 freshly cooked vegan meals during the months immediately following the tsunami, along with medical care, water, clothing, and shelter. In the fall of 2023, Food for Life Global deployed volunteers, resources, and aid to those suffering from the floods that devastated many lives in Morocco, while committing to help humanity, in addition to their other core mission of reducing animal suffering globally.

Impressively, Food for Life Global makes the following claims, assessing their positive impact on the environment: with every vegan meal served, Food for Life Global estimates that at least 1 animal is spared, 20 pounds of CO_2 is offset, 30 square feet of the forest is saved, 46 pounds of grain is redirected from animal feed to direct human consumption, and 1,116 gallons of water is preserved. When you multiply that by the actual number of meals being served daily by Food for Life Global volunteers (over one million and counting), it shows a tremendous impact on animals and our planet, which they track and measure through their blockchain system. Many of their affiliates and grant recipients complement their feeding programs with vegan education, which includes gardening and nutrition advice. Since their mission is to *unite the world through pure food*, they are moving more and more toward increasing their vegan advocacy as a long-term solution to issues like world hunger.

The US-based nonprofit provides grants, typically ranging from $500 to $20,000, to affiliated partners in sixty-five countries, where the US dollar stretches incredibly far in places like Africa. To facilitate this, they rely on donations from individuals and companies in the developed world. As an example, a vegan-owned and operated sports nutrition company, Clean Machine, created by Geoff Palmer, donates a percentage of their proceeds to Food for Life Global to help them carry out their mission of feeding as many vegan meals to hungry children as possible. Moved by Food for Life Global's commitment to supporting animals and children in need, I have committed to donating a vegan meal to a hungry child *with every copy of this book that is sold*.

Beyond individual donors like me, and company donors like Clean Machine, and plant-based supplement company Complement (which you read about in chapter three), Paul created a vegan food product to sell to customers in the developed world, to help provide financial resources for Food for Life Global's worldwide campaigns. An idea Paul had for a vegan snack bar in the early 1990s was put on hold while he grew Food for Life Global into one of the most robust animal charities, and the world's leading plant-based meal provider to hungry children in need. However, he would revisit the idea many times, aiming to bring a commercial product to the market to further support the primary causes his organization contributes to (hunger relief, sparing animal lives, and planting trees).

In 2016, Paul had an epiphany: while the snack bar was still a great idea, it was important to understand that the social impact attached to the sale of the product was equally valuable. Thus was born the OM Guarantee certification of social good (omguarantee.com), a B-lab social enterprise focused on providing a convenient and cost-efficient way for companies to give back in a measurable way that was also tracked on the blockchain. The three social impacts serviced by OM Guarantee are feeding children, feeding rescued animals, and planting trees.

Early in 2022, Paul approached Pure Bliss Organics, a successful vegan and organic food company that operates all over the United States, to create snack bars for Food for Life Global. It was then that Paul had another epiphany where he could combine the value of the OM Guarantee and its diversified and measurable social impact products with vegan snack bars. The Impact for Life energy bars project was launched in August 2023 with three specific, measurable social impacts right in the name of the bars themselves: *Save a Child*, *Help an Animal*, and *Plant a Tree*. Every purchase of an Impact for Life Bar goes directly to the particular cause listed on the label. This is one more way that Food for Life Global fulfills their mission of creating a more compassionate world. Though it took Paul decades to build up an organization that has fed billions, he now has a variety of strategic partners and supporters that helped bring his latest creation to life. It's a classic case of conscious capitalism, where his commercial products are designed to do good, directly supporting his nonprofit commitment to feeding vegan meals to hungry children, and improving the environment we live in.

NEXT LEVEL BURGER

Next Level Burger is America's first all-vegan national burger joint chain. Founded in 2014 in Bend, Oregon, by Matt and Cierra de Gruyter, the married couple set out on a mission to create a healthier world. Like most small businesses, they sank their own money into the new venture, but luck would strike when early Twitter employee Alex Payne stopped in for a plant-based burger shortly after opening day. He loved the concept of Next Level Burger so much that he made a substantial investment into the company. That enabled Next Level Burger to open restaurants in what has often been referred to as the "vegan capital of the world," Portland, Oregon. When they opened their doors in Southeast Portland in 2015, they had lines out the door for days. The restaurant was so popular that they ran out of food just eight days into operating out of their newest location.

Little did Matt and Cierra know that the Global Chef for Whole Foods Market lived just a few blocks away, and when he learned of Next Level Burger, he let his executives know about it. The word made it up the chain of leadership all the way to Whole Foods Market cofounder and then CEO John Mackey. A partnership was born and, in the ensuing years, Next Level Burger opened up restaurants inside of numerous Whole Foods Market locations from Portland, to Seattle, to San Francisco, to Brooklyn, to the Whole Foods Market flagship and corporate headquarters in Austin, Texas.

In August 2022, Next Level Burger opened its ninth restaurant nationwide in Denver, Colorado. Shortly after opening the new Denver location, Next Level Burger made the announcement that they had successfully completed a round of $20 million in fundraising, led by Whole Foods Market; original investor Alex Payne and his wife, Nicole Brodeur; and others, to continue their national expansion. Their ultimate goal is building one thousand Next Level Burger locations from coast to coast.

When the de Gruyter family set out for a change of pace and change of scenery with their move from Southern California to Bend, Oregon, with them came the goal of doing something more altruistic, to help our planet, the animals, and our fellow citizens. They wanted to create change. They set out to make a difference. They were committed to giving back. Not only have they done all of those things, but they also have become more successful, in every sense of the word, than the venture capital days of Matt's previous employment in the oil and gas industry.

They traded in the "American Dream" for a better one that they found by following their heart and intuition, not by following the money. In their case, following their passion to create an organic, vegan, sustainable national restaurant chain worked. They have since opened up more locations, including a second location in Seattle and a third location in the Portland metro area. Matt said that Next Level Burger has succeeded because of their amazing team, and because of their ability to reach a mainstream audience, claiming that more than 50 percent of their customers are non-vegans. They focus on treating their team members with respect and paying them well, while cultivating a collaborative winning attitude, knowing that every day they show up to work they are making a positive impact on our planet. Being early to market has served them well, and earning investments from influential people and corporations has enabled them to scale their business beyond the modest single location they started with. Their big dreams led to big results, and they're the first to admit that they are just getting started. In January 2024, Next Level Burger acquired Veggie Grill, effectively making Next Level Burger that largest vegan restaurant operator in the country, and one of the largest in the world.

GREENER BY DEFAULT

Greener by Default is a forward-thinking organization that puts plant-based meals in the spotlight as the default option in order to decrease animal consumption. They work with hospitals, universities, and corporations to apply behavioral science to menus in order to make plant-based the easiest and most appealing option for all diners, shifting the paradigm that vegetarian food is just for vegetarians, and flipping the norm so that the norm is a plant-based meal and that people have to opt in to a meat option. This strategy helps institutions meet climate commitments, save on food costs, serve healthier and more inclusive food, and protect freedom of choice.

The beauty in Greener by Default is its simplicity and its effectiveness. It is a research-backed strategy that helps diners make healthier choices without requiring extra time or willpower, and without taking options off the menu. The core concept is simple: make plant-based food the default, while giving diners the choice to opt into meat or dairy. When it's not possible to implement a fully plant-based default, Greener by Default uses other behavioral science strategies like increasing the ratio of plant-based to animal-based dishes, placing plant-based options first on menus and in buffet lines, and giving plant-based dishes mouthwatering names. For instance, instead of calling a dish "Vegan Risotto," naming it "Caramelized Butternut Sage Risotto" makes omnivores much more likely to choose it.

Some of the institutions incorporating Greener by Default practices are NYC Health + Hospitals, Harvard Business School, Stanford School of Medicine Prevention Research Center, Oxford University's Uehiro Centre for Practical Ethics, Northwestern University's Donald Pritzker Entrepreneurship Law Center, the media and event company GreenBiz, and many others.

Greener by Default cofounder Ilana Braverman conducted a study with researchers from Harvard and UCLA looking at the meal choices of students at catered on-campus events. In the control condition, like at most events, meat was the default option and students could select if they wanted to stick with the default meat option or switch to a plant-based meal. In the experimental condition, plant-based meals were the default option and students could select if they wanted to stick with the default plant-based option or switch to a meat-based meal. They found that only 18 percent of students requested a vegan meal when meat was the default, but 66 percent of students stuck with vegan when it was the default—that's an almost 50 percentage point increase in the amount of people eating vegan meals simply by switching the language on registration forms. Many omnivores are not going to go out of their way to specially request a plant-based meal, but they're happy to stick with it when it's delicious and when that's what most other people around them are eating.

In New York City's eleven public hospitals, they have verbal menus. Patients are first offered two daily chef's specials, and if they don't want either of those, there are a variety of other options. Prior to the pilot, they had vegetarian options on Mondays, but every other day of the week the two specials were meat-based. So someone would have to really go out of their way to request a vegetarian or vegan option. For the pilot, Greener by Default worked with Sodexo and NYC Health + Hospitals to make both chef's specials plant-based. If patients don't want either of those, then they can choose from other meals with animal protein. They found that more than 50 percent of patients ordered one of the plant-based chef's specials, and the vast majority of patients who chose the plant-based option were satisfied with their meal. Because it was so successful, they've now expanded the plant-based default to lunches and dinners across all eleven hospitals, which is expected to transition about eight hundred thousand meals per year from meat-based to plant-based.

In other environments where it's more complicated to implement a true default, they use other behavioral nudges like placement, naming, and the ratio of plant-based to animal-based products. This was their approach to a pilot at LinkedIn's San Francisco office. Before the pilot, they had three stations that always featured plant-based entrées, and five stations that always featured meat entrées. What happens with this type of setup is the vegetarians go to the plant-based stations, and omnivores go to the "normal" meat stations. So they slowly started incorporating veg entrées into the stations that had previously served meat, until the ratios were reversed—instead of five meat and three veg options every day, there were five veg and three meat options. But they kept the focus on the flavors and provenance of the dishes, not the fact that they're plant-based; for example, instead of "Vegan Tamales" they were "Ecuadorian Fresh Corn Tamales." What they found was the amount of meat served dropped in half, with no change to diner satisfaction. They also implemented an oat milk default in their coffee bar, which also cut the amount of dairy milk served in half.

Success stories like these make a compelling case for providing plant-based meals as the default options at catered events, parties, gatherings, company picnics, and in other scenarios where the diner can make it through their day with a plant-based meal without feeling like they must overhaul their entire diet. If you're going to a work banquet for a couple of hours, surely a plant-based option will suffice with little resistance, and it could increase receptiveness to future plant-based-by-default entrées elsewhere, such as at weddings, parties, and holiday gatherings.

CHEF AJ

Chef AJ is a chef, an author, a YouTuber, an event organizer, a public speaker, a comedian, an online influencer, a recipe developer, and she hosts many online summits, of which I have been a part. Chef AJ has created a personal brand that has become her full-time career. She makes a great living hosting a daily YouTube show where she interviews interesting people that are doing amazing things in the world, while also recommending products and programs, referring customers to discover solutions via collaborative partners. And, of course, she's selling lots of books and putting on her own hugely popular events that have a profound impact on improving the lives of participants. Chef AJ has been vegan for longer than nearly anyone I know, since 1977, and has contributed greatly to the reduction of animal suffering, through the example that she has set.

As someone who was formerly obese, and a serious food addict, Chef AJ now helps thousands of people learn how to lose weight and keep it off, improve their body image and their relationship with food, as well as overcome their food addictions. Chef AJ collaborates with clinical psychologist Doug Lisle, TruthNorth Health Center founder Dr. Alan Goldhamer, and pioneering plant-based physician Dr. John McDougall to support her work with a range of experts in related fields, ensuring that her audience will get the most helpful, well-rounded information to transform their own lives. In doing so, with a health-first approach, Chef AJ's work is sparing countless animals from being used in the food system, because personal health concern is the number one driver bringing people to a plant-based diet. Though Chef AJ is an animal rights advocate at heart, and she is and always has been "vegan for the animals," she knows that to make the biggest impact, you have to meet people where they are with a message they are willing to receive. Chef AJ accomplishes this with plant-based food, with health, and with weight loss. Within Chef AJ's community, her audience tends to stay plant-based for a very long time. This is largely owing to the fact that she has a never-ending supply of support for her community, given her daily health show, titled *Chef AJ LIVE!*, on YouTube, and her highly engaged community members, supporters, and fans that help nurture a group of passionate individuals looking to improve their lives and enhance their longevity.

After working as a pastry chef for a decade, followed by releasing her first book, *Unprocessed*, and organizing her own plant-based health conferences, Chef AJ realized that her talent for performing as a stand-up comedian, guest speaker, and presenter at many large conferences could transfer over into a video show that she launched during the start of the Covid-19 pandemic. As it turns out, her audience was craving what she was offering, and her show exploded in popularity, gaining hundreds of thousands of YouTube subscribers and millions of unique visitors, creating a new full-time job as a daily YouTube live video host that she has embraced for years.

To give herself a bit of a break (from years of hosting a daily show without missing a day), and to amplify some of her favorite professionals within the plant-based health and fitness industries, she gave dozens of experts a platform to have a monthly show on her popular YouTube channel. I was one of those lucky recipients, hosting my own show, *Vegan Conversations with Robert Cheeke*, on Chef AJ's YouTube channel, featuring my interviews with special guests being viewed tens of thousands of times. This creative approach not only gave Chef AJ a bit more time to write yet another book (*Sweet Indulgence*), but it was a smart and thoughtful approach to tap into the audiences of dozens of colleagues, further growing her platforms and creating a sustainable career with no signs of slowing down, while also generously sharing her platform with some of her favorite advocates for plant-based living.

Chef AJ really leaned into her STRONG V characteristics with the formation of her daily show. She is one of the most well-connected professionals within the entire plant-based community, which she called upon to secure hundreds of guests for her show, spanning more than two thousand episodes to date. She also relied on her inherent talents as a natural performer, as well as her learned skills in production, marketing, and communication, which made her show possible. Furthermore, she leaned into her resources, understood what she wanted to accomplish, and assembled a team around her to make it all work. She has multiple assistants who handle digital production, marketing, copywriting, and management of her media platforms. That allows Chef AJ to do what she does best, which is to host, build relationships, network with others, entertain, and deliver a message to the masses. All of this leads to impactful and fulfilling work that makes a difference for animals. It also pays well, and shows us all what consistent hard work can lead to when we lean into our strengths and follow our intuition. Much of Chef AJ's success is the result of small, daily, deliberate actions that compound over time, creating a career that not even she thought was possible just five years ago.

Today, Chef AJ is the author of multiple bestselling books, including the aforementioned *Unprocessed*, *The Secrets to Ultimate Weight Loss*, and *Sweet Indulgence*, and she makes regular guest appearances at one of the top health retreat centers in the world, Rancho La Puerta in the Baja California region of Mexico, just forty-five minutes from San Diego. Her daily *Chef AJ LIVE!* show is also going stronger than ever, with some videos attracting hundreds of thousands of viewers. Chef AJ effectively used the online platforms that made a career as a personal brand possible, showing others that with a collection of the right talents, skills, and other strengths, we, too, can be a powerful voice for animals, while making a living at it.

PLANT BASED NEWS

Cofounded by Klaus Mitchell and Robbie Lockie, Plant Based News is the world's leading plant-based and vegan media organization, currently reaching ninety million unique readers per month. They are a mission-driven, impactful media company focused on amplifying the plant-based diet and vegan lifestyle to benefit all of us who share this planet together. Plant Based News is often the first media organization to release breaking news in the vegan world, such as announcing when a highly anticipated product is released, when a new animal protection law is passed or goes into effect, when a major celebrity goes vegan (or announces they are no longer vegan), when a major company stops testing their products on animals, or other newsworthy topics including natural disasters and other tragedies impacting animals that many other news outlets might not cover. Think of them as a plant-based, online version of CNN, *People*, and TMZ, combined.

In addition to sharing news, they also provide incredible resources on plant-based nutrition, led by a team of nutritionists, physicians, and other medical experts; content for children; recipes; and plenty of articles curated for vegan lifestyle, culture, health and fitness, and the environment, which is a large part of their focus during our ongoing climate crisis. They also elevate plant-based organizations, nonprofits, companies, products, individuals, and campaigns, such as the monthlong vegan challenge Veganuary. Much like Rich Roll in the plant-based podcasting space, Plant Based News is usually the most sought after platform for authors like me to get our stories featured to a massive, dedicated audience. In fact, it's highly likely that many of you discovered this book because of Plant Based News.

With a firm grip as the leader in the plant-based news media and a team of more than twenty-five, Plant Based News is an organization that could be a great landing spot for potential team members eager to have their work contribute to the solutions to some of our world's environmental sustainability concerns, with an established leader in the industry. With positions in social media, advertising, video and design, editing, operations, technology, graphic art, writing, research, content, science, and engineering, and even more from advising to legal, joining established companies like Plant Based News, or learning from them and modeling your own media platforms after them, could be a wise move for many people. There won't be a shortage of vegan or plant-based news anytime soon, and popularity in this space is likely to grow with huge potential, especially as plant-based foods usher in a new era with cultivated meat, which will be discussed for years to come. Their mission is clear, as they exclaim: "If we're not working to make our planet a more just, equitable, and sustainable place, we won't have a planet at all!" To be part of the change you wish to see in the world, explore the possibility of modeling your mission-focused work after Plant Based News, or consider joining the team to bring your unique set of skills, talents, connections, ideas, and resources to their award-winning, leading organization.

VEGA

You don't have to be vegan to have a massive influence on helping animals. When I think of non-vegans who have created a significant impact on reducing animal suffering, one of the first examples that always comes to mind is Charles Chang, the founder of the sports nutrition brand Vega. Charles originally founded the company Sequel Naturals, which would later become Vega, in 2001. The Vancouver, BC, resident partnered with professional Ironman triathlete and product formulator Brendan Brazier to officially bring Vega to the market in 2003. Brendan, a plant-based athlete of more than thirty years, used a variety of superfoods, such as hemp seeds, maca, spirulina, chlorella, and others, to make a nutritional shake in a blender to fuel his professional triathlete career. Living in the same city where Sequel Naturals was originally founded in Charles's garage, Brendan was purchasing his high quality ingredients, including maca and chlorella, from local health food stores. Brendan reached out to Charles one day via email, telling him about the nutritional shake he had been making with Sequel Naturals products, with the concept of possibly bringing his shake to market. The two Canadians met, and the rest is history. They created Vega, an all-in-one nutritional shake that would change the plant-based sports nutrition industry forever.

Vega sparked a revolution in plant-based living, spearheaded by an omnivore, while having one of the greatest impacts on plant-based product consumption in modern history. Not only does Charles deserve credit for the millions of meals that Vega replaced that would have otherwise been consumed as animal protein, but the impact that Vega had on the emergence of other plant-based sports nutrition products, from powders, to bars, to shakes, to snacks, from dozens of other companies, further contributes to his legacy of replacing billions of animal-based meals with plants. Today, there are hundreds of plant-based sports nutrition companies. In fact, if you follow even a small number of vegan fitness social media influencers online, you will notice that many of them have their own brands and products they'd like to sell you. Charles started that cascade of events two decades ago when his vision to bring quality plant-based ingredients to the market was noticed by one of the best vegan athletes in the world at the time, and together they innovated a new sector of the market and created a movement that lives on today.

I often use Charles as an example when I have conversations with others about the impact that for-profit companies can have on helping animals, even if there is not an altruistic effort to help animals coming from the top of the company. The reality is, Charles helped reduce animal suffering in more significant ways than many vegan organizations combined, and he did it in a way that had long-lasting staying power. When you go to any grocery or sports nutrition store in the US or in Canada today, and look around at an entire wall, or at many aisles, shelves, towers, and end caps of plant-based products, you now know that twenty years ago a non-vegan from beautiful British Columbia paved the way for today's plant-based sports nutrition landscape. Further still, you will likely notice that it is not just plant-based brands, but nearly every store brand, and even the largest sports nutrition companies in the world, all have vegan options for protein powders, bars, drinks, or other supplements—and much of that started with Charles, a non-vegan, wanting to bring healthy plant-based foods to the masses. What started with a vision for a healthier future that began in Charles's garage turned into a company that he ultimately sold for $550 million, making it one of the largest plant-based company sales to date. Furthermore, Charles has offered some of his profits from his company sale to invest back into the plant-based movement, giving back to the community that embraced his company and shared in the success that he experienced.

YVES VEGGIE CUISINE, GARDEIN, AND KONSCIOUS FOODS

Charles is not alone as an omnivore making waves in the plant-based food industry. Fellow Canadian Yves Potvin is the founder and former president of Yves Veggie Cuisine, a brand that nearly every longtime vegan is well familiar with. Yves is not vegan, and has described himself as a flexitarian with an omnivorous family. Not only did Yves innovate the plant-based meat space with his original brand that debuted in 1985, which he sold to Hain Celestial Group many years ago, but he also founded the company Gardein, one of the most popular plant-based meat companies in the world. Gardein was also acquired, in a sale to Pinnacle Foods for more than $150 million in 2014.

Yves has used his culinary background to create plant-based foods for decades, and he is still at it. In 2022, he secured a $15 million investment from a variety of Canadian food companies to launch a vegan sushi company named Konscious Foods. As an omnivore who recently purchased a prominent culinary school in Vancouver, BC, Pacific Institute of Culinary Arts, Yves is one of the most influential people in the plant-based meat industry. Just as Charles was an innovator in the plant-based supplement and sports nutrition industry as an omnivore, Yves is another example, showing that there is room at the table for everyone who contributes to the reduction in animal suffering, whether or not that is part of their altruistic mission. Results matter most, and a couple of Canadian entrepreneurs have made that unmistakably clear, cementing their legacies within the plant-based food revolution.

There are plenty of vegan entrepreneurs worth recognizing and celebrating, too, of course, such as Seth Tibbott, the founder of Tofurky; Ethan Brown, the founder of Beyond Meat; Miyoko Schinner, the founder of Miyoko's Creamery; Josh Tetrick and Josh Balk, the cofounders of Eat Just; and many others we have already recognized throughout this book, but it's well worth mentioning the role that omnivores have played in the growth of the plant-based food industry, because vegan allies help bring more people into the movement, which is what this movement desperately needs to make continued forward progress.

I added the Vega story because, though vegan athlete Brendan Brazier was the formulator of the products, Vega, as a company, never would have made it without Brendan's partner, Charles Chang, who was the business founder. There are actually many "vegan" and "plant-based" companies today that took lots of outside funding, guidance, and mentoring from non-vegans, but we just consider those to be "vegan companies," like Beyond Meat, despite the countless non-vegan investors that made Beyond Meat possible, including many celebrities, athletes, musicians, and entrepreneurs.

Perhaps you have an idea for a vegan product, company, or service, but you don't have the business background, the start-up capital, or the connections to bring your idea to market. Would you be willing to partner with those outside the vegan community? Some worry about a conflict of interest, a standard of ethics potentially being overlooked, or future products being compromised (which does happen sometimes), but if your idea can have a measurable impact on reducing animal suffering, it could be worth exploring many different options, including partnering with people outside of the vegan community, which many "vegan" companies have done.

With all the examples shared throughout this section, I hope it helps you find some direction as you think about your own career and how you interpret your passions. To dive deeper into finding a career that is a good "fit" for you, there is an organization, cofounded by MacAskill, that is dedicated to helping people find the best careers that match their goals and interests. That organization is called 80,000 Hours, named for the approximate number of hours you will work during your professional career. As MacAskill puts it, "Your choice of career is a choice about how to spend more than eighty thousand hours over the course of your life, which means it makes sense to invest a considerable amount of time in the decision." Surely there are heavy considerations to ponder. What do you want to do with your life, and how can you lead a fulfilling career while still doing the most to help others? Visit the 80,000 Hours website to see if there is some insight there to help steer your decisions.

Ultimately, whether you embark on a journey to start your own vegan business or organization, prioritize building your own personal brand that becomes a full-time job, or decide to work for an established organization with a proven track record, you will have the opportunity to lean into your strengths to help others in meaningful ways. Working for yourself is hard. Working for someone else is hard. Choose your hard.

CHAPTER 9

REACHING THE RIGHT AUDIENCE

FIND YOUR FOLLOWING FOR THE GREATEST IMPACT

"How will you serve the world? What do they need that your talent can provide? That's all you have to figure out. The effect you have on others is the most valuable currency there is."
—Jim Carrey, 2014 Commencement Address at Maharishi International University

Though this book examines a lot of questions about how to best help animals, it also provides solutions. From creating our own personal brands to using our talents to help existing companies, we possess a lot of potential to create massive positive change. We must also acknowledge our intentions, as well as our flaws, and be open to criticism, suggestions, recommendations, and feedback so we can see things from outside of our confirmation bias. Melanie Joy, psychologist and cofounder of the

Center for Effective Vegan Advocacy, points out four key obstacles to effective vegan advocacy:

1. Not knowing your audience, and not being familiar with the psychology of eating animals
2. Underdeveloped advocacy skills
3. Emotional reactivity
4. Lack of information about veganism, animal rights, and systems of oppression

When trying to reach your right audience, Dr. Joy also advises not to over-inform people, and that "people need just a few takeaways from a conversation." Oftentimes, our passion for veganism and animal rights can get in the way and we could find ourselves overly enthusiastic, spewing out facts and opinions while losing the attention of our interlocutor. Once we understand our audience, Dr. Joy recommends that we focus on these key areas in order to increase our effectiveness advocating on behalf of animals:

1. Know when *not* to advocate.
2. Develop relational literacy.
3. Focus on process over content.
4. Don't expect facts to sell the ideology.
5. Highlight common ground.
6. Share your story.
7. Illuminate animal-cruelty defenses.
8. Focus on the positive.
9. View non-vegans as allies.
10. Avoid all-or-nothing thinking.

Dr. Joy highlights more than just these ten points in her effective vegan advocacy online course, which you can access on veganadvocacy.org, but these ten points were some of the most important to draw attention to. In her online course, she describes each of these points in detail, while providing examples for each one as well. I found them to be incredibly helpful in assessing my own efficacy in various areas of animal advocacy. When it comes to analyzing behaviors and solutions that help animals, Dr. Melanie Joy and her partner at the Center for Effective Vegan Advocacy, Tobias Leenaert, are as good as they come. Tobias's book, *How to Create a Vegan World*, is one of the best on the subject. Their deep knowledge of veganism, animal rights, and psychology make them highly effective in their work, and I recommend that you explore the many resources they have available online, and in their numerous books.

Let's go back to reaching the right audience. When it comes to who will most likely reduce animal suffering—men, women, and others; old, young, and somewhere in the middle—are all audiences the same? I will argue that resonating with some audiences is far more effective than others when it comes to impacting the actions that individuals will take to reduce animal suffering.

OUR IDEAL AUDIENCE TO REACH TO GROW THE VEGAN MOVEMENT

Since 80 percent of household purchases are made by women, and 80 percent of grocery store purchases also are made by women, we should take this demographic as seriously as possible because of the tremendous influence women have on the foods that an entire household will eat.[31] The same survey reported that, in addition to 80 percent of grocery store purchases, women also prepare more than 70 percent of household meals.

We have to ask ourselves: How does veganism, and a campaign to reduce animal suffering, resonate with women? How can we position our advocacy, activism, and outreach to influence that highly influential targeted audience? Which messages make the greatest impact? Should we take approaches based on compassion, health, nutrition, taste, cost, convenience, or something else? Or should we take a combination of those approaches? Which combination is most effective? A similar survey revealed that 91 percent of women feel like advertisers don't understand them. It appears that it's high time we start becoming better listeners. Since there are far more vegan women than there are vegan men, sometimes we conclude that we should spend our time, energy, and effort to reach men with the vegan message, to balance things out. Statistics and evidence show that's not the best approach to take. Men are just far less likely to stop eating animals. It's akin to evaluating our strengths and weaknesses as individuals and deciding where to put our efforts for improvement.

Instead, what has been much more popular over the past decade or so is the advice to double down on your strengths and pretty much ignore your weaknesses. Who cares if you're not good at drawing, golf, public speaking, or figuring out math equations? If you're really good at building a community, writing, baking, or building a brand, then focus even more on that and become great at it. This is similar to how we approach the promotion of veganism to different audiences, and also ties in to our STRONG V approach to really understanding our own skills, talents, resources, other strengths, network, generosity, and our volunteer work. Don't be afraid to lean into your greatest character traits and really shine.

Women are much more likely to become vegan than men, and younger people, such as college students, are more likely to become vegan than seniors who have decades of habits built up and less motivation to change in their later years.[32] Even if we remove the word "vegan" and replace it with "reduce animal suffering," which is the actual goal of this book, it becomes even more clear. Women and young people, such as college students, are more likely to reduce animal suffering than middle-aged men, who through some biological flaw, perhaps, tend to find more enjoyment from contributing to animal suffering (by hunting, fishing, grilling, cooking, and eating animals). Given this clear reality, we should spend considerable time contemplating how to most effectively engage with women about reducing animal suffering, and we will get closer to a vegan future. Or we could do something radical. Rather than spending time contemplating, and pondering—brainstorming how to effectively influence women—we could experiment with the novel idea of communicating with women, asking them questions, and listening to them to learn more about what drives their purchase decisions.

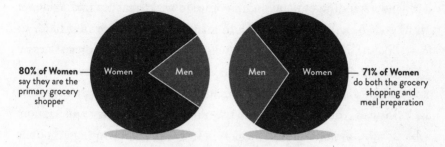

Ideal Audience
(Purchasing Power of Women in the US Ranges from $5 to $15 Trillion Annually)

80% of Women
say they are the
primary grocery
shopper

Women | Men

Men | Women

71% of Women
do both the grocery
shopping and
meal preparation

Data from "Statistics on the Purchasing Power of Women,"
Girlpower Marketing, accessed November 2023, https://
girlpowermarketing.com/statistics-purchasing-power-women.

Introducing plant-based foods to women, mothers, families, college students, and those who make household purchases, and who are most likely to actively reduce animal suffering through their actions, reaches an audience that can affect supply and demand of products in our collective food system. Encouraging these audiences of women and young people to support plant-based food purchases on an ongoing basis can make a serious impact on our primary goal of reducing animal suffering, and that is where our attention and our marketing efforts should go.

Furthermore, reaching this same demographic within the Black community is even more effective, since Black Americans represent the fastest growing vegan community in the country right now, which we'll describe a bit later on. From the biggest and best vegan festivals in America, to the most popular books, to the most famous and successful athletes, Black vegans have been powering the vegan movement forward for years. By knowing this data, and discovering more nuanced information about particular cities, states, countries, and communities that have the highest vegan population density, which host the most events, or are home to the most vegan restaurants, we can apply that data and use that momentum to help bolster the vegan movement. We can also, importantly, identify which communities are underserved and neglected with little access to vegan foods, information, and events, and bring veganism to those communities through a number of outreach programs.

Understanding our audience in order to make real progress is something that *New York Times* bestselling author of *The Korean Vegan Cookbook*, Joanne Molinaro, embraces with her brand, The Korean Vegan. She told me, "You have to meet your audience where they are. If you try and convince a jury of something that they aren't already open to, good luck. Instead, you have to get into the minds of your jurors to understand what sort of misconceptions, stereotypes, biases, and other baggage they bring to the table. Understand *why* they have those misconceptions, stereotypes, biases, and other baggage, in order to deconstruct them. Which means treating them with respect and trusting in their intelligence and compassion. Most people don't like being told what to think; but, if you guide them to draw their own conclusions, they will not only appreciate the assistance, but will be far less likely to waver from those conclusions when tested."

Interestingly, in her quest to make a difference for animals, which she is passionate about, Joanne doesn't actually focus on that outcome when she creates systems to help people reduce their intake of animals. She said, "I honestly don't focus on what does the 'most good' because 'most' and 'good' are such subjective terms. I'd rather know that I'm attacking the problem in multiple ways: (a) build a brand that will have incredible reach, in order to spread the 'good word' on veganism; (b) create tools that allow that community to implement what they're learning (e.g., my book or The Korean Vegan meal planner or YouTube instructional videos); and (c) stay engaged with my community to ensure that they feel seen and heard.

"Given this perspective, there are two really effective ways to promote veganism: (a) by example, and (b) by effective and respectful debate. The first is very nonconfrontational and appeals directly to a person's innate sense of compassion and inquisitiveness. You plant seeds by showing them, 'Hey, look, I can do it and so can you!' The second is more challenging—you confront people with their biases and show them a potentially different way of thinking. I think Earthling Ed [Winters] is the champion at this. It's a style that I could never adopt, which is why I'm extra glad he does."

YOUNG VOICES

Let's look at another example of what we can learn about reaching the right, and wrong, audiences. I talked with a vegan graduate student at Colorado State University named Rae in December 2022 about successful methods of promoting vegan advocacy aimed at college students, and she shared some interesting perspectives. One comment she made that I found particularly provocative was that "her generation" (college students at the present time) are not impacted by seeing video footage of animal suffering, such as slaughterhouse videos, because they see so much violence (including death) on social media platforms every day. She said that they have become desensitized to it. She made that remark in relation to factory farmed video footage that was being shown on her college campus by the vegan advocacy group Anonymous for the Voiceless, which I was volunteering with at the time we met.

Rae didn't believe that undercover animal cruelty footage would appeal to a sense of compassion or empathy from observers, particularly the college-aged students on campus. She reiterated her claim that college students are desensitized to violence they see in videos because they've grown up with it. She also expressed alternative ideas for effective activism tailored to college students specifically, such as providing free vegan foods and educational materials to a budget-conscious and impressionable audience.

Furthermore, she recommended that a vegan outreach group promote and support regional vegan options around campus and all over town, such as creating a local vegan-friendly restaurant guide for the city (which many cities have). Or something less formal, yet still effective, such as simply sharing with members of the community where to shop for vegan foods in the area (such as the grocery co-op near campus, vegan-friendly grocery stores on the main street that runs through the university, or restaurants that have vegan menus, such as the many international cuisines available in the college town).

Rae also suggested setting up a vegan advocacy table inside the student center, with literature, free food samples, and more, managed by fellow students who tend to be more approachable than an older demographic (like me) who are not as relatable to current college students. Rather than being outside in the plaza where students walk from class to class, not having a whole lot of time for a conversation about animal rights, she suggested that being inside, where students are eating meals, studying, socializing, and otherwise hanging out indoors, in large numbers, would be a better option for increasing student engagement. The student center contains the campus food court and student store, among many other facilities, and there would be higher foot traffic and a more welcoming environment for discussion about veganism. That approach would make for a more effective and inviting way to promote the vegan lifestyle, and achieve greater results for reducing animal suffering.

These, of course, are not new ideas. If this feedback from one particular college student is coming in, imagine the amount of neglect in effective animal advocacy that is happening nationwide, and undoubtedly, worldwide. There are vegan organizations that specialize in distributing vegan literature on college campuses, particularly one aptly named Vegan Outreach, which they have been doing for decades, and many colleges and universities have animal rights student groups, but could we do more?

Rae's feedback suggests that our potential to help animals at the college campus level is not being met to the degree that it could be, and perhaps more resources should be invested into reaching that incredibly influential demographic of college students. This audience represents "the future" and they are at an age where they form a lot of their philosophical beliefs and build new habits. Why not encourage them to a greater degree to help reduce animal suffering?

I must say that so far, in my initial discussion with Rae, I have to agree with every point she made. After all, she spends five days a week on campus, and I hadn't been on a college campus, aside from attending sporting events, in years. Furthermore, the animal rights group that she was providing constructive criticism for is only on campus (doing that type of vegan advocacy) a few times per year.

Rae had a different perspective and worldview compared to those I had been interviewing for this book, who have been vegan for decades, and who paved the way for the growth of the vegan movement and the plant-based food and beverage category's meteoric rise in recent years. It was, quite frankly, refreshing to hear some different perspectives unique to a demographic that should be one of the highest on our list of priorities of individuals to try to influence if we expect to be successful at reducing animal suffering in more significant ways.

Aside from reaching women, particularly mothers, who to a large degree determine the dietary consumption of an entire household, college students are some of the most likely individuals to embrace veganism and other efforts to reduce animal suffering. I met with Rae at a coffee shop on campus to learn more.

I described The Vegan Strong Method for Rae, including our fitness expo outreach tour, and even supplied her with two large tote bags filled with vegan products and cookbooks for her to enjoy and distribute within her community. I shared with her that if we were to distribute products on a college campus, they would need to be foods and beverages that resonate with that particular demographic, such as snacks, bars, nut butters, teas, coffees, breakfast cereals, full-size meals and foods (such as packaged pasta and soup), and other foods that college students commonly consume. If we were to have the ability to distribute "prepared" (unpackaged) foods, with the right health permits and campus approvals, then plant-based burgers, pizza, burritos, tacos, sandwiches, and international cuisine would all be very popular and appropriate to that demographic, more so than protein drinks, muscle recovery drinks, and pre-workout drinks targeted to the fitness audience on our Vegan Strong tour.

I like the idea of applying The Vegan Strong Method and getting involved in product distribution at college campuses in ways Rae described, with a table inside a high foot traffic area like the student center. It would be an interesting approach to engage in such an experiment to test the efficacy of this style of vegan outreach on a college campus, given the potential resources available by leveraging The Vegan Strong Method.

When it comes to distributing plant-based foods on college cam-puses, a skeptic might ask, "Why not just pass out healthy foods like apples, oranges, and bananas to students who are strapped for cash and looking for healthy options when they are thrust into the real world to fend for themselves, rather than having meals prepared for them by their parents?" The answer is perhaps a predictable one—that our mis-sion is to reduce animal suffering by replacing animal-based foods with plant-based options. Most people consume fruits as snacks, so more fruit wouldn't necessarily be replacing animal-based foods. Ultimately, we're also trying to reduce animal suffering by introducing plant-based replacements to animal-based foods, not just promote a healthy diet of fruits and vegetables. Most people already know that fruits and vegeta-bles are the cornerstones of a healthy diet, but they might not be aware of plant-based meats, cheeses, milks, eggs, and other products traditionally coming from animals. That's where we come in.

If college students can learn (and experience firsthand) that they can enjoy a plant-based version of some of their favorite foods, such as mac and cheese, pizza, burgers, cookies, and snacks, this makes a bigger impact for animals, since everyone already knows that garden produce exists. And it might be more effective if these foods are being distributed by students, to their fellow students, rather than from outsiders who don't match the age, lifestyle, or mindset of a college student. This may seem obvious, but how often do we put ourselves in a position for others to see themselves in us, because they can relate to us as being similar to them? If we put this into practice often, what kind of influence could it have on those we interact with? That's what reaching the right audience is all about, which includes acknowledging when you're not the right messenger.

Just as so many others do, from politicians, to business owners, to marketers, to entertainers, we need to spend our efforts going after the low-hanging fruit—the people who are on the fence, already open to veganism as a result of their stage in life. College students are low-hanging fruit, just as vegetarians and environmentalists are, too, as well as people who follow particular diets and remain open to new health and fitness approaches. Those audiences, and others, are where we will find the most success in our pursuit to reduce animal suffering, by knowing the best demographics of communities to reach to elicit the most change in diet and lifestyle habits.

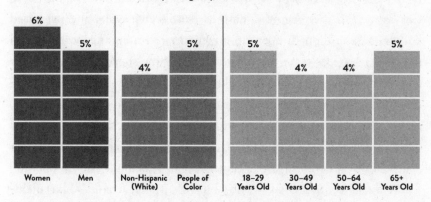

Percent of People Who Identify as Vegetarian
(By Subgroup of US Adults)

Women	Men	Non-Hispanic (White)	People of Color	18–29 Years Old	30–49 Years Old	50–64 Years Old	65+ Years Old
6%	5%	4%	5%	5%	4%	4%	5%

Data sources: Jeffrey M. Jones, "In US, 4% Identify as Vegetarian, 1% as Vegan," Gallup, August 4, 2023, https://news.gallup.com/poll/510038/identify -vegetarian-vegan.aspx; "What Percent of Americans Are Vegan? The Latest Statistics," CookUnity, March 30, 2023, https://www.cookunity.com/blog/what -percent-of-americans-are-vegan; Edouard Mathieu and Hannah Ritchie, "What Share of People Say They Are Vegetarian, Vegan, or Flexitarian?" Our World in Data, May 13, 2022, https://ourworldindata.org/vegetarian-vegan.

BLACK VEGANISM

There is another demographic to reach, as referenced earlier, because it is the fastest growing vegan community in America. I am referring to the Black community, which, for a number of years, has been contributing to the growth of veganism more than any other demographic in the US.

According to a Pew Research Center survey, 8 percent of African Americans identify as vegans compared to just 3 percent of the general population. Some of the most popular and most successful individuals in the vegan community are also in the Black community, including Tabitha Brown, an award-winning actress, *New York Times* bestselling author, restaurant owner, and TV show host, widely known as "America's Mom." Tabitha's social media following is nearly twenty million, making her one of the most influential vegans in the world.

Another African American vegan making huge waves is Pinky Cole, who has built a more than $100 million brand with her chain of Slutty Vegan restaurants, food products, and her bestselling book, *Eat Plants, B*tch*, among other entrepreneurial endeavors. She just raised another $25 million to open up dozens more restaurant locations and she doesn't appear to be slowing down anytime soon. Cities that have already been established as new Slutty Vegan destinations include Harlem and Brooklyn, New York; Birmingham, Alabama; Athens, Georgia; and Baltimore, Maryland, with many other locations to be rolled out soon, to go along with four Atlanta-area restaurants. In September 2023, Pinky announced that a Slutty Vegan restaurant will be opening a permanent location at the world's busiest airport, Atlanta's Hartsfield-Jackson International. The highly anticipated Slutty Vegan location will be in Concourse B, for those who are eager to indulge in a fully vegan experience before a flight (though at the time of this writing, an opening date hasn't been announced). Cole claims that 97 percent of her Slutty Vegan customers are non-vegans, which contributes greatly to the growth of the plant-based food market, and to the advancement of veganism. She has her own Pinky Cole Foundation, which is focused on empowering generations of people of color to win in life, financially, and in the pursuit of their entrepreneurial dreams. Along with her celebrity allies who help amplify her brand, such as Shaquille O'Neal, we'll likely see many more Slutty Vegan locations opening up soon.

Historically influential African American vegans, including the late Dick Gregory and Jim Morris, who helped grow the community, and contemporary pioneers of the modern African American vegan movement in America, such as nutritionist Tracye McQuirter, author Bryant Terry, four-time NBA champion John Salley, and chef and restaurant owner Babette Davis, are just some of the Black vegans powering the movement. Formula One champion Lewis Hamilton, cardiologist Columbus Batiste, New York City mayor Eric Adams, New Jersey senator Cory Booker, and thousands of other influencers are inspiring millions of Black vegans. There are vegan NBA players including Chris Paul, JaVale McGee, and DeAndre Jordan, among others, as well as Black vegans in many other professional sports, such as pioneering tennis player Venus Williams and NFL quarterback Cam Newton.

Within the fitness industry, where I have spent more than two decades of my career, vegan bodybuilders Torre Washington, Korin Sutton, Will Tucker, Dr. Harriet Davis, Jehina Malik, and others have all become champions in their sport, effectively giving a powerful voice to veganism in a typically meat-dominated industry. Athletes, influencers, and entrepreneurs John Lewis, Dominick Thompson, Berto Calkins, and Koya Webb have contributed to the growth of veganism within the Black community for many years, with books, classes, brands, products, and a massive social media presence that has attracted millions of followers. Actress Hayley Marie Norman has been normalizing veganism in Hollywood for well over a decade.

Whereas vegan festivals, or "VegFests" as they are often affectionately called, have been historically white, in recent years Black-owned and operated vegan festivals, and those managed by people of color, have quickly emerged as the most popular vegan festivals in America, including arguably the "world's largest vegan festival," the LA Vegan Street

Fair, organized by Jessica Cruz and her team. There is even a festival aptly named Black VegFest, which takes place in Brooklyn, New York, where entrepreneur and touring speaker Will Tucker had the most memorable speaking engagement of his career. He told me, "For the first time in a decade that I've been vegan, I could stand onstage and stare out to a massive audience of people who looked like me. It was such an incredible feeling that is hard to describe. I felt a rush, a surge, talking with people who have the same challenges, roadblocks, and experiences. To have significant Black representation at a vegan festival, and to reach a community that can relate to me and my story, is something I will never forget."

Veganism is gaining momentum within the Black community, but especially in the Southeast in places like Atlanta and Miami, according to Will. The influence that Black vegans are having in America stretches far beyond South Beach and the Peach State, though, and that is evident to anyone who tours the national vegan festival scene. Will mentioned that one of his most memorable experiences took place in South Central Los Angeles, just a five-hour drive from where he lives in Phoenix, Arizona. Los Angeles is undoubtedly one of the vegan capitals of the world, and the Black community there is strong, with actresses, actors, athletes, authors, restaurant owners, chefs, artists, and others who bring much-needed diversity to the vegan movement as a whole. Within lower socioeconomic communities in South Central LA, Will, along with other Black vegan activists, volunteered his time to help people in the inner city shop for healthy foods. Will told me that it felt empowering, knowing he was making a difference in the lives of others, especially in underserved communities.

My conversation with Will lasted for a couple of hours, covering everything from his introduction to veganism when he found my first book in a Borders bookstore more than a decade ago, when he, too, was a competitive bodybuilder, to what life was like for him growing up in East St. Louis, Illinois, which has a 98 percent Black population. He had met very few vegans before he moved out to Phoenix, where he was working in the corporate world, and later opened up multiple vegan gyms in the area. But by the time I moved to Phoenix in 2016, Will was the most well-connected and recognized vegan in the city. It was my friendship with Will that contributed to my desire to move to the desert, and it was rewarding to watch the vegan movement grow and diversify during my time there. Will co-organized a monthly vegan street fair that lasted for years. He was the host, emcee, or guest speaker at many other yearly vegan festivals in not only the Phoenix valley but in nearby Southern California and Las Vegas as well.

Will credits the growth of the vegan movement within the Black community to increased representation. When people are able to relate to others within a given movement, representation plays a major role in making people feel welcome. And he suspects that the current rise in Black veganism also has to do with the "cool" factor, which Pinky Cole also credits to the rapid increase in Black vegans. It's akin to the rise of the hip-hop movement, and in many ways, the two are intertwined. Many notable Black vegan hip-hop artists, such as Stic from Dead Prez, RZA from the Wu-Tang Clan, KRS-One, and Jermaine Dupri, are just some of the rappers who made veganism popular within their communities. My favorite Black vegan rapper, Grey, has also made a name for himself within veganism for years with a viral Vegan Thanksgiving free-style rap, numerous albums, and his Plant Based Drippin brand. In the summer of 2023, Vegandale, a vegan festival that takes place in six major cities in North America, hosted Rick Ross and other Black entertainers as headliners at their event, which saw crowds of thousands of people surrounding the stage, while enjoying foods and beverages from more than 150 vegan vendors.

Another major vegan festival, Vegan Street Fair, organized by the aforementioned woman of color Jessica Cruz and hosted by Black entrepreneur John Lewis, is a large vegan street fair taking place in nine US cities, including New York, Atlanta, Austin, Seattle, Las Vegas, and Miami. In recent years, it has become the new reality that the largest vegan festivals in America are organized and/or hosted by Black vegans. There are plenty of other events hosted by Black vegans, from block parties in South Beach, to food festivals and plant-based educational programs nationwide. I suspect this will be the case for quite some time, given the momentum veganism has within the Black community, and in popular sports and music cultures.

When I asked Will what he thought about the idea that the Black community is powering the vegan movement, considering they are the fastest-growing demographic and most likely to become vegan, he simply replied, "It's happening." With regard to representation with the vegan community, he added, "Be a role model if you can't find one." That is how I have always viewed Will—as a role model, and someone I look up to for many reasons. Will didn't know any Black vegans when he became vegan more than twelve years ago, and now he is a role model for the next generation who are inspired by his tenacity, grit, and his championship bodybuilder physique, which he maintains even after the age of fifty. With his competitive bodybuilding and gym-owning days behind him, though still in incredible shape, Will is reinventing himself as an entrepreneur working to advance the vegan movement. But his passion, where he feels most alive, is helping people who are suffering the most, like those in underserved communities in South Central LA, and he plans to lend his expertise in plant-based nutrition and exercise to help those in the greatest need within the Black community.

There are clearly many different audiences to reach when promoting veganism, including those who are statistically more likely to embrace veganism as a daily practice. Engaging with those audiences is one way to be an effective and efficient vegan advocate. As Dr. Joy, Joanne, Rae, and Will all alluded to, leading by example will be one of the most powerful steps you can take to wear veganism on your sleeve and welcome more people to the movement.

Understand that just because a specific form of vegan activism "worked" on you to "convert" you or inspire you to adopt a vegan lifestyle, it doesn't mean that same approach will work on every individual you meet. In fact, it is unlikely to be the catalyst that inspires someone else to go vegan, since there are many ways to reach that same conclusion of ethical consistency and compassionate living. Sure, some forms of activism might be statistically likely to be more effective in having an influence on someone else becoming vegan, but it doesn't necessarily mean that even greater likelihood of persuasion will lead to influential change. Evaluating the situation on a case-by-case basis will help guide you to advocate for animals in the most effective ways for each given situation, rather than using a one-size-fits-all approach to promoting veganism.

Dr. Joy encourages us to find reason for hope—to look at the progress that has been made to improve the lives of animals over the past couple of decades in particular—and to understand that when we connect with the right audience, we increase our likelihood of having the greatest impact on reducing animal suffering. Look for the best opportunities to progress toward a more compassionate world. Use your strengths to help others and lead by positive example. Know your audience, engage with your community, and provide resources that support your mission. Success in reducing animal suffering can be a motivational tool to inspire you to keep moving forward, and that momentum can carry you through the struggles that exist within the social costs associated with veganism—having to constantly defend yourself, and animals, in somewhat awkward conversations. I encourage you to explore Dr. Joy's effective vegan advocacy online course to better understand which vegan outreach approaches are most likely to connect with your friends, family, and colleagues, and to equip yourself with the knowledge to effectively answer questions and lead by positive example. You can find all of Dr. Joy's psychology courses centered around effective vegan outreach on veganadvocacy.org.

EMBRACING OR REJECTING THE VEGAN LABEL AND THE SOCIAL COSTS OF VEGANISM

One of the controversial decisions we face is determining which labels we will identify with, which could be anything from religious affiliations to sports teams that we support, to, you guessed it, deciding whether or not we introduce ourselves as a "vegan." To be clear, you don't have to identify with a specific label, or a variety of labels, that define your lifestyle, such as "vegan" or "effective vegan altruist," in order to make a difference for animals, so long as you practice the principles and behaviors associated with those labels. Whether you actually resonate and identify with a particular label or not, you will still be making an impact simply by adhering to actions and lifestyle decisions that support the mission that you care about. Even if you don't want to label yourself to avoid feeling boxed in or pigeonholed into a particular identity that might have some preconceived notions about reputations associated with the group as a whole, you can feel confident that your daily actions still contribute to doing good.

Some people really enjoy having labels to identify with, in many areas of life, from a particular religion or lack of religion; a sports team, college alma mater, or school mascot associated with one's education, or labels common in the animal rights movement such as activist, advocate, vegan, environmentalist, empath, or altruist. There is often a sense of belonging when identifying with particular labels. "They're like me." Or, "I'm like them." We naturally feel safe in numbers and enjoy being part of a community of like-minded people. Think about other areas where this is common in any niche community where people of a certain feather flock together, like comic book collectors, motorcycle riders, bird watchers, RV drivers, stamp collectors, or members of a book club. Of course, many people live fulfilling and happy lives without identifying with any labels, and some people are even anti-label, so ultimately, it's up to you as to how you choose to identify, and whether "vegan," "plant-based," or "altruist" is part of your identity moving forward.

There are many pros and cons associated with labels, including being categorized into a group and absorbing whatever positive and negative reputations a given group experiences. In today's social media world, one benefit of labeling oneself could be business opportunities that come your way as a result of identifying with a particular label that leads to companies or individuals interested in compensating you for your services. Conversely, if identifying with a label makes you uncomfortable, and negatively impacts your life, it is best to leave labels behind, even while you still contribute positively to the world. Many of the great influencers in various movements have been successful without particular labels, so it certainly isn't a requirement and falls solely onto personal preference.

When it comes to the social cost of veganism as it relates to labels we're either associated with, or are prescribed by others, we may feel part of a community or a sense of isolation. Either way carries social implications. Many vegans are no strangers to the dilemma of how to self-identify within a movement that is praised by some and loathed by others—much like an organized religion in that regard, where there is no universally consistent popular opinion of such a group.

Paul Shapiro, the president of The Better Meat Co., who first initiated this conversation with me about the social cost of veganism, wrestles with the vegan label in similar ways that I do. We've been vegan for nearly an identical length of time, are nearly identical in age, and we have formed many of the same views from decades of living altruistic vegan lives. Paul is just more eloquent and experienced than me, and articulates some powerful messages that I often overlook. He shared with me, "Too many vegans act like being right is sufficient for animals; that if we just made stronger arguments, or had better statistics, we could be more effective. But humans are often irrational, and we don't tend to base our behavior on logic. Rather, we do what we enjoy and what we think will enhance our status within our social group.

"Sadly for animals, humans tend to really enjoy eating meat, and there's usually a steep in-group social cost to becoming vegan. What's important isn't merely being 'right.' We must actually be *effective*. That doesn't mean 'winning an argument with a meat-eater.' It means winning over meat-eaters. Vegans often talk about the triumvirate of reasons to be vegan: animals, planet, and environment. But when you look at the reasons most people actually make their food choices, those three choices are nowhere near the top of their motivating reasons. Rather, most of us choose foods based on taste, price, and convenience. We need to compete on the factors that actually drive most food decisions rather than just being content that we're 'right' while animal consumption keeps skyrocketing. That's what The Better Meat Co. is trying to do."

Paul told me that his company, which harnesses the power of fermentation to make delicious, versatile mycoprotein ingredients for food companies to use as the basis of their blended and fully animal-free meats, has already displaced the need for four hundred thousand chickens to be farmed and slaughtered, by selling all-plant-based formulas that food companies then blend into their chicken nuggets and other ground chicken products. He told me, "This approach may not be popular with all vegans, but it's great for animals. The goal is to find ways to reduce the number of animals used for food, and helping meat companies use fewer animals accomplishes that, perhaps even more efficiently than many other strategies."

Let's back up for a moment. What is mycoprotein again? It might sound like a confusing (though fermented and easier to digest) mouthful, so here's another explanation of what The Better Meat Co. produces: Rhiza mycoprotein is a whole-food, complete protein ingredient, made primarily from fermented potatoes and other common agriculture commodities, that's versatile, allergen-free, neutral in taste, and has the texture of animal meat. Rhiza mycoprotein contains more protein than eggs, more iron than beef, more fiber than oats, more potassium than bananas, and naturally contains vitamin B12. This does sound pretty incredible, so I wanted to learn more. Paul shared his vision with me. "The whole reason I cofounded The Better Meat Co. was to help find ways for the food industry to slash the number of animals it uses. Right now, alt-meats are much more expensive than animal meat, and they typically don't fool carnivores in blind taste tests either. Our strategy has been to 'meat' people where they're at. We all agree that it's great to put plant proteins in the meat aisle at the supermarket. Our strategy is to put them directly into the animal meat itself. We only manufacture animal-free ingredients, but by selling them at affordable prices to food companies, we enable them to slash their demand for animal slaughter."

I knew nothing about mycoprotein before my interview with Paul for this book. I knew he had written a book, *Clean Meat*, and I knew he was working in an interesting and innovative space within the food industry. He continued, "I became vegan in 1993 and have devoted my life since then to trying to give animals a better shake in our world. It's been painful for me to see that almost everyone who becomes vegan stops being vegan (nearly nine out of ten people who go vegan stop, according to animal movement research [from Faunalytics]). Even worse is that per-person demand for meat has continued going up to the point where Americans are now eating more meat per capita than ever before. None of these sobering facts have anything to do with 'capitalism.' Humans just really like to eat meat, regardless of what political system they're living in. The task before us must be to find ways to allow humanity to continue enjoying the experience of eating meat without the need to use animals. The Better Meat Co. is betting on mycelial fermentation as a way to do just that."

According to Paul, the solution to stagnant plant-based meat sales, which is a reality in the post-pandemic climate, is to think outside the plant-based meat box and, as he says, "meat people where they're at." Paul concluded that "the key to growth is to bring down prices and bring up the sensory experience. In other words, the products have to taste better and be more affordable. Both are very hard to do, but I do think that mycelium (as opposed to plant protein isolates) offers a promising pathway. Mycelium—the rootlike structure of fungi—is hard to grow industrially, but that's what we need to do. That means making real scientific and technological breakthroughs, and increasing our fermentation capacity. Neither is a small feat, but it's feasible with enough resources. So, to put it bluntly, the space needs more capital."

If you're curious to learn more about the potential of these fermented plant proteins to save animals, or would like to invest in their pursuit of a more compassionate food system, visit BetterMeat.co.

When price parity for vegan meats is widely accessible, and taste becomes indistinguishable, we will likely experience the alleviation of those particular social costs of veganism, while also reaching the right audience at the right time. Cultivated meat, made from animal cells, but without the need for animal slaughter, has already been approved in Singapore and in the United States, and is available to consumers now. It's still a gray area as to whether it is "vegan" or not to consume cultivated meat, because of the fact that it is made from real animal cells, and there is still a level of exploitation involved, but it certainly does reduce animal suffering on a massive scale, which is our ultimate goal. The general consensus is that cultivated meat is not vegan, but it is also not marketed to, or created for, vegans. It is designed to reach the masses and disrupt the food industry to spare animals (and preserve our natural resources and protect our planet).

When it comes to knowing your audience and absorbing the social costs associated with veganism, Dr. Michael Klaper is as experienced as they come. Dr. Klaper, a vegan for more than four decades, echoed the social costs and challenges that vegans face, and shared his thoughts on why some people might not stick with veganism for the long term: "Most people revert to flesh eating due to social pressures—they tire of being the 'odd man out' in restaurants and family gatherings, they tire of defending their food choices to others, they are weary of family strife and rifts over their diet, and they feel it's just too inconvenient to continue being vegan in a non-vegan world. It's sad, but understandable. If you feel compassion in your heart for all living beings who love their lives as much as you do—and you remember there is an innocent creature facing the butcher's knife if we order and pay for that burger—choosing the plant-based meal becomes the only option for the person who wants to decrease violence and suffering on this planet. I know 'the animals are always watching,' and that their fate is in my hands."

And now, here is Dr. Klaper with his physician coat on: "After a fifty-year career as a primary care physician, it has become blazingly clear to me that adopting a diet based on whole plant foods is the most effective way to arrest and reverse the most common lethal diseases that Western physicians spend their careers treating: obesity, clogged arteries, type 2 diabetes, high blood pressure leading to heart attacks, strokes, and kidney failure, and a host of inflammatory diseases. Yet, most young doctors graduate after four years in medical school with essentially zero formal training in nutrition and are generally clueless as to how the patient's daily diet affects their health, for good or ill. Through our Moving Medicine Forward Initiative, I have devoted the rest of my career to reaching as many medical students, faculty teachers, practicing physicians, and allied health professionals as possible with the message of disease reversal through plant-predominant diets.

"As a physician, I know this one understanding, if acted upon by doctors, patients, and the medical system, will immeasurably relieve suffering of millions of people, save trillions of health care dollars, vastly reduce 'burnout' among doctors, and revolutionize human health and health care around the world. It would even benefit planet Earth and the future of humanity as widespread adoption of plant-based diets would require so much less land to grow food for humans that the forests would return on previous grazed lands—and as the trees grow, they will turn global-warming carbon dioxide in the air into solid wood. However, as revolutionary as these changes will be for human health around the world, as a forty-two-year vegan, I know in my heart that if every doctor recommended a plant-based diet to every patient at every visit—and adopted the same diet themselves—the most suffering-relieving benefit of all would be to the billions of cows, pigs, chickens, ducks, fish, and other creatures currently living misery-filled lives in the world's factory farm systems. Every plant-based meal consumed means less demand for 'rape racks' and slaughterhouses. So I am working to have as many humans as possible evolve their diets toward plant-based nutrition because contributing to the ending of the suffering of these billions of innocent creatures gives me the greatest satisfaction of all. It is the best way I can live up to the adage that guides all physicians—'Do no harm.'"

As Dr. Klaper clearly communicates, from his position as a vegan and physician for more than four decades, there are opportunities to relieve the social costs of veganism, while also relieving the health care, environmental, and animal-suffering costs associated with our current food system. We really can be the change we wish to see in the world, and Dr. Klaper is a living legend, personifying that truth and setting an example for generations to come.

"As a physician with a 'Bodhisattva' approach to life, my role is to relieve suffering wherever I may find it," he said. "I don't know if that is altruism, but avoiding the causing of suffering is key to my moment-to-moment decisions, and that starts with what I choose to eat. I encourage others to strive to be the vegan with compassion for all. We are all on this learning journey of life together, and we all deserve compassion from our fellow travelers, and so we need to extend the same compassion to others."

What Paul and Dr. Klaper reveal is that there will always be social costs involved in going against the grain, and there will likely be mountains to climb and obstacles along the way. But the pursuit is worth it for the altruistic reasons they each shared—that animal lives intrinsically matter—and that we can live healthy and fulfilling lives without contributing to animal suffering. Furthermore, rather than the vegan label being a burden in our lives, we can embrace it and join some of the best communities of people in the world, bonded together for a common goal of alleviating suffering and elevating compassion.

I started this chapter with a quote from one of my favorite actors, Jim Carrey, and I'll close with another quote from his 2014 commencement address at Maharishi International University: "All there will ever be is what's happening here, and the decisions we make in this moment, which are based in either love or fear. So many of us choose our path out of fear disguised as practicality. What we really want seems impossibly out of reach and ridiculous to expect so we never ask the universe for it. I'm saying, I'm the proof that you can ask the universe for it."

So many of us long for a more compassionate future, but we often fear putting ourselves out there to contribute to the future we want to see in the world because we worry about judgment from others. Jim has some encouraging words to free you from that concern: "You can fail at what you don't want, so you might as well take a chance on doing what you love." Sure, there can be a social cost that comes with being vegan, and sometimes we do fail, but everything has a cost, so you might as well follow your heart, your intuition, and your compassion to do the most good for animals, even if at times it feels discouraging or isolating. As you'll read in the next chapter, there are reasons to be hopeful about the direction the vegan movement is going in.

CHAPTER 10

DON'T LET PERFECT BE THE ENEMY OF THE GOOD

OUR SHARED VEGAN FUTURE

"Meat tastes good. We're probably genetically wired to enjoy meat, because evolutionarily, we needed it to survive. Today we don't, but it's still in our programming. You can't escape animal-based food in our current food environment. Sit down at any restaurant, and over 90 percent of the entrees have animal products in them. But that can change. I think compassionate, non-judgmental, non-absolutist vegans get the most done. They spread the word that every creature is worthy of our compassion and deserving of a decent life, and they gently make the point that the human race will not further itself until we expand our compassion beyond just humans. Thus, we look to the growth of the plant-based food movement for forward progress."

—Dan Buettner, *New York Times* Best-selling Author of *The Blue Zones* ontrary to popular belief, veganism is not a set of rules that one must follow exactly. Theoretically, one might argue that every decision made must be decided with empathy and compassion toward animals in order to be morally and ethically consistent with the core values and tenets of veganism's opposition to animal cruelty.

But in no other area of discourse do we hold ourselves to this impossible standard. Are we polite and considerate of others, including our parents, our siblings, our friends, and in other relationships 100 percent of the time, without fail? Of course we're not. Are we in a perfectly happy mood every day of our lives, making the absolute most of this one life we have, seizing every minute of the day? Not a chance. Are our diets consistently free of alcohol, refined sugars, processed oils, junk foods, and artificial colors and flavors, amounting to a perfect daily calorie intake based on our optimal caloric needs? Keep dreaming. The reality is, we're all imperfect beings.

If you accidentally eat a piece of cheese that was inadvertently included in your otherwise plant-based fast-food meal, are you now a contributor to animal suffering, because the one calorie you just ate from a sliver of cheese was the result of a baby calf being taken from his mother so that she could be milked in order to make cheese, and for her baby to be killed at eighteen weeks of age and served as veal at a restaurant downtown? No, you're not a willing contributor to such atrocities.

We all make mistakes in our communication, in relationships, in friendships, in our work, in our advocacy, in our education, and in our everyday actions, and holding ourselves to an impossible set of rules is not an effective way to practice veganism. *The goal of veganism is to prevent and reduce animal suffering, whenever possible.* Are you a hypocrite every time you drive your car because of the insects you might smash, or every time you drive past a farm and don't cut the fences down to free all the animals? I don't think so. As vegans, we're also individuals with our own sets of personality traits, characteristics, preferences, behaviors, habits, and tendencies, and we'll likely react to animal exploitation differently from one another. We're motivated by compassion, not by an inflexible set of rules.

The pursuit of perfection can be paralyzing, often leads to stress and anxiety, and is ultimately unsustainable. It can also lead to unhappiness because you'll always feel like you're not doing enough. And, importantly, trying to be perfect will not help animals any more than being an imperfect vegan, because aiming for perfection leads to higher rates of recidivism from veganism, which ultimately hurts animals. So don't strive for perfection, but strive to live in alignment with your moral values, and if those values extend compassion to nonhuman animals, that is an excellent form of vegan advocacy, without having to follow a specific set of rules. When I became vegan in 1995, I basically followed what I believed were the "vegan rules." I often didn't even know *why* I couldn't eat this or that, but there was an understanding that being vegan meant that you don't do this or that, don't eat this or that, don't wear this or that, don't use this or that product, and I followed that model because "those were the rules." It was dogmatic and uncomfortable at times as I navigated my way through my early years of veganism.

Those perceptions of rules led me to live a very compassionate and ethically consistent life, but I also didn't always understand why I was avoiding eating honey, or why I should be boycotting a particular clothing company. I had some basic understandings that consuming any animal by-product must come from some sort of exploitation of that animal, and if I was boycotting a company because they test their products on animals, I should boycott the whole line of products or the whole industry. I was also just a teenager, so my perceptions of veganism, and my understanding of what it meant to be vegan, was likely vastly different than it is today. Those early years of veganism, regardless of my age at the time, revealed experiences that many new vegans go through, and that's another reason why having vegan mentors, coaches, role models, and supporters could be very valuable. Even today, when veganism is at an all-time high in acceptance rate and popularity, there is still a lot of gray area about what it means to be an ethical vegan. One of my goals is to focus on being an impactful vegan, which could have different ethical interpretations and underpinnings than what was previously established in a more dogmatic system of veganism from the twentieth century.

Being a little more flexible, focusing on impact rather than purity, will reduce the most suffering in the long run. We have seen this in many circumstances, from the Forks Over Knives Effect of eating a plant-based diet even if one is not philosophically vegan, to the vegan kaizen system of taking small, incremental steps toward veganism rather than an all-or-nothing approach, to recognizing progress for what it is, not for what it should be in a perfect world.

My hope for you is that you can recognize all the ways to live a happy, healthy, compassionate life even in a non-vegan world, while still achieving all of your hopes and dreams, and leading by example every step of the way. Remember that animals don't care why you're vegan, and they don't care about your purity or perfection in ways that don't impact them; they just care to live their lives free of fear, pain, and suffering, as much as possible. We have the ability to help with that cause, with every decision we make. So embrace veganism and all that it has to offer, and be flexible, go out and eat with your friends, and be social, exuding confidence, showcasing how practical a vegan lifestyle can be.

It doesn't cost anything to be kind, and for many of us, especially for farmed animals, kindness is the greatest gift to receive. We also experience our greatest gift when spreading kindness to others. So here's the question: What can you do to create change that aligns with your inner compassion? That's the question to answer to move forward confidently as a vegan, despite your non-vegan surroundings.

DON'T SWEAT THE SMALL STUFF

One of the ways to avoid becoming overwhelmed is by not worrying about the little things. I embrace veganism in all its forms to the extent that is possible and practical, but I've also learned not to sweat the small stuff. This is not to say that one should make exceptions and compromise vegan ethics, but it means not stressing about things that don't contribute to additional animal suffering, even if those actions don't initially seem in line with vegan morals.

An example might be renting a car only to find out that it has leather seats. Rather than stressing and worrying about the uncomfortable reality that you're sitting on the skin of what was once an animal who wanted to live, understand that though it's uncomfortable, it doesn't cause any additional animal suffering. The car was already made to be used as a rental, and you're just one of hundreds, or perhaps thousands, of people who will likely borrow the car for a period of time. Since you're not buying the car and voting with your dollars to create more demand for cars with leather seats, it's not something to dampen your vegan spirits.

There's also power in listening to opposing viewpoints to better understand those who hold differing opinions about how the world ought to work. Asking questions and trying to discover a deeper understanding of someone's positions could be a very important step in connecting with someone you would otherwise not find common ground with. Rather than focusing on the little things that could bother you or slow you down, how about embracing some of these little things instead?

These are some small things that you *can* do every day to help animals:

- Follow a plant-based diet and make food choices that are consistent with ethical veganism.
- Tell others about the health, wellness, or fitness success you have experienced by following a plant-based diet.
- Share plant-based foods with others, introducing them to meals that would have otherwise been animal-based foods in their diet.
- Talk about ethical veganism with friends and family, answering questions and having meaningful discussions about compassion.
- Vote with your dollars by making compassionate purchases for food, clothing, self-care, and other products, impacting the supply and demand for such items.

- Wear vegan-themed clothing to act as an advertisement for the lifestyle.
- Donate to effective animal charities.
- Volunteer to help animals in shelters, on farm animal sanctuaries, or in other capacities.
- Give of your time, resources, or talents to help animals in need.
- Support vegan activists, companies, organizations, and individuals.

These are some things to *remove* your attachment from. Let go of these small things:

- **Old clothing that is made from animals (leather, wool, silk, etc.):** It doesn't cause any additional animal suffering to continue to use shoes, belts, gloves, coats, wallets, or apparel that contains animal by-products, even if it does feel hypocritical or kind of gross to wear another animal's skin, hair, feathers, or something that involved their exploitation. Often, it's better to get the full use of these items before purchasing replacements, to reduce overall consumerism, while saving financial resources that could be donated to the most effective animal charities to prevent future animal exploitation.
- **Cross contamination in restaurants:** It happens everywhere. Accept it, embrace it, and don't let it ruin your experience. Slight cross contamination doesn't lead to any additional animal suffering, so let it go. It also shows that veganism is something that can be embraced socially and is flexible, without compromising ethics.
- **Leather seats in rental cars or borrowed vehicles:** You're simply borrowing the car for a brief period. You're not buying the car. Don't let it drive you crazy.
- **Playing sports that use leather balls and equipment:** Get your own non-leather basketballs, footballs, soccer shoes, or baseball gloves to use at home, but don't quit the sport you love just because your school or your league uses a leather ball.

- **Watching sports like football, which exploit animals in many ways:** Yes, animals are killed for the footballs themselves, as well as for the athletes' sports equipment and clothing. The reality is that 99 percent of football players, fans, sponsors, vendors, and others associated with the game exploit animals and contribute to their suffering. The amount of animals eaten by football fans on any given Sunday is astronomical, but it doesn't mean you need to boycott football and not watch it, if you like watching football. Prepare your own vegan dishes and snacks and enjoy game day knowing that you are voting with your dollars in so many other areas of life that help reduce animal suffering.

- **Having a cat, which needs to be fed hundreds or thousands of animals to sustain just one cat's life over a lifetime:** One could make the argument that vegans shouldn't have cats, since cats are obligate carnivores and need to eat meat (whereas dogs do not). This gets into that gray area again about the "rules of veganism." Is it ethically consistent with the tenets of veganism to have a cat as a pet if you need to feed other animals to your pet? At the end of the day, that will be up to each individual. There are often more pressing issues to concern ourselves with within the greater scope of reducing animal suffering.

- **Supporting or boycotting plant-based fast-food options:** Don't sweat it. If you like the taste and convenience of fast food, and there are plant-based options, you're not contributing to an evil corporation by spending a few dollars on a vegan fast-food meal.

- **Non-vegan soaps and shampoos in hotels when you're just staying for one or two nights:** In a perfect world, all hotels would carry cruelty-free body care products that are not tested on animals, but since we don't live in a perfect world, and if you don't want to haul your own soaps and shampoos everywhere you go (though there is nothing wrong with doing so), just use what is available, knowing it's just a small drop in a big bucket of soapy water.

- **Feathers in pillows in hotel rooms:** Like non-vegan soaps and shampoos, some hotels are going to have feathers in their pillows and there's not a whole lot you can do about it, unless you travel with your own pillow (which doesn't impact the fact that feathers are used in hotel pillows anyway). Don't get a stiff neck about it.

- **Driving a vehicle and smashing bugs:** Unless you want to be like Fred Flintstone and power your own mode of transportation with bipedal force, the reality is that you're likely going to drive a vehicle, unless you're in a major city and exclusively use public transportation (which will also likely smash lots of bugs). When it comes to suffering, bugs have a much shorter life span than most animals, and their impact with a vehicle is immediate, likely resulting in little to no actual suffering, and it is another unfortunate necessary evil if we plan to commute in any sort of efficient way.

- **Animal manure as fertilizer to grow plants:** It might be a crappy situation, but using animal manure as fertilizer to grow plants is a necessity for most of us. It doesn't have to involve animal exploitation in order to acquire manure, since it can be naturally produced on a small farm. But, in our society, most things are produced on an industrialized scale, and using a manure-based fertilizer to grow plants shouldn't be something that ties your stomach in a knot.

- **Eating at non-vegan restaurants (rather than at only all-vegan restaurants):** Though many of us enjoy the idea of our money going to exclusively vegan companies, especially when we're ordering food, we must also acknowledge that rarely does any purchase go solely to vegans. Nor can we control what a vegan does once they receive our money. It will likely go toward paying bills to non-vegan companies such as landlords and energy companies. Any non-cash transaction has a portion of that payment going to major credit card companies in the form of transaction fees, interest, or otherwise. Furthermore, it could be more

effective at reducing animal suffering to eat at non-vegan restaurants, giving support and amplifying their vegan options. So pull
up a seat and enjoy a plant-based meal, regardless of what type of
restaurant you're at.

- **Having non-vegan friends:** Some of my best friends in the
  world are non-vegans, and I would be willing to bet that is the
  same for many of you. We can love our friends, but we don't have
  to love their actions. There are many things that bond family and
  friends beyond the actions we take and the foods we eat, and we
  can honor those relationships without letting them go sour over a
  difference in worldview. Yes, our actions have consequences, but
  there was very likely a time when you were not vegan, so don't
  be so quick to judge others who are not currently traveling down
  the same path as you. Lead by example and pave a road for your
  friends and family to follow.

- **Working for a non-vegan company:** Even with the demographic of readers I suspect I'm reaching with this book, chances
  are most of you do not work for a fully vegan company. And
  that's okay. As we've discussed throughout, it's what you do with
  your actions, how you vote with your dollars, and how you give
  to effective animal charities that matters the most in our quest
  to reduce animal suffering. In fact, sometimes working for a
  non-vegan company can create an opportunity to have a positive
  influence on others, leading to an increase in compassion toward
  animals. Also, embracing the idea of "earning to give," which is
  basically working a high-paying job that you might not love in
  order to give more to the most effective charities than you would
  be able to by doing a more altruistic job that you enjoy, is often
  worth exploring.

As you can see, there are many areas of our life that are not in perfect
alignment with veganism, but if we get hung up on those issues, and
countless others that could have been listed, we're not serving ourselves,

or animals, in meaningful ways. Seeking perfection is a recipe for disaster because it is impossible to attain, and furthermore, it can actually slow or completely halt forward progress. I learned the hard way, as someone who was obsessed with being "the perfect vegan" for more than twenty years before I looked at the bigger picture of animal suffering and realized I wasn't making the impact I thought I was. Now, using evidence and data, rather than emotion and speculation, I've been able to be a more effective voice for animals. Changing behaviors and habits is hard, but it's also liberating to let go of purity and let the small stuff roll off your shoulders. It also gives you an opportunity to "choose your hard." Pursuing perfection is hard. Changing habits is hard. Choose your hard.

CHOOSE YOUR HARD

This expression, "choose your hard," came across my radar when I learned it from Leif Arnesen, cofounder of The Vegan Gym. You heard from him earlier when we discussed the vegan kaizen method of small, deliberate steps toward desired forward progress. Leif was speaking in a podcast interview when he discussed the crossroads that we often find ourselves in, which results in having to make hard decisions. Some of the examples he shared from the popular quote included, "Marriage is hard. Divorce is hard. Choose your hard." "Being in debt is hard. Being financially disciplined is hard. Choose your hard." And, "Obesity is hard. Being fit is hard. Choose your hard." Clearly, this *choose your hard* scenario works well within their fitness coaching business, but I also think it applies to promoting veganism, too, such as taking the time to learn evidence-based approaches that lead to the most impactful results, admitting when we're wrong, learning to become a beginner again, and in many other areas of advocacy.

Sometimes, we need to make hard decisions, like acknowledging that we don't know as much as we think we do, and that it's okay to ask for help and feedback in order to grow into an effective vegan advocate. We must remain open to critique and criticism if we want to learn how to do the most good for animals, since techniques, approaches, and tactics are always changing, and therefore the data and evidence is constantly changing, too. During the process of writing this book, I had a lot of my own preconceived notions about effective animal advocacy challenged by experts that I interviewed. And as you have seen throughout the evolution of this process, I applied many new strategies and approaches that I previously would have scoffed at or dismissed. That's the power of being open-minded, realizing that we don't know what we don't know. And sometimes accepting that is hard—but it's much harder for the animals if we don't accept and adopt more effective advocacy approaches. Animal activism is hard. Watching animals suffer is hard. Choose your hard.

Therefore, I encourage all of you to choose your hard, and decide how you will make the greatest impact for animals. The famous anonymous quote that Leif referenced finishes by saying, "Life will never be easy. It will always be hard. But we can choose our hard. So pick wisely." I always thought the quote should end with "so *choose* wisely" since every expression is about choosing. But we're not going to get caught up in perfectionism here, right? Let's discuss food instead.

Since we know that we don't live in a perfect vegan world and that we will find ourselves at all sorts of different restaurants throughout our life—some vegan but mostly non-vegan establishments—let's take a look at our dining options. This is your chance to embrace imperfection by choosing to be effective, keeping the reduction of animal suffering top of mind, even if some of these ideas seem counterintuitive. Eating at only purely vegan restaurants is hard. Eating at non-vegan restaurants is hard. Choose your hard.

VEGAN FAST-FOOD NATION

In addition to nearly all of the major corporate fast-food giants offering plant-based options these days, from McDonald's to Burger King, and from Taco Bell to Pizza Hut, we have also seen fully vegan fast-food restaurants pop up around the country lately, particularly in progressive-leaning California, by companies embracing the idea that Americans are addicted to fast food and therefore feeding them what they want. The American appetite for sugary, greasy, salty, fried food that's fast, convenient, and relatively inexpensive probably isn't going to change anytime soon. Consequently, many conscious entrepreneurs have created exclusively vegan fast-food restaurants for the growing number of people who are switching to a plant-based diet, but who still enjoy fast food, including those who would rather have an all-vegan experience than have to constantly request substitutions for items ordered from Burger King or McDonald's. Next Level Burger, Plant Power Fast Food, and PLNT Burger are notable plant-based fast food restaurant chains with locations from coast to coast across America.

You already learned about Next Level Burger, the 100 percent vegan burger joint, established in 2014, which now has 27 locations after their recent acquisition of Veggie Grill, in Oregon, California, Washington, Texas, New York, Massachusetts, and Colorado, with immediate plans to open many more locations throughout the country within the next few years. But Next Level Burger is just one of many all-vegan fast-food restaurants. PLNT Burger has thirteen restaurants in Washington, DC, Maryland, Virginia, Pennsylvania, New York, and Massachusetts. Plant Power Fast Food has ten locations throughout California, and one in Nevada. Hart House, a vegan fast-food restaurant created by comedian Kevin Hart, opened multiple restaurants in Southern California in 2022 with plans to roll out ten other locations in the near future, with four locations already experiencing great success.

Slutty Vegan, an Atlanta-based vegan comfort food restaurant by serial entrepreneur Pinky Cole, which you learned about earlier, has bold plans of opening twenty more locations after raising $25 million in 2022. Many of her new locations opened up in 2023, in four different states, with more doors opening soon.

HipCityVeg has eight locations throughout the Washington, DC, and Philadelphia areas, Monty's Good Burger has five locations throughout

Southern California, and the list goes on, from Washington, to Texas, to Florida. These are just vegan fast-food restaurant chains, of course.

There are plenty of independent vegan fast-food spots with single locations, or two or three locations throughout the country, too, such as Honeybee Burger's three locations, Stand-Up Burgers' three locations, Meta Burger's three locations, Burgerlords' two locations, and Romeo's two locations, among many others, including, statistically more and more likely, a vegan fast-food restaurant somewhere near you. From New Mexico to New Hampshire, vegan restaurants are here to stay and more money has been invested into the vegan food space than ever before, as evident from Next Level Burger and Slutty Vegan each raising at least $20 million in 2022 alone.

Clearly, plant-based fast food is on the rise, all across America, and retail sales data supports that notion, as you saw from the Good Food Institute's state of the industry report. Some other vegan restaurant chains boast hundreds of locations, such as Loving Hut, with more than two hundred locations in thirty-five countries, including dozens of restaurants spanning fifteen US states. Veggie Grill and Native Foods, along with Loving Hut, are vegan casual restaurants amassing more than fifty combined locations in the United States.

Nearly every US state has multiple all-vegan restaurants (Alaska is the only state with just one all-vegan restaurant at the time of this writing—though that could change with the help of ambitious readers who are restaurateurs, seeking expansion), and some states, like California and New York, are home to hundreds of all-vegan restaurants. There are approximately 2,200 vegan restaurants in America,[33] with more popping up every month, and more than 30,000 vegan-friendly restaurants, particularly those offering international cuisines, such as Indian, Thai, Ethiopian, and Mexican cuisine. Perhaps soon, we'll be able to include the largest fast-food restaurant chains in the world under the "vegan-friendly" umbrella with their continued expansion of plant-based menu options. This is all very encouraging to vegans everywhere, and my examples, largely based in the US, where I live, are just representative of one particular geographical location. The US is not the most vegan-friendly nation in the world—in fact, it's not even close.

While walking in the town of Chiang Mai, Thailand, for example, checking my HappyCow app (created by Eric Brent and his team to help users identify vegan restaurants, vegetarian restaurants, and restaurants that have veg options within a geographical area) to identify vegan-friendly restaurants based on my location, there were approximately one hundred vegan-friendly dining options within walking distance revealed on my phone. Sure enough, when I looked up as I walked down the sidewalk, the streets were in fact lined with vegan and vegan-friendly eateries. You likely won't find that in Houston or Chicago. While traveling in major cities in Australia, vegan options were more the norm in places like Sydney, Melbourne, and Adelaide. Then there's the UK, where the term "vegan" was coined by Donald Watson in 1944, with hundreds upon hundreds of vegan restaurants just in London and surrounding areas alone. Yet another city in the UK, Brighton, which was designated as one of the top vegan-friendly cities in the world, boasts more vegan fame in the UK, as does Bristol, Manchester, and Leicester, and it's not just vegan food in the UK that shines. They even have an entirely vegan professional soccer team (Forest Green Rovers F.C.), a massive animal rights movement, and are the home of the Vegan Camp Out, VegfestUK, and numerous other vegan festivals.

The United Kingdom really is one of the greatest vegan places on Earth.

Though the UK often steals the show, relevant to many readers in North America, Canada, even with its relatively low population, celebrates more than 400 all-vegan restaurants, an additional 350 vegetarian restaurants, and 3,250 more that have "veg options," such as a vegan or vegetarian menu.

Most of these locations are predictably in Ontario, with the dense population of Toronto, followed by British Columbia where iconic cities Vancouver and Victoria are home to many vegan eateries. Also relevant to readers in North America, Mexico is home to more than 450 all-vegan restaurants, including over 100 vegan spots in Mexico City alone, with another 275 vegetarian restaurants and more than 1,000 restaurants with "veg options."

Depending on where you live, you will certainly have a skewed perspective of the vegan food landscape. There could be vegan options on seemingly every corner in parts of Jamaica, as standard menu items in Israel, or you could be in a complete vegan oasis in some German towns. You might witness plant-based diets as part of a trend in Santa Monica, as part of the cultural norm in Taiwan and in rural Asia and Africa, or as a popular restaurant theme in New York City or Vancouver. You could also view veganism as a fringe lifestyle in Amarillo, as an obnoxious moral agenda being pushed in Alberta, or a not-so-culturally-accepted lifestyle in Buenos Aires or Havana. A plant-based diet might not even be practical in some remote parts of the world. Your perception of veganism, and of plant-based food, likely has a lot to do with where you live in the world, what your cultural eating habits have been throughout your life, and which foods you have been exposed to. We need to keep that in mind as we engage in vegan conversations with non-vegans. Most of us eat what we eat and do what we do because of the experiences we had when we were young, which we still embrace today. Let's go back to my primary vegan food experience in the United States for a moment.

There is no denying that we live in a fast-food nation, and though I had never gone through a drive-thru as an adult until recently, there is no question that those establishments feed America. According to the Centers for Disease Control and Prevention (CDC), more than one-third of American adults eat fast food daily (37 percent),[34] and according to a survey posted by NBC, 80 percent of Americans consume fast food weekly.[35] So it behooves us to recognize that and create a higher demand for plant-based options at Subway, McDonald's, Starbucks, KFC, Burger King, Pizza Hut, Domino's, and beyond. This same approach goes for family diners, sit-down restaurant chains, independently owned restaurants, and other food establishments, pubs, bars, and food trucks. The greater demand we create for plant-based food options within the mainstream food culture, the greater impact we have as vegans in a non-vegan world. This, of course, applies to whatever restaurant chains are in your part of the world, too, and is not unique to America. We all have the capacity to create change right in our own neighborhoods, in our towns, and in our countries, and it all adds up to making a difference for animals. It all starts with you and what you will decide to put on the end of your fork. Every bite counts.

My assumption is that many of you reading this are already vegan or considering a vegan lifestyle or plant-based diet, and like me, you're genuinely curious as to what actions, including food choices, do the most to help animals. It's also my assumption that even if you are vegan, you're very likely in a friend or family circle with plenty of people who are not vegan. Consequently, you'll likely find yourself at many non-vegan restaurants for family gatherings, parties, meetups with friends, lunch or dinner with colleagues, when traveling, or in countless other situations, especially when invited out by others to a location that has already been determined. If you do happen to have a say in where your group goes, know that there are plenty of totally mainstream restaurants that cater to both vegans and non-vegans alike, by having clearly marked vegan items on their menu, such as at P.F. Chang's, Olive Garden, Mellow Mushroom, The Cheesecake Factory, Sweet Tomatoes, Chipotle, and yes, even at Cracker Barrel.

So whether you're celebrating at a restaurant with family, out to lunch with coworkers, or at dinner with friends, know that there are plenty of vegan meals available to you, across the country and around the world, at major restaurant chains that have answered the call for an increased demand for vegan foods. There are thousands of independently owned restaurants that cater to vegans as well, which can make for a fun experience exploring the local food scene in small and large cities across the country. Get out there and create a greater demand for plant-based options in your community.

When I graduated from high school in 1998, a neighbor gave me the book *Don't Sweat the Small Stuff*, which had the subtitle *And It's All Small*

Stuff: Simple Ways to Keep the Little Things from Taking Over Your Life and was published the year prior. Though it had a very basic premise, kind of like a pep talk, perhaps aimed at recent graduates like me, encouraging readers to "live in the present moment," "trust your intuition," and "live each day as if it might be your last," which are all incredibly overused clichés as we know them today, the book sold more than twenty-five million copies and the words became an anthem for my generation. As I reflect on the theme of not sweating the small stuff, I'm hung up on the subtitle that the book chose—*And It's All Small Stuff.* From an effective altruism perspective, some things are small things, and some things are very big things—like the importance of reducing as much suffering as possible. As Nick Cooney reminds us in *How to Be Great at Doing Good,* "There is an unfathomable amount of very real misery and suffering going on just outside the borders of our comfortable lives. Every charitable decision we make should be based on one question and one question only: Which choice will reduce as much of that suffering as possible?"

As you move forward as an imperfect vegan, consider the various ways you can tap into your STRONG V characteristics to amplify veganism, while letting go of the minutiae that no longer serves your mission to help animals. Most importantly, though, always keep your goal within arm's reach and never lose sight of the big picture. You'd like to see a vegan future someday, right? Or at least as close to a vegan future as we can get. Let's evaluate how to get there.

TOWARD A VEGAN FUTURE

Many vegans like to imagine a vegan future, or at least more of a vegan future than we currently live in. So what might a vegan future look like?

Since the treatment of animals raised for food is perhaps the easiest way to view veganism on a mainstream scale, what a vegan future would look like would be a complete overhaul of the types of foods available in grocery stores and at restaurants around the world. It would include changing nutritional habits based on supply and demand, making animal protein harder to come by, and having plants as a plentiful source of nutrition, that would naturally alter the way future generations eat. And, as presented throughout the book, it would mean fundamentally changing how meat is made.

In order to actually create a vegan future, we have to start with addressing food production, which is a monumental task that involves evaluating agricultural practices, government subsidies, land use, generational family farmers, corporate animal producers, and the supply chain from farm to store, in an effort to change the way the entire food system views animal and plant production. This effort would need to confront governmental policies, state and national legislatures, the public school system, a national and global food education program, and many more components of education aimed at giving farmers, politicians, educators, and the general public confidence that plants are adequate sources of nutrition that are also tasty, affordable, convenient, and overall satisfying.

Luckily, we have intelligent organizations like the Good Food Institute (GFI) working on such issues. We also need to prepare all of those entities for the future of meat, made from cells and fermented plants, so that we're in a position to completely transform the food system. In the meantime, making people more comfortable with eating plants—including plant-based meats, dairy, and eggs—in higher numbers is going to be of paramount importance to address our global food crisis in the present.

It appears that creating a vegan future would see people adopt lifestyle habits that would have little to do with "veganism," and would have much more to do with diet, supply and demand, cost, and perhaps even health care implications. But, as I've argued throughout, it doesn't matter *why* someone stops harming animals. Their actions are much more consequential than their reasons behind their actions.

Given this observation that our fellow humans tend to lack empathy toward animals, and are more persuaded to not eat animals because of dietary or health preferences (or because of taste, cost, and convenience), we should put our efforts there. Recognizing that, in our current position within the growth of the vegan movement, most people join the community for personal health reasons, we need to embrace that reality and support people where they are. There have been numerous studies showing that, by and large, personal health is the primary entry point to plant-based living, even if we know that "veganism" represents a moral philosophy, not a diet.

In the early years of the animal rights movement, around fifty years ago, many people were vegan for the animals, and there was a strong ethical undertone to abstain from animal exploitation. Over the years, the vegan movement has somewhat morphed into a diet and lifestyle campaign that has much more to do with personal health, wellness, and food preferences than a concern for the suffering of animals. That was inevitable, given the growth of the movement—expanding to many other niche communities—and considering the motivations that many people have for their own self-interests. A vegan future might still be possible one day, at least within particular communities, but it won't be because of a shared ethical perspective to reduce animal suffering.

THE POWER OF THE POSITIVE VEGAN

The power of positive thinking and optimism is paramount as an effective vegan altruist because the reality of animal suffering is so grim and can lead to depression and sadness if we're unable to focus on the positive impact our work has on animals. There are perceptions of "angry vegans" and "militant vegans" and those are likely accurate interpretations by non-vegans based on their interactions with passionate vegan advocates. I've asked the following question for decades: "Are you angry because you're vegan, or are you happy because you're vegan?" I certainly realize that you can be both angry and happy as a vegan, because of the cruelty animals are subjected to and the reduction of that cruelty as a result of your veganism, and perhaps all of us share a bit of both strong emotions.

The question is designed to get people thinking of how they feel about being vegan, how those feelings are expressed, and how others perceive their expressions. I think it's an important question, and obviously (based on their observations and comments) many people still hold a view of vegans as "angry" or "militant" or "superior" to non-vegans because of an aggressive way that some people choose to represent veganism.

Will leading with positivity, optimism, and happiness draw more people to veganism than by leading with anger, aggression, and with a pessimistic worldview? I think that question is worth thinking about from a variety of angles, evaluating the net result of our actions, and the impact those results have for animals. Beyond how we portray veganism to others, we also need to maintain a positive relationship with our personal vegan lifestyle to avoid burnout, sadness, and depression as a result of our awareness of the constant suffering going on around us, and the emotional wear and tear that has on our psyche.

Even though veganism is a moral baseline for many of us to strive for, we all have family or friends who just don't want to embrace veganism and are unlikely to ever be vegan. I am sure you can think of various people in your life (often family members) that fit this description. Since these people are unlikely to be vegan, they won't be embracing the moral foundation of veganism by preventing unnecessary cruelty as a result of adhering to vegan philosophical principles, but there are still many ways that our non-vegan loved ones, friends, and colleagues can contribute to reducing animal suffering. This is achieved largely by donating to the best animal charities—many of which we've covered already—and by being a vegan ally, supportive of your lifestyle. Of course, omnivores can, and often do, support plant-based products and vegan companies, making some of their voting dollars count toward reducing demand for animals as food.

Whenever we have the opportunity to live in alignment with our core beliefs, we should embrace them fully. We don't want to discourage our omnivorous friends from contributing to animal rights causes by making it sound like being vegan is the only way to help animals. Progress for animals as quickly and effectively as possible is our goal as effective vegan altruists, so we should represent veganism as positively as we can, to attract other people to our movement.

A vegan future often starts with the small steps you take today. My advice for people taking the first steps toward veganism is to determine why you want to be vegan, and to always keep those reasons at the top of your mind. Discover your favorite plant-based foods and incorporate them into your lifestyle consistently to build up plant-based eating habits. Understanding why you're deciding to become vegan, supported by a plant-based diet with your favorite foods, is a recipe for a long-lasting vegan lifestyle. Joining a vegan or plant-based community, either online or in person, is another great way to connect with like-minded people to learn from, and to lean on for support. Any significant change requires time to adapt to a new lifestyle. Taking small steps, such as eating your favorite plant-based meals and connecting with a vegan community, will help you ease into your newfound vegan lifestyle. Donating to effective animal charities can also give you a sense of purpose, and is a contribution to the type of future you believe in. A vegan future is possible.

When I interviewed vegan experts for this book, I asked each one to speculate about whether or not they think we will one day experience a vegan future. To close our final chapter, I'd like to share some of their thoughts with you.

> "I do believe there will be a vegan world, but I'm not certain that we'll see it in our lifetimes, although I remain optimistic. While the number of vegans in the US has increased from 3 percent in 2020 to 5 percent in 2022, according to data from the Vegetarian Resource Group and Statista, there are people who refuse to give up meat, dairy, eggs, and/or fish in favor of plant-based alternatives. However, with the advent of cultivated

meat and precision fermentation, there soon won't be a valid excuse. Once the price point and availability can match that of traditional animal foods, there won't be a reason to choose the crueler, less environmentally friendly options. I also suspect that knowledge of the impending climate crisis may provoke governments to pour more money into the development of cultivated meat and plant-based alternatives, expediting the shift away from animal agriculture. After all, while it's not the only thing we can do to combat climate change, it is a necessary weapon in that fight, as illustrated by the latest IPCC climate report."

—Dr. Matthew Nagra, researcher,
author, and vegan athlete

"I am not sure if a vegan world will ever be a reality. I do think we will always have good versus evil on this planet as we know it, but I do believe we can make great change for the good while we are here, and honestly, not fighting for the lives of the voiceless is simply not an option for me."

—Dotsie Bausch, Olympian and
founder of Switch4Good

"I think the most realistic path to a vegan world in terms of no longer exploiting animals involves the use of cultivated meats and other animal products such as fermentation to create certain proteins like whey. While more and more people may become more open to ethical veganism, many will refuse to relinquish their habit of meat consumption. It will likely be the gradual replacement of animal meat with these products as they outprice animal products that could collapse animal farming entirely. While many people's gut reaction to cultivated meat is that it is unnatural, gross, or somehow more harmful to consume, the reality is that the population has demonstrated thoroughly that they don't care where their meat comes from, as is evident by factory farming, which provides virtually all meat in terms of volume produced. It took testing Subway's chicken breast to discover that it was only 50 percent chicken. Additionally, the properties of these meats can be tweaked to be healthier than competitors such as removing cholesterol, saturated fat, etc."

———————

—*Mike Dearborn*
(Mic the Vegan on YouTube)

"When it comes to long-term veganism, it's a decision that requires commitment, and if you don't commit to eating vegan for one or more reasons, there will be no purpose. When I was pregnant with our first daughter in 2000, I sat in doctor's offices with a sense of dread whenever the topic of diet came up. And, after she was born, I can't count how many disapproving looks I received from peers and professionals when they learned I ate plant-based—and planned the same for our children. But my heart and gut told me that I had researched information that they did not. Now, I see our daughters thriving and happy, truly loving their food, understanding the atrocities of animal agriculture, and never asking to eat anything with meat, dairy, or eggs. Eating vegan is now their norm as it is mine. When people see their peers in a vegan light, it's very powerful, and that contributes to a brighter vegan future."

———————

—*Dreena Burton, author of* Dreena's Kind Kitchen
and vegan for more than twenty-five years

"I don't think there will be a vegan future, but I do believe meat will become a luxury item and veganism or a plant-based diet will be part of a social norm. I believe this because there are companies that are creating cultivated meat, and our environment cannot sustain the pollution from the creation of infinite animal production for human consumption."

—Korin Sutton, author and twenty-eight-
time champion pro vegan bodybuilder

"While I would love a vegan future, I'm not sure if we'll see it in our lifetime. I do believe that it will happen, though, and just because we won't be around to see it, that shouldn't stop us from working hard to make it happen. There is often a lack of solidarity in the vegan movement, which I believe slows forward progress. At the end of the day, the animals don't care why we're vegan. They don't care if we follow a vegan ketogenic diet, or if we follow a raw vegan diet, or if we are going to identify with veganism for our health, for the community, or for the animals. The animals only care that we're not assisting or aiding in their suffering and death. So the infighting about how people self-identify with their brand of veganism as being superior to someone else's perceptions of veganism is not helping the long-term goal of making the world vegan."

—John Lewis, entrepreneur, and
author of Badass Vegan

"I anticipate a rise or even an explosion of plant-based product acceptance in the coming years. I have been a plant-based proponent since the early 1980s and I have witnessed a palpable increase in interest in all things plant-based over several decades. Sometimes, I have to pinch myself when I see the options in stores and restaurants. Non-vegetarians are far more open to trying these options than they once were. Recently an omnivorous friend told me that he thought the new plant-based burgers were so good he no longer feels he needs to eat meat burgers. This is progress. I believe that the plant-based sector is on an exponential growth curve. The thing that influences my perspective on this the most is the climate crisis. People are beginning to make the connection between their food choices and climate change, and they are beginning to make choices that they believe will reduce their carbon footprint."

—*Brenda Davis, RD, author, speaker, and vegan for more than forty years*

"As much as I want to remain positive, I think we are headed toward a sixth mass extinction on this earth. The harm we are causing the planet—animal agriculture being one of the leading culprits—is devastating, and I don't think our efforts to slow and reverse the damage are enough. I do feel intuitively that, as a collective, our consciousness is elevating and that love and compassion is our natural state of being from a soul-perspective. I believe that we are navigating this life, trapped inside a human form, with a human ego and all the programming that comes along with it that causes us to feel separate, when in reality, we are all one. The spiritual path I'm on brings me both comfort, and also allows me to continue playing the role of animal advocate from a place of profound curiosity, fierce compassion, and a deep connection with all living beings. I don't know what will happen, when, but I know my purpose here is to spread love, and so spreading love I shall continue to do until the day I die!"

—*Ella Magers, author, trainer, and vegan for more than twenty-eight years*

"Taking veganism into the future requires leading by example. There will sadly always be a heightened scrutiny on vegans, so being vegan in a non-vegan atmosphere bears the responsibility of being informed and in tune with my body. I take great pride in not being what people would expect a vegan to look like. When I became vegan many years ago, the options and acceptance were nowhere near what they are today. I believe 'what's right' will shine through in the end, and I have no doubt that veganism is 'what's right.'"

—*Joseph Blair, NBA Assistant Coach*
for the Washington Wizards

"I don't think that we'll see a vegan future, but we will have a *more-vegan* future. Eating meat is so ingrained in our culture. We're going to need a huge cultural shift, and the problem is there is so much money in animal agriculture. Until that is changed, unfortunately, we're stuck in the status quo. We have to make vegetables so enticing and so affordable because they are competing against government-subsidized meat. But we have to do something, and if we don't, we're going to procrastinate our way out of a planet someday."

—*Chef AJ, author, host of* Chef AJ LIVE! *on* YouTube, *and vegan for more than forty-seven years*

"Once we get to the point where cultivated meat products are as affordable as regular animal products, and can be produced on a mass scale without the loss of an animal's life, I truly believe we will see a massive shift toward veganism."

—*Carleigh Bodrug,* New York Times *bestselling author of* PlantYou

"Let's say that 2 percent of the world population is vegan, and 98 percent consume animal products. If we define a 'vegan future' as being the reciprocal of today's meat-to-vegan percentage, in other words, 98 percent vegan and 2 percent of the world eating animal products, then yes, I do believe that we will see a vegan future. I doubt our world will reach those percentages in my lifetime (I'm thirty-one), but I do think I will see a predominantly vegan world in my lifetime (meaning more than 50 percent of the world population).

There are a few main drivers that I believe will contribute to this vegan future: 1) the economics of plant-based products versus animal-based products, 2) growing vegan awareness, and 3) a dire need to reduce large-scale fishing and factory farming practices to save our planet. Those last two are pretty self-explanatory, so I'll just touch on the first in more detail. The economics of plant-based products versus animal-based products:

Most people buy food based on taste, price, and convenience. I don't think vegan food is inherently more expensive—after all, rice and beans are vegan—but if you directly swap animal products with plant-based meat and dairy substitutes, then, in general, most people will spend more money per calorie or gram of protein. But soybeans will always cost less per gram of protein than beef, so as demand for plant-based products increases, the price of those products relative to their animal-based counterparts will continue decreasing. Once the average consumer:

1.   Cannot taste the difference between plant-based products versus their animal-based counterparts (I think we're already there for some products, and we're just years away from this being true for most types of meat and dairy products), and

2. Spends less by filling their grocery cart with 100 percent
    vegan items,

then I think the shift to plant-based eating will accelerate. As
this shift happens, the price of meat and dairy products will
spike in response to falling demand. This is simple supply and
demand economics.

One final reason why I believe we will see a predominantly vegan world (future) in this century is the fact that
good always triumphs over evil. As Gandhi once said, 'When I
despair, I remember that all through history, the way of truth
and love has always won. There have been tyrants and mur-
derers, and for a time, they seem invincible, but in the end,
they always fall.'"

———————————

*—Leif Arnesen, author and
CEO of The Vegan Gym*

Whether or not we'll actually experience any type of vegan future
will likely come down to technological advancements in food production, not a logical, emotional, or philosophical opposition to unnecessary
animal suffering. As Paul Shapiro points out in his book, *Clean Meat*,
and in many articles, it wasn't our desire to improve the lives of horses
that moved us away from using horses for transportation. It was the
invention of bicycles and automobiles that made exploitation of horses
for transportation obsolete.

In a 2023 blog post that was both a book review of Peter Singer's
updated *Animal Liberation Now* and an article about the state of the
animal rights movement, nearly fifty years after Singer's original *Animal Liberation* was published, Paul further made his point that technology will win in the end. "Geese are no longer live-plucked for their
quills not because anyone made persuasive arguments for the birds,
but because metal fountain pens were invented. Whales are no longer

harpooned for their oil not because 19th century social reformers gave whales a voice, but because kerosene offered a cheaper, cleaner way to light our homes." He provided many other examples, too, showing how technology has made what was once a common practice of animal exploitation obsolete because those methods are no longer efficient in today's world. We could very well experience a future where meat is made from plants and from animal cells, and as Bruce Friedrich said, "that's just how meat is made."

CONCLUSIONS ABOUT HOW TO BE THE MOST IMPACTFUL VEGAN

"It's not enough to tell people there is a problem. You have to tell them that there is a solution. Oftentimes, I meet a lot of folks in the vegan space that heavily focus their lives around the problem. Yes, we're all aware that industrialized animal agriculture produces 99 percent of the animal products in the world—and that there is untold, undue suffering every second of every day—but for us to be successful as a movement, we have to become an industry, too."

—Jennifer Stojkovic, author and founder
of Vegan Women Summit

After not only reading this book, but having written this book, and having conducted many more interviews about this topic, my recommendations for being an impactful vegan are the following:

- Support the Animal Charity Evaluators Top and Standout Charities.
- Lead by example and connect with the right audiences to influence.
- Donate to effective organizations abroad where dollars stretch the furthest.
- Apply the vegan kaizen system of taking small, incremental steps to build consistent habits.
- Incorporate The Vegan Strong Method into your life by introducing plant-based products to non-vegan audiences.
- Volunteer your strengths, talents, skills, connections, time, and resources to help animals in ways that are most effective.
- Deliberately support vegan menu items at non-vegan restaurants.
- Actively patronize vegan businesses.
- Amplify others in the vegan community.
- Invest in the type of future you would like to see by voting with your dollars.
- Take courses about effective vegan advocacy and apply what you learn.
- Teach others what you know about helping animals.
- Remember why you became vegan and let that fuel your advocacy.
- Stay positive to avoid burnout, while maintaining a sustainable routine.
- Look at studies to learn which advocacy techniques most effectively help animals.
- Write pro-vegan articles for newspapers, websites, and magazines.
- Utilize social media to engage in conversations about reducing animal suffering.
- Identify your STRONG V characteristics and avail them to help animals.
- Attend conferences to learn from leaders in the vegan and effective altruism movements and apply what you learn.

- Connect with others to grow your support network, and support others too.
- Let go of your biases and follow the evidence in your quest to make the biggest impact for animals.
- Celebrate all wins for animals, and don't sweat the small stuff.

SPECIFIC ACTIONS THAT I AM TAKING AS A RESULT OF WRITING THIS BOOK

My goal with this book is to not only share the most effective methods of reducing animal suffering but also to make the greatest impact for animals. The intent is that this book becomes an informative tool for effective vegan altruism. My personal commitment to supporting effective vegan outreach and reducing animal suffering includes the following:

- A monthly donation to the Good Food Institute
- A monthly donation to The Humane League
- A monthly donation to Dharma Voices for Animals
- A monthly donation to Luvin Arms Animal Sanctuary, plus yearly donations to other animal sanctuaries
- Feeding a vegan meal to a hungry child with every sale of this book
- Recruiting plant-based products to distribute to primarily non-vegan audiences, by applying The Vegan Strong Method
- Leveraging social media platforms to amplify other vegans, vegan companies, and animal charity organizations
- Patronizing vegan-friendly and vegan restaurants
- Donating a portion of book sales to the most effective animal charities in the world, as well as donating book proceeds to other effective animal organizations, particularly those outside America

- Sharing information about effective vegan altruism on podcasts, in magazine interviews, in online articles, and on social media, in order to raise awareness of strategies to do the most good for animals
- Attending animal advocacy and effective altruism conferences to share ideas with other highly motivated individuals who are committed to creating positive change for animals
- Donating copies of this book to vegan organizations and others who are already invested in reducing animal suffering, with the intent this book will give them additional ideas and strengthen their commitment to helping animals
- Using my personal brand and likeness to help advance the vegan movement within the fitness industry and within other communities

Those are the actions I am taking on a daily, weekly, monthly, and yearly basis to make the most effective impact I can for animals. The goal is not to try to play hero and give more than you can, but to be effective with your contributions and adjust those amounts based on the resources you have available. Making small donations, even just $10 a month to a single organization, likely will not cause any measurable disruption in your lifestyle.

It might seem like a $10 per month donation won't change much, but if The Humane League, for example, can spare three chickens per dollar, a simple $10 a month donation to their organization could spare thirty chickens per month and 360 chickens per year. Other effective animal organizations have similar levels of impact, so with just $50 contributed per month, you could spare more than one hundred animal lives each and every month, and more than a thousand per year. Imagine what you could accomplish with monthly donations of $100, $500, $1,000, or more. In the meantime, if everyone reading this book pledged just $10 per month to one of the recommended animal charities, or an animal charity of your choosing, imagine what we could accomplish for animals together. Who's with me? Which animals do you want to spare from abuse and suffering, and how many are you committed to helping?

As you reflect back on the book, which organizations were you most compelled to contribute to? Can you make the decision right now to go to their website and make your first donation? Which method, system, or strategy of reducing animal suffering resonated with you the most? Are you ready to send your first email to request plant-based products to distribute while you embrace The Vegan Strong Method? Are you prepared to create small, achievable goals to set the wheels of the vegan kaizen system in motion to build consistent habits that achieve results? Are you motivated to write articles for major newspapers, websites, and magazines, or call politicians to advance policies to help animals? Or do you feel moved to put your money where your mouth is and support the vegan and vegan-friendly restaurants in your town so that they not only stick around but also have the potential to grow? Those are just some ideas, of course, and everything else, including leading by example, teaching others, supporting others, taking courses, joining communities, and volunteering your time, are additional ways to help animals, as discussed throughout this book.

Fully embracing effective vegan altruism means discovering ways to do the most good for animals. You now know which organizations are most effective at reducing animal suffering, which methods of advocacy inspire the most people to reduce their animal consumption, which for-profit companies are most important to support, and how to most effectively connect and communicate with the right audiences to advance veganism. It is my sincere desire that whether you strive to do the most good, or to simply get started on your path to being an effective vegan altruist, that you will play an active role in improving the lives of our fellow animals. Let's take action and make it happen.

Impactful Vegans

Vegan D

Vegan C

Vegan B

Vegan A

Does not donate to
any animal charities

Donates $200 to
their preferred
animal charities

Donates 5% of annual
income* to the most
effective charities

*(based on median
US salary ranges)

Donates 5% of annual
income* to the most
effective charities
and incorporates The
Vegan Strong Method
to distribute plant-based
products to omnivores
throughout the year

*(based on median
US salary ranges)

**365
animals**
spared per year

**1,000
animals**
spared per year

**7,115–8,615
animals**
spared per year

**9,000–10,000
animals**
spared per year

APPENDIX
THE MOST EFFECTIVE
ORGANIZATIONS TO SUPPORT

Ranked by Animal Charity Evaluators as the Top Charities and Standout Charities (listed alphabetically)

Animal Charity Evaluators—animalcharityevaluators.org

Top Charities

Faunalytics—faunalytics.org

Good Food Institute—gfi.org

The Humane League—thehumaneleague.org

Wild Animal Initiative—wildanimalinitiative.org

Standout Charities

Ciftlik Hayvanlarini Koruma Dernegi—kafessizturkiye.com

Compassion USA—ciwf.com

Dansk Vegetarisk Forening—vegetarisk.dk

Dharma Voices for Animals—dharmavoicesforanimals.org

Federation of Indian Animal Protection Organizations—fiapo.org/fiaporg/

Fish Welfare Initiative—fishwelfareinitiative.org

Material Innovation Initiative—materialinnovation.org

Mercy For Animals—mercyforanimals.org

New Harvest—new-harvest.org

Sinergia Animal—sinergiaanimalinternational.org

Xiaobu Vegan—instagram.com/vegansofshanghai

Charity Navigator Recommended Charities—charitynavigator.org

American Bird Conservancy—abcbirds.org

Blue Ridge Humane Society—blueridgehumane.org

Colorado Feline Foster Rescue—coloradofelinefosterrescue.org

Hoof or Paw—hooforpaw.org

Nassau Humane Society Inc.—nassauhumane.org

The Anti-Cruelty Society—anticruelty.org

The Marine Mammal Center—marinemamalcenter.org

Also recommended were The Humane League, Mercy For Animals, and the Good Food Institute, previously recommended by Animal Charity Evaluators.

Other Vegan and Animal Welfare Charities

A Well-Fed World—awellfedworld.org

AfroVegan Society—afrovegansociety.org

Animal Legal Defense League—aldf.org

Animal Outlook—animaloutlook.org

Better Food Foundation—betterfoodfoundation.org

Black Veg Society—blackvegsociety.org

Center for Effective Altruism—centerforeffectivealtruism.org

Center for Effective Vegan Advocacy—veganadvocacy.org

Farm Animal Rights Movement (FARM)—farmusa.org

Food for Life Global—ffl.org

Food Systems Innovations—fsi.org

Global Federation of Animal Sanctuaries—sanctuaryfederation.org

Greenbaum Foundation—greenbaumfoundation.org

Greener by Default—greenerbydefault.com

Impactful Animal Advocacy—impactfulanimaladvocacy.org

In Defense of Animals—ideausa.org

Legal Impact for Chickens—legalimpactforchickens.org

Let Live—let-live.org

Material Innovation Initiative—materialinnovation.org

New Roots Institute—newrootsinstitute.org

Nutritionfacts.org—nutritionfacts.org

OM Guarantee—omguarantee.com

People for the Ethical Treatment of Animals (PETA)—peta.org

Plants-4-Hunger—plants4hunger.org

Pro Veg International—proveg.com

Physicians Committee for Responsible Medicine (PCRM)—pcrm.org

Reimagine Agriculture—reimagineagriculture.org

Sentient Media—sentientmedia.org

Shrimp Welfare Project—shrimpwelfareproject.org

Switch4Good—switch4good.org

The American Vegan Society—americanvegan.org

The Center for Nutrition Studies—nutritionstudies.org

The Humane Society of the United States (HSUS)—humanesociety.org

The Life You Can Save—thelifeyoucansave.org

The Open Sanctuary Project—opensanctuary.org

The Vegan Society—vegansociety.com

Thrive Philanthropy—thrivephilanthropy.org

Vegan Outreach—veganoutreach.org

Veg Fund—vegfund.org

Animal Sanctuaries and Rescues

Aimee's Farm Animal Sanctuary—aimeesfarmanimalsanctuary.org

Animal Place—animalplace.org

Austin Farm Sanctuary—austinfarmsanctuary.org

Barn Sanctuary—barnsanctuary.org

Best Friends Animal Society—bestfriends.org

Broken Shovels Farm Sanctuary—brokenshovels.com

Catskill Animal Sanctuary—casanctuary.org

Cedar Row Farm Sanctuary—cedarrow.org

Center for Great Apes—centerforgreatapes.org

Charlie's Acres—charliesacres.org

Chimpanzee Sanctuary Northwest—chimpsnw.org

Chimp Haven—chimphaven.org

Ching Farm Rescue & Sanctuary—chingsanctuary.org

Edgar's Mission—edgarsmission.org.au

Farm Animal Refuge—farmanimalrefuge.org

Farm Sanctuary—farmsanctuary.org

Global Sanctuary for Elephants—globalelephants.org

Goats of Anarchy—goatsofanarchy.org

Happy Compromise Farm + Sanctuary—happycompromise.org

Here With Us Farm Sanctuary—herewithusfarmsanctuary.org

Hogs and Kisses Farm Sanctuary—hogsandkisses.org

Humane Society of Fremont County—fremonthumane.com

Indraloka Animal Sanctuary—indraloka.org

Juliana's Animal Sanctuary—julianasanimalsanctuary.org

Kanda Farm Sanctuary—kandafarmsanctuary.org

Karen Elephant Habitat—elephantnaturepark.org

Lancaster Farm Sanctuary—lancasterfarmsanctuary.org

Life With Pigs Farm Sanctuary—lifewithpigs.com

Lighthouse Farm Sanctuary—lighthousefarmsanctuary.org

Little Woods Animal Sanctuary—littlewoodssanctuary.com

Little Steps Matter—littlestepsmatter.org

Living with Pickles—livingwithpickles.com

Luvin Arms Animal Sanctuary—luvinarms.org

New Hope Animal Rescue—nhanimalrescue.org

Oinking Acres Farm Rescue & Sanctuary—oinkingacres.org

Orphaned Wildlife Rehabilitation Society—owlrehab.org

Pawsitive Beginnings—pawsitivebeginnings.org

Rancho Compasión—ranchocompasion.org

Road to Refuge Animal Sanctuary—roadtorefugeanimalsanctuary.com

Rooster Sanctuary at Danzig's Roost—roostersanctuary.org

Rosie's Farm Sanctuary—rosiesfarmsanctuary.org

Rowdy Girl Sanctuary—rowdygirlsanctuary.org

Sale Ranch Animal Sanctuary—saleranch.org

Save The Chimps—savethechimps.org

Sleepy Pig Farm—spfanimalsanctuary.org

Sowa Goat Sanctuary—sowagoatsanctuary.com

Sunrise Sanctuary—sunrisesanctuary.org

Surge Sanctuary—surgesanctuary.org

Tamerlaine Sanctuary & Preserve—tamerlaine.org

The Elephant Sanctuary—elephants.com

The Gentle Barn—gentlebarn.org

The Happy Herd Farm Sanctuary—happyherd.org

The Kangaroo Sanctuary—kangaroosanctuary.com

They All Want To Live—theyallwanttolive.org

Tikkun Olam Farm Sanctuary—tofsanctuary.org

Uncle Neil's Home—uncleneilshome.org

Winnipeg Humane Society—winnipeghumanesociety.ca

Woodstock Farm Sanctuary—woodstocksanctuary.org

RECOMMENDED
RESOURCES

Books on veganism, animal rights, ethics, and philosophy

Get Lean with Plants by Leif Arnesen

What a Fish Knows by Jonathan Balcombe

How to Be Great at Doing Good by Nick Cooney

Goodbye Autoimmune Disease by Brooke Goldner

Goodbye Lupus by Brooke Goldner

Why We Love Dogs, Eat Pigs, and Wear Cows by Melanie Joy

How to Create a Vegan World by Tobias Leenaert

Badass Vegan by John Lewis

Doing Good Better by William MacAskill

Food is Climate by Glen Merzer

Vegan For Life by Jack Norris and Virginia Messina

The Joyful Vegan by Colleen Patrick-Goudreau

Eating Animals by Jonathan Safran Foer

Clean Meat by Paul Shapiro

Animal Liberation by Peter Singer

The Most Good You Can Do by Peter Singer

The Future of Food Is Female by Jennifer Stojkovic

This Is Vegan Propaganda by Ed Winters

How to Argue With a Meat Eater (And Win Every Time) by Ed Winters

Vegan and plant-based cookbooks

Unprocessed by Chef AJ

Sweet Indulgence by Chef AJ

PlantYou by Carleigh Bodrug

PlantYou: Scrappy Cooking by Carleigh Bodrug

Cooking From the Spirit by Tabitha Brown

The Blue Zones American Kitchen by Dan Buettner

The Fiber Fueled Cookbook by Dr. Will Bulsiewicz

Dreena's Kind Kitchen by Dreena Burton

PlantPure Comfort Food by Kim Campbell

The China Study Cookbook by Leanne Campbell

Sweet Potato Soul by Jenné Claiborne

Eat Plants, B*tch by Pinky Cole

Plant-Powered Protein by Brenda Davis, Vesanto Melina, and Cory Davis

The Plant-Based Diet Revolution by Dr. Alan Desmond

Be a Plant-Based Woman Warrior by Jane and Ann Esselstyn

Plant-Strong by Rip Esselstyn

The Sprout Book by Doug Evans

The No Meat Athlete Cookbook by Matt Frazier and Stepfanie Romine

Best of Vegan by Kim-Julie Hansen

Your Super Life by Michael Kuech and Kristel de Groot

America Goes Vegan by Glen Merzer and Tracy Childs

The Korean Vegan Cookbook by Joanne Lee Molinaro

Unbelievably Vegan by Charity Morgan

Veganomicon by Isa Chandra Moskowitz and Terry Hope Romero

Fake Meat by Isa Chandra Moskowitz

The Plant Power Doctor by Dr. Gemma Newman

Plant-Based on a Budget by Toni Okamoto

Plant-Based on a Budget Quick & Easy by Toni Okamoto

The Joyful Vegan by Colleen Patrick-Goudreau

The Joy of Vegan Baking by Colleen Patrick-Goudreau

31-Day Food Revolution by Ocean Robbins

The Vegan Meat Cookbook by Miyoko Schinner

The Homemade Vegan Pantry by Miyoko Schinner

The Forks Over Knives Cookbook by Del Sroufe

Afro-Vegan by Bryant Terry

Flavor! by Darshana Thacker

Craving Vegan by Sam Turnbull

Vegan Fast Food by Brian Watson

Recommended listening (YouTube, podcasts, etc.)

Are You Ready with Joanne Molinaro

Brown Vegan with Monique Koch

Cheap Lazy Vegan on YouTube

Chef AJ LIVE! on YouTube

Chew On This: Bite-Sized Stories about Nutrition with Dr. Brooke Bussard

Derrick and Tanya's Highway to Health

Fit Rich Life with Justin David Carl

Food for Thought: The Joys and Benefits of Living Vegan with Colleen Patrick-Goudreau

Health Science Podcast

Hidden Brain

Highway to Health with Tanya O'Callaghan and Derrick Green

Lifting Vegan Logic on YouTube

Main Street Vegan with Victoria Moran

Mic the Vegan on YouTube

Moby Pod

Muscles by Brussels Radio!

No Bullsh*t Vegan with Karina Inkster

No Meat Athlete Radio

Nutrition Facts

Our Hen House

Perfectly Planted with Dr. Daphne Bascom

PLANTSTRONG Podcast with Rip Esselstyn

Plant Yourself: Embracing a Plant-based Lifestyle with Howard Jacobson

Real Men Eat Plants

Rise and Thrive with Ella Magers

SoFlo Vegans Podcast

Sweet Potato Soul on YouTube

Switch4Good with Dotsie Bausch and Alexandra Paul

The Brain Health Revolution Podcast with the Drs. Sherzai

The Disclosure Podcast with Ed Winters

The Doc & Chef on YouTube

The Exam Room Podcast with Chuck Carroll

The Health Science Podcast with Dr. Frank Sabatino

The Plant-Based Morning Show with Matt Frazier and Doug Hay

The Plant Based News Podcast

The Proof with Simon Hill

The Rich Roll Podcast

The Sonya Looney Show

The Vegan Good Life with Miyoko on YouTube

The Vegan Gym Podcast

The VegNews Podcast

Unnatural Vegan on YouTube

Vegans Who Lift

Documentaries

A Prayer For Compassion

Blackfish

Cowspiracy

Dominion

Earthlings

Eating Our Way to Extinction

Eating You Alive

Forks Over Knives

Meat Me Halfway

Milked

PlantPure Nation

Racing Extinction

Seaspiracy

Speciesism: The Movie

The Cove

The Game Changers

The Smell of Money

They're Trying to Kill Us

UnSupersize Me

What The Health

You Are What You Eat: A Twin Experiment

Websites

Earthling Ed—earthlinged.org

Enrich Creative—enrichcreative.com

Fit Vegan Chef—fitveganchef.com

Fit Vegan Coaching—fitvegancoaching.com

Forks Over Knives—forksoverknives.com

Happy Cow—happycow.net

Institute of Plant-Based Medicine—iopbm.com

Joyful Ventures—joyful.vc

Live Kindly—livekindly.com

Moving Medicine Forward—movingmedforward.com/about

Perfectly Planted—perfectlyplanted22.com

Plant Based News—plantbasednews.org

Plant-Based on a Budget—plantbasedonabudget.com

Plantrician Project—plantricianproject.org

Sexy Fit Vegan—sexyfitvegan.com

The Game Changers—gamechangersmovie.com

The Vegan Gym—thevegangym.com

Vegan.com—vegan.com

Vegan Bodybuilding & Fitness—veganbodybuilding.com

Vegan Calculator—vegancalculator.com

Vegan Printer—veganprinter.com

Vegan Strong—veganstrong.com

Vegconomist—vegconomist.com

VegNews—vegnews.com

80,000 Hours—80000hours.org

Vegan and plant-based events and conferences

American College of Lifestyle Medicine Conference—lmconference.org

Animal and Vegan Advocacy Summit—avasummit.com

Black VegFest—blackvegfest.org

Food Revolution Summit (virtual only)—summit.foodrevolution.org

Holistic Holiday at Sea Vegan Cruise—holisticholidayatsea.com

International Animal Rights Conference—ar-conference.org

National Health Association Conference—healthscience.org

Plant-Based Nutrition Healthcare Conference—pbnhc.com

Plant-Based World Expo—plantbasedworldexpo.com

Plant-Stock—plantstrong.com/plantstock

Planted Expo—plantedlife.com

Reducetarian Summit—reducetarian.org

The Vegan Superhero Retreat—thevegangym.com/retreat

Vegan Block Party—veganblockparty.com

Vegan Camp Out—vegancampout.co.uk

Vegan Women Summit—veganwomensummit.com

Vegan Street Fair—veganstreetfair.com

Vegandale—vegandalefest.com

VegFest Expos—vegfestexpos.com

World Vegan Bodybuilding & Fitness Championships—vhfexpo.com

Effective for-profit conscious companies

All Y'alls Foods—allyallsfoods.com

Alt Protein Careers—altproteincareers.com

Better Meat Co.—bettermeat.co

Beyond Meat—beyondmeat.com

Clean Machine—cleanmachineonline.com

Complement—lovecomplement.com

Dandies—dandies.com

DEVA Nutrition—devanutrition.com

Fair Wind Cruises—fair-wind.com

FYTA—fyta.com

Impact for Life Bars—impactforlife.shop

Impossible Foods—impossiblefoods.com

Loving Hut—lovinghut.us

Meati—meati.com

Munchy Crunchy Protein—munchycrunchyprotein.com

Next Level Burger—nextlevelburger.com

No Cow Bar—nocow.com

Only What You Need (OWYN)—liveowyn.com

Outstanding Foods—outstandingfoods.com

Pnuff Crunch—pnuff.com

Rise Brewing—risebrewingco.com

Unisoy Jerky—unisoyjerky.com

Upton's Naturals—uptonsnaturals.com

Vegan Essentials—veganessentials.com

Veggie Grill—veggiegrill.com

Wicked Kitchen—wickedkitchen.com

ACKNOWLEDGMENTS

This was by the far the most difficult book-writing process I have gone through. All of my other books were about the vegan fitness lifestyle, which I have lived for decades, and can easily write about. This book, however, challenged me in many ways. I had much to learn throughout the journey of bringing this topic of effective vegan altruism to a mainstream audience, trusting that it would be embraced and accepted by vegan supporters and critics alike. My longtime friend Jordan Baskerville walked this path with me, helping me uncover solutions to the most pressing problems that inflict suffering on our fellow animals. Jordan helped me, and this book, more than anyone, and he stuck with me during the multi-year writing process that was anything but easy. Jordan, what can I say? It has been quite the adventure, navigating through the philosophical discussions about what it means to believe that we can change the world, and to develop the confidence to act on those beliefs. You dedicated years of support to this book, and to me, challenging me to create my most effective work yet. I believe we achieved that goal together, and for that, I am grateful.

To my agent, Janis Donnaud—without your feedback, this book would have never taken off, and would just be another one of those ideas in my head, left for me to ponder about what might have been if I had pursued it. You helped me find my voice in what proved to be a grueling undertaking to get to the finish line. You weren't satisfied by my initial drafts, and rather than bending in the light of my enthusiasm to pursue this dream, you never settled, and that forced me to grow as a writer. Thank you for believing that I was capable of creating great work, and for giving me the space to unleash my creativity and tell meaningful stories.

To BenBella founder and CEO Glenn Yeffeth, thank you for taking a chance on me, and for personally offering me a book deal to bring *The Impactful Vegan* to the masses. The enthusiasm you displayed during our first conversation, supported by your immediate understanding of what I was aiming to accomplish with this book, gave me confidence that by accepting an offer from BenBella, I was part of your publishing family. Without you and your talented staff of smart, compassionate, and creative team members, this book would not be as influential as we all believe that it will be. Thank you for trusting the process and for giving me the platform to voice my concerns about the plight that animals go through, which I hadn't yet expressed in book form, until now. Thank you to the BenBella team: Claire Schulz for being the project manager, working closely with me on this book for more than a year, helping me get to the finish line, and making me feel so proud of what we accomplished together. Also thanks to Madeline Grigg, Adrienne Lang, Heather Butterfield, Morgan Carr, Kellie Doherty, Kim Broderick, Sarah Avinger, Susan Welte, Alicia Kania, Monica Lowry, Michael Fedison, Sarah Vostok, Jenny Bridges, and Amy Murphy. You all shaped this book into what it has become, and I appreciate you. I also want to express deep gratitude to Gregory Newton Brown, whose brilliant editing helped me find my strongest voice during the final rounds of rewrites and revisions, making this book feel whole. Greg, thank you for your invaluable contributions to this book, helping it read so much more clearly, communicating the stories more powerfully in memorable ways.

To my wife, Karen, here we go again. Round five of being by my side during a long and strenuous book-writing adventure. Perhaps this is the one that makes the greatest impact on the world around us. Thank you for believing in me, and for encouraging me to lean in with my heart and to grow as a writer, and as a person. I love you, and I appreciate your patience, your understanding, your support, and all the meals you prepared for me while I sat in the basement and wrote from morning until night. We did this together, and I thank you for being a pillar of support for me to lean on.

To the Vegan Strong Team—Susan Peters, Dani Taylor, Giacomo Marchese, and Korin Sutton—thank you for taking the lead while I needed to step back to write this book full time. Your willingness to step up and carry on The Vegan Strong Method and legacy made this book possible. You are some of my favorite people, and you're helping change the world, particularly making the world a more compassionate place for animals.

To my executive assistant and amazing friend, Alex Hays, thank you for your unrelenting passion for helping others, and for your unwavering support of me, and of this book. I am so grateful for the friendship we have built, and I love that you are from my hometown. We did it. We followed our passion, and we made it happen. I'm already predicting that this book will become a bestseller, and you played one of the most important roles in that pursuit. Thank you.

To my parents, Peter and Edna, thank you for embracing my creativity at a young age, allowing me to pursue such a dream of someday being a professional writer. The journey has been long, and anything but straightforward, but you have supported me every step of the way. I love you, and I thank you for encouraging me to blaze my own trail and carve out my own path of self-discovery and creative expression. I hope you're proud of what this book will accomplish in the world.

To my sister, Tanya, I wouldn't be doing any of this if it weren't for your guidance, your leadership, your support, and for paving the way for me to follow in your footsteps as a compassionate vegan all those years ago, in the mid-'90s in our hometown of Corvallis, Oregon. For anything that I have accomplished within the vegan community, I credit you for lighting that spark, and for helping keep that flame burning for animal rights three decades later.

To my family, my friends, and my supporters, thank you for helping make this dream come true, for taking the recommendations in this book to heart, and for applying effective strategies to help animals in your own lives. Thank you for all you do for others.

To everyone who contributed to this book with an interview, a story, a quote, or an endorsement, which shaped my writing, enhanced my storytelling, and ultimately made this book what it is today, I am grateful for all of you. Thank you to those who assisted in the interviews, bringing these powerful stories to light. Thank you to Dreena Burton; Toni Okamoto; Paul Shapiro; Bruce Friedrich; Matt de Gruyter; Carleigh Bodrug; Will Bulsiewicz; Shaleen Shah; Joanne Molinaro; John Oberg; Dotsie Bausch; Gene Baur; Chef AJ; Mike Dearborn; Rae McDowell; Dr. Michael Klaper; Dr. Matthew Nagra; Dr. Vicky Bond; Brenda Davis, RD; John Lewis; Dani Taylor; Jennifer Stojkovic; Leif Arnesen; Anders Arnesen; Korin Sutton; T.K. Pillan; Matt Tullman; Dan Buettner; Dr. Melanie Joy; Will Tucker; Ella Magers; Joseph Blair; Josh Balk; Paul Rodney Turner; Juliana Castaneda Turner; Katie Cantrell; Bob Isaacson; Julia Wisner; Jennifer Barckley; Karen Hirsch; Rich Roll; Dr. Doug Lisle; Dr. Ayesha Sherzai; Dr. Dean Sherzai; Tracy Tong; Robbie Lockie; Kathy Freston; Dr. Brooke Goldner; Ocean Robbins; Rip Esselstyn; James Wilks; Phil Collen; Tabitha Brown; Chuck Carroll; Julieanna Hever, Isa Chandra Moskowitz; and Mike Gasca.

To Amy Esch for taking my headshot photos, and for helping me feel more like a professional writer and speaker.

To Bruce Sachs and Suzanne Duval d'Adrian from Enrich Creative for creating all of the images for the book, which helped me share stories more powerfully, making an even stronger impact, as we carried out our mission to effectively help animals. Thank you for being in the right place, at the right time, when I really needed your expertise.

To Satish Karandikar, Shawn Kowalewski, Charles Chang, and Sheryl and Bob Greenberg for your continued support of my writing career. I wouldn't be here without you, and I am eternally grateful for your generosity, and for your belief in a shared vision for a more compassionate future.

To our rescue dogs, Benny and Ellie, who have followed a plant-based diet for as long as we've had them (twelve-plus years for Benny at age eighteen, and seven-plus years for Ellie at age eight), thank you for the constant reminder that all animals share a desire to live a life free of fear, pain, and suffering. I love you so much.

To Ed Winters, for being, in my view, the most logical and reasonable voice for animals today, for engaging in meaningful debates to shed light on the abhorrent lives farmed animals are subjected to, and for inspiring me to amplify my voice for the voiceless.

To Alex O'Connor for piquing my interest in philosophy, which drove much of my inquisitiveness as I pursued the topic of learning how to most effectively reduce animal suffering.

Lastly, to Peter Singer and William MacAskill for captivating my interest in effective altruism, and for helping me evaluate my own priorities, inspiring me to contribute in more meaningful ways. Thank you for all you do for animals.

ENDNOTES

1. Humane Society of the United States, "More Animals Than Ever Before—92.2 Billion—Are Used and Killed Each Year for Food," June 2023, https://blog.humanesociety.org/2023/06/more-animals-than-ever-before-92-2-billion-are-used-and-killed-each-year-for-food.html.

2. National Library of Medicine, "Factory Farming and Public Health: How Industrial Animal Agriculture Harms Communities, Humans, and Animals," November 2020, https://www.ncbi.nlm.nih.gov/pmc/articles/PMC7596793/.

3. Peter Cheeke, "Confessions of a Closet Vegan," (unpublished manuscript, sent July 17, 2023), Microsoft Word file.

4. National Geographic Education, "Dead Zone," https://education.nationalgeographic.org/resource/dead-zone/.

5. Animal Equality, "Factory Farming Facts," October 2022, https://animalequality.org/blog/2022/10/14/factory-farming-facts/.

6. Sentience Institute, "United States Factory Farming Estimates," https://www.sentienceinstitute.org/us-factory-farming-estimates.

7. Chartr, "Vegging Out," September 3, 2023, https://read.chartr.co/newsletters/2023/9/3/vegging-out.

8. Cheeke, "Confessions of a Closet Vegan."

9. United States Department of Agriculture, "Fluid Milk Consumption Continues Downward Trend, Proving Difficult to Reverse," June 2022, https://www.ers.usda.gov/amber-waves/2022/june/fluid-milk-consumption-continues-downward-trend-proving-difficult-to-reverse/.

10. Food Dive, "Plant-Based Food Sales Hit $8 Billion in 2022," accessed September 22, 2023, https://www.fooddive.com/news/plant-based-2022-sales-8b/647315/.

11. JustFood, "Meat Consumption in Germany Falls to 34-Year Low Trough, Led by Pork," accessed September 22, 2023, https://www.just-food.com /news/meat-consumption-in-germany-falls-to-34-year-low-trough-led-by -pork.

12. Michael Goodier and Viktor Sunnemark, "UK meat consumption at lowest level since records began, data reveals," *Guardian*, October 24, 2023, https:// www.theguardian.com/environment/2023/oct/24/uk-meat-consumption -lowest-level-since-record-began-data-reveal.

13. Against Malaria Foundation, "Why Nets?" https://www.againstmalaria .com/WhyNets.aspx.

14. William MacAskill, *Doing Good Better* (New York: Avery, 2015), 13.

15. United States Department of Agriculture, "U.S. Population Consumes More Poultry Than Beef, Pork, or Fish," https://www.ers.usda.gov/data-products /chart-gallery/gallery/chart-detail/?chartId=103505; Sentient Media, "Battery Cage," https://sentientmedia.org/battery-cage/; United Egg Producers, "Facts & Stats," https://unitedegg.com/facts-stats/.

16. Farm Sanctuary, "2021 Impact Report," https://assets.farmsanctuary.org /content/uploads/2022/03/28161739/2021-impact-report.pdf.

17. National Library of Medicine, "The Environmental and Public Health Impacts of Factory Farming: A Review," May 2017.

18. Harvard T.H. Chan School of Public Health, "What's Behind Shocking U.S. Life Expectancy Decline—and What to Do About It," accessed September 22, 2023, https://www.hsph.harvard.edu/news/hsph-in-the-news/whats -behind-shocking-u-s-life-expectancy-decline-and-what-to-do-about-it.

19. Ben & Hish, "Why People Go Vegan: 2019 Global Survey Results," VOMAD Life, March 3, 2019, https://vomad.life/survey/.

20. Nils-Gerrit Wunsch, "Leading motivations that led people to take part in Veganuary worldwide in 2022," Statista, January 30, 2023, https://www .statista.com/statistics/1264382/top-motivations-for-veganuary/.

21. Jo Anderson, "Going Vegan or Vegetarian: Motivations & Influences," Faunalytics, December 8, 2021, https://faunalytics.org/going-veg-motivations -and-influences/.

22. Karine Lacroix, Matthew Goldberg, Jennifer Marlon, Seth Rosenthal, Matthew Ballew, Xinran Wang, Martial Jefferson, Jillian Semaan, and Anthony Leiserowitz, "Understanding differences in Americans' motivations for eating plant-rich foods," Yale Program on Climate Change Communication, April 7, 2022, https://climatecommunication.yale.edu/publications

/understanding-differences-in-americans-motivations-for-eating-plant
-rich-foods/.

23. United States Department of Agriculture, "Fluid Milk Consumption Continues Downward Trend, Proving Difficult to Reverse," June 2022.

24. United Nations News, "World Population Projected to Reach 9.7 Billion by 2050, Says UN," December 2022.

25. Faunalytics, "What Influences People to Go Vegan?" https://faunalytics.org/what-influences-people-to-go-vegan/.

26. University of Oxford, "Sustainable Eating Cheaper and Healthier: Oxford Study," November 11, 2021, https://www.ox.ac.uk/news/2021-11-11-sustainable-eating-cheaper-and-healthier-oxford-study.

27. US Bureau of Labor Statistics, "Percent Change in Average Weekly Wages by State, December 2022," https://www.bls.gov/charts/county-employment-and-wages/percent-change-aww-by-state.htm.

28. Faunalytics, "Relative Effectiveness of Strategies to Reduce Meat Consumption," https://faunalytics.org/relative-effectiveness/.

29. Good Food Institute, "2022 Plant-Based State of the Industry Report," Accessed September 22, 2023, https://gfi.org/wp-content/uploads/2023/01/2022-Plant-Based-State-of-the-Industry-Report.pdf.

30. William MacAskill, *Doing Good Better* (New York: Avery, 2015), 150.

31. *Forbes*, "20 Facts and Figures to Know When Marketing to Women," accessed September 22, 2023, https://www.forbes.com/sites/forbescontentmarketing/2019/05/13/20-facts-and-figures-to-know-when-marketing-to-women/; Girl Power Marketing, "Statistics on the Purchasing Power of Women," accessed September 22, 2023, https://girlpowermarketing.com/statistics-purchasing-power-women/.

32. BBC Future, "The Mystery of Why There Are More Women Vegans," February 14, 2020, https://www.bbc.com/future/article/20200214-the-mystery-of-why-there-are-more-women-vegans.

33. HappyCow.net, "Vegan & Vegetarian Restaurants in USA," August 10, 2022, https://www.happycow.net/north_america/usa/?filters=vegan.

34. "Fast Food Consumption Among Adults in the United States, 2013–2016," CDC.gov, August 10, 2022, https://www.cdc.gov/nchs/products/databriefs/db322.htm.

35. "80% of Americans Eat Fast Food Once a Week," Local 3 News, August 10, 2022, https://www.local3news.com/80-of-americans-eat-fast-food-once-a-week/article_0b86cb76-6407-540d-8ba8-329bae49009f.html.

INDEX

plant-based diet. *See also* meat,
  alternative; milk alternatives;
  protein, alternative
  affordable, 29, 30
  barriers to, 126
  convenience and, 10-11
  fast food restaurants and, 10
  health and, 25, 198-199
  land required for, 199
  number of humans following, xxi
  prolonging adherence to, 75, 87, 110-
    111, 167-169
  taste and, 30
  vs. veganism, 23-24, 113
plant-based foods. *See also* meat,
  alternative; protein, alternative
  access to, 64-66
  in convenience stores, 65
  cost of, 126, 228, 229, 230
  as default option, 164-167
  distributing on college campuses, 186
  donating, 48
  food spending and, 63-64
  names of, 165, 166
  sales of, 123
  taste of, 28, 229
Plant-Based on a Budget (Okamoto), 29
Plant-Based State of the Industry Report
  (GFI), 123
Planting Seeds (Faunalytics), 97
PlantYou, 139, 228
PLNT Burger, 214
policy
  Farm Sanctuary and, 9
  Farm System Reform Act, 14
  of food companies, 66, 67
Polis, Jared, 107
politicians, 106-107
pollution, xvii, xx
population growth, xvii, xxi
pork, 104, 105
positive thinking, 221-223
positivity, 221-223
Potvin, Yves, 173-174
Prabhupada, Srila, 160
presentations, 44
priorities, 19
proceeds, donating, 53, 161
processes, efficient, 78
profits, vs. beliefs, 92
progress, 8, 80, 82. *See also* kaizen system
  recognizing, 206

protein, alternative, xxii, 61, 122. *See also*
  meat, alternative; plant-based diet;
  plant-based foods
  availability of, 127
  companies, 123
  cost of, 125
  GFI and, 122-127
  levels of adoption of, 126
protests, 97, 98-99, 101
proximity bias, 69
Pukel, Sandy, 49
purchases, 8, 22, 35-36, 211, 218. *See also*
  financial resources
  alternative proteins and, 127
  compassion and, 30-31
  non-vegans and, 210
  women and, 179-181
Pure Bliss Organics, 162
purity, vegan, xxiii, 35, 206. *See also*
  perfection

R

Rae (student), 183-185, 192
raffle tickets, 49
recidivism from veganism, 87, 88, 89,
  198
recommendations, openness to, 177
regional bias, 2
Reis, Marlon, 107
relationship-building skills, 40, 49
relationships, 49, 169
representation
  advocacy and, 191
  Black vegans and, 192
  of food choices, 8
reputation, 50. *See also* personal brand
rescues, 42, 43. *See also* sanctuaries
research, 97. *See also* Faunalytics
resources, on veganism, 245-252
resources, personal, 38. *See also*
  STRONG V characteristics
  inefficiency with, xx
  reaching mainstream audience and, 99
  using, 51, 180
restaurants, 213-218. *See also* fast-food
  restaurants; food companies;
  individual restaurants
  caged animals and, 105
  cross contamination in, 208
  HappyCow app, 216
  international cuisines, 215
  location and, 214

ABOUT THE AUTHOR

Photo by Amy Esch.

Robert grew up on a farm in Corvallis, Oregon, where he adopted a vegan lifestyle in 1995 at age fifteen, weighing just 120 pounds. Today he is the author of the books *Vegan Bodybuilding & Fitness*, *Shred It!*, *Plant-Based Muscle*, and the *New York Times* bestseller *The Plant-Based Athlete*. He is often referred to as the "Godfather of Vegan Bodybuilding," growing the industry from its infancy in 2002 to where it is today.

As a natural bodybuilding champion, Robert is considered one of *VegNews* magazine's Most Influential Vegan Athletes. He tours around the world sharing his story of transformation from a skinny farm kid to champion vegan bodybuilder. Robert is the founder and president of Vegan Bodybuilding & Fitness and maintains the website VeganBodybuilding.com. He is a regular contributor to Forks Over Knives, the Center for Nutrition Studies, The Vegan Gym, No Meat Athlete, and Vegan Strong; is a former multi-sport athlete; and has followed a plant-based diet for more than twenty-eight years. Robert lives in Fort Collins, Colorado, with his wife and two rescued Chihuahuas.